A-Z WAL

CW00531526

Regional Road Atlas

CONTENTS

REFERENCE

MOTORWAY _____ **M1**

   Under Construction _____

   Proposed _____

MOTORWAY JUNCTIONS WITH NUMBERS _____ **4**

   Unlimited interchange **4**

   Limited interchange **8**   **8**

MOTORWAY SERVICE AREA   **FERRYBRIDGE**   Ⓢ

MAJOR ROAD SERVICE AREAS   **LEEMING**   **GRASBY**

   with 24 hour Facilities _____ Ⓢ   Ⓢ

PRIMARY ROUTE _____ **A19**

PRIMARY ROUTE DESTINATION _____ **DOVER**

DUAL CARRIAGEWAY (A & B Roads) _____

CLASS A ROAD _____ **A614**

CLASS B ROAD _____ **B6422**

MAJOR ROAD UNDER CONSTRUCTION _____

MAJOR ROAD PROPOSED _____

GRADIENT 1:5(20%) & STEEPER _____ «

   (Ascent in direction of arrow)

TOLL _____ *TOLL*

MILEAGE BETWEEN MARKERS _____ 8

RAILWAY AND STATION _____

LEVEL CROSSING AND TUNNEL _____

RIVER OR CANAL _____

COUNTY OR UNITARY AUTHORITY BOUNDARY _____

NATIONAL BOUNDARY _____

BUILT UP AREA _____

VILLAGE OR HAMLET _____

WOODED AREA _____

SPOT HEIGHT IN FEET _____ • 813

HEIGHT ABOVE SEA LEVEL 400' - 1,000'

               1,000' - 1,400'

               1,400, - 2,000'

               2,000' +

NATIONAL GRID REFERENCE (Kilometres) _____ 100

TOURIST INFORMATION

AIRPORT _____ ✈

AIRFIELD _____ ✈

HELIPORT _____ ✈

BATTLE SITE AND DATE _____ ✕ *1408*

CASTLE (Open to Public) _____

CASTLE WITH GARDEN (Open to Public) _____

CATHEDRAL, ABBEY, FRIARY, PRIORY, CHURCH

   (Open to Public) _____ †

COUNTRY PARK _____

FERRY (Vehicular) _____ (Foot only) _____

GARDEN (Open to Public) _____

GOLF COURSE _____ 9 HOLE _____ 18 HOLE

HISTORIC BUILDING (Open to Public) _____

HISTORIC BUILDING WITH GARDEN (Open to Public) _____

HORSE RACECOURSE _____

INFORMATION CENTRE, VISITOR CENTRE OR

   TOURIST INFORMATION CENTRE _____ 🅸

LIGHTHOUSE _____

MOTOR RACING CIRCUIT _____

MUSEUM, ART GALLERY _____

NATIONAL PARK OR FOREST PARK _____

NATIONAL TRUST PROPERTY (Open) _____ *NT*

           (Restricted Opening) _____ *NT*

NATURE RESERVE OR BIRD SANCTUARY _____

NATURE TRAIL OR FOREST WALK _____

PLACE OF INTEREST _____ *Monument* •

PICNIC SITE _____

RAILWAY (Preserved, Miniature, Steam or Narrow Gauge) _____

TELEPHONE _____ PUBLIC (Selection) _____ AA OR RAC _____

THEME PARK _____

VIEWPOINT _____

WILDLIFE PARK _____

WINDMILL _____

ZOO OR SAFARI PARK _____

SCALE

| 0 | 1 | 2 | 3 | 4 | 5 | 6 Miles |

| 0 | 1 | 2 | 3 | 4 | 5 | 6 | 7 | 8 | 9 | 10 Kilometres |

1:158,400
2.5 Miles to 1 Inch

Geographers' A-Z Map Company Ltd

Head Office : Fairfield Road,
Borough Green, Sevenoaks, Kent TN15 8PP
Telephone : 01732- 781000
Showrooms :
44 Gray's Inn Road, London, WC1X 8HX
Telephone: 0171-242 9246

INDEX TO SELECTED PLACES OF INTEREST

KEY TO MAP PAGES

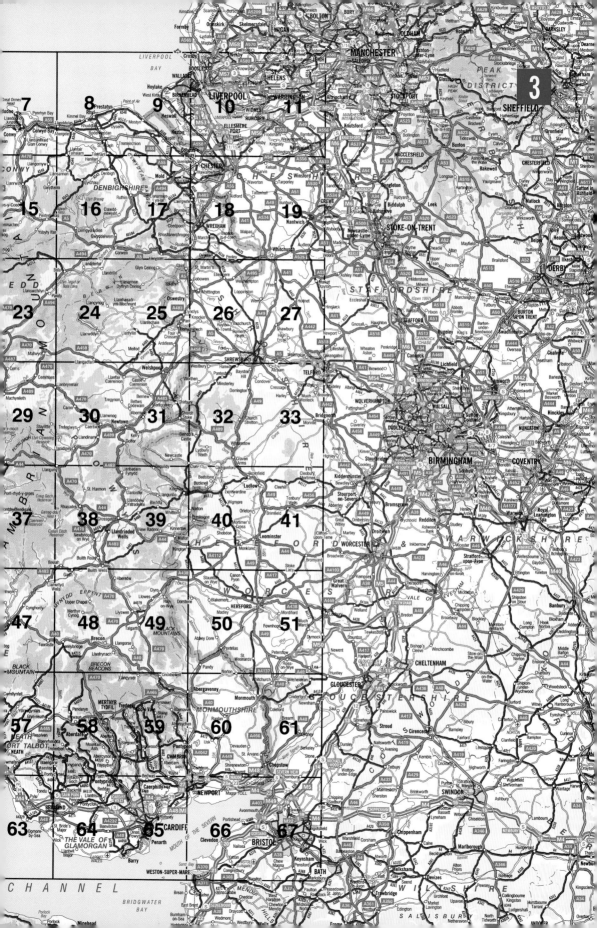

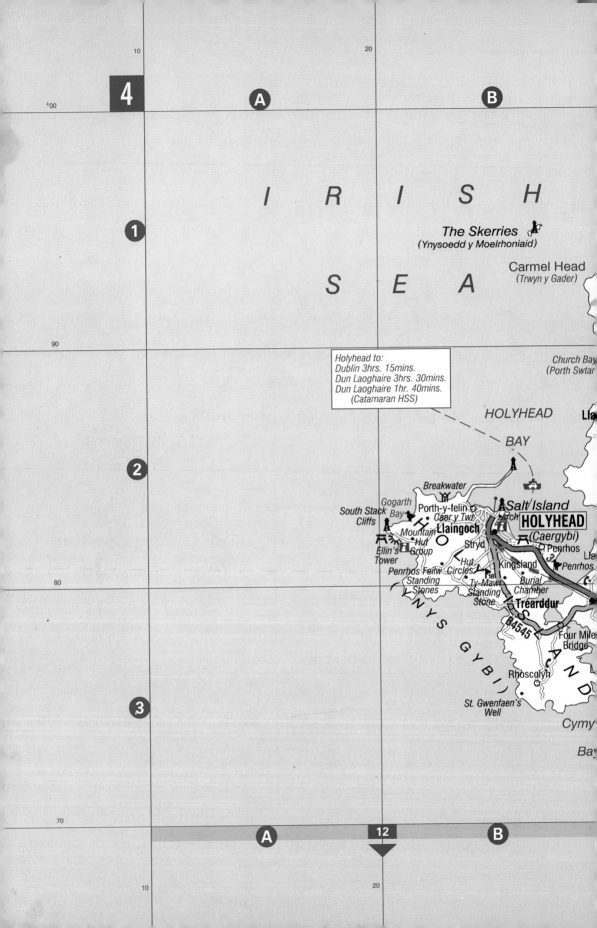

4

10   20

⁴00

①

I R I S H

The Skerries
(Ynysoedd y Moelrhoniaid)

S E A

Carmel Head
(Trwyn y Gader)

90

②

Holyhead to:
Dublin 3hrs. 15mins.
Dun Laoghaire 3hrs. 30mins.
Dun Laoghaire 1hr. 40mins.
(Catamaran HSS)

Church Bay
(Porth Swtar

HOLYHEAD   Lla

BAY

Breakwater

Salt Island

Gogarth
Bay
Porth-y-felin

South Stack
Cliffs

Caer y Twr

Arch
HOLYHEAD
(Caergybi)

Mountain
Hut
Group

Llaingoch

Penrhos

Ellin's
Tower

Stryd

Kingsland

Penrhos

Hut
Circles

Penrhos Feilw
Standing
Stones

Lla

80

Ty-Mawr
Standing
Stone

Burial
Chamber

Trearddur

B4545

Four Mile
Bridge

③

YNYS GYBI

Rhoscolyn

St. Gwenfaen's
Well

Cymy

Bay

70

▼

10   20

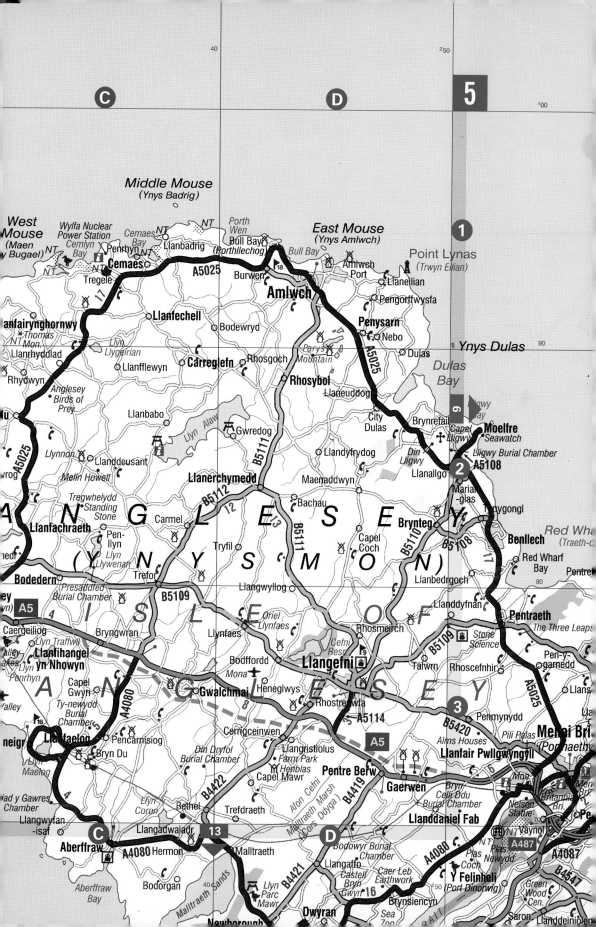

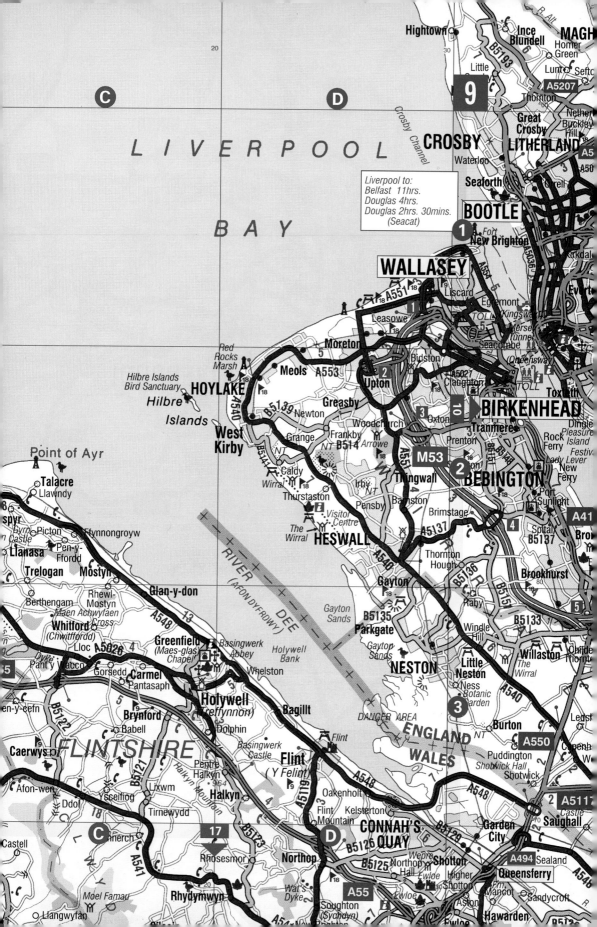

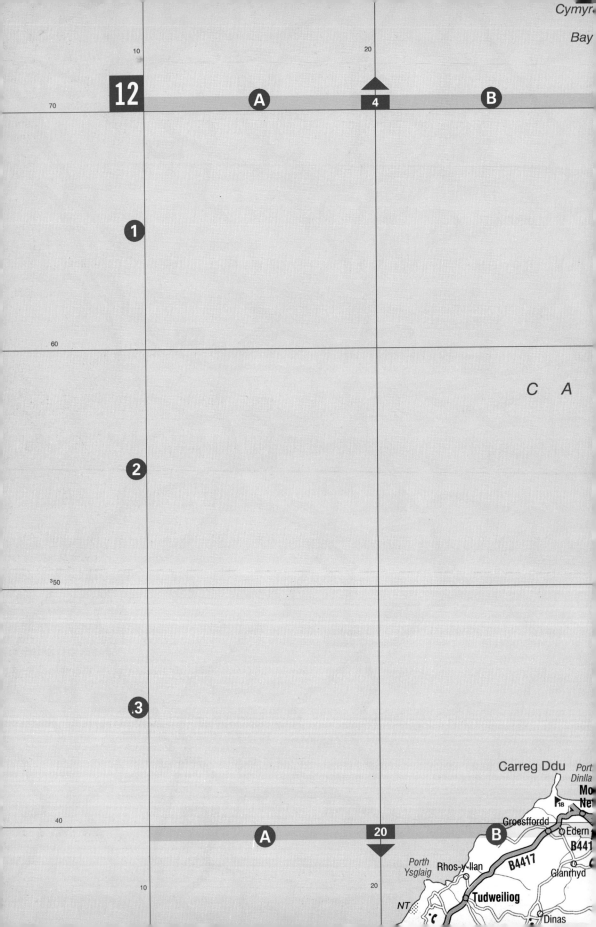

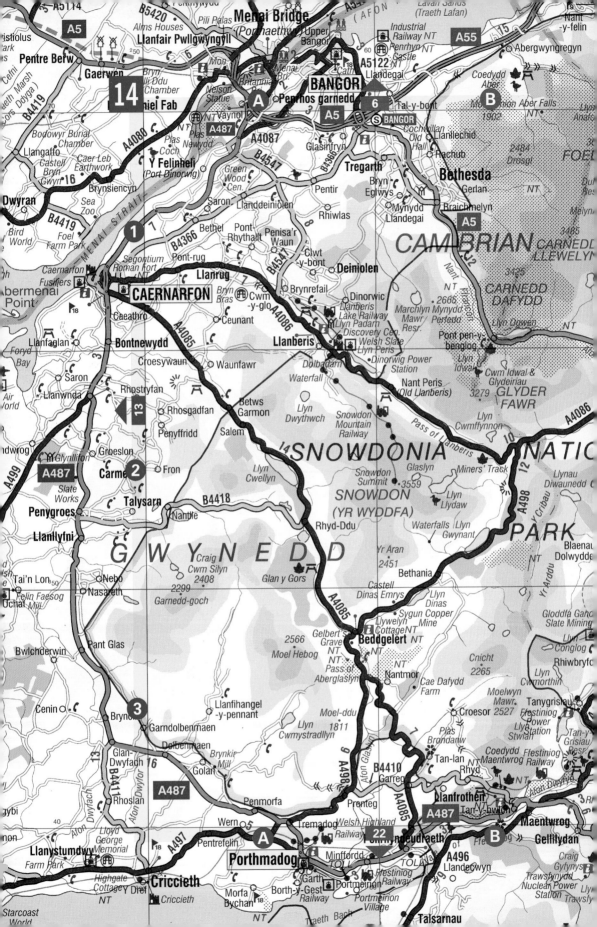

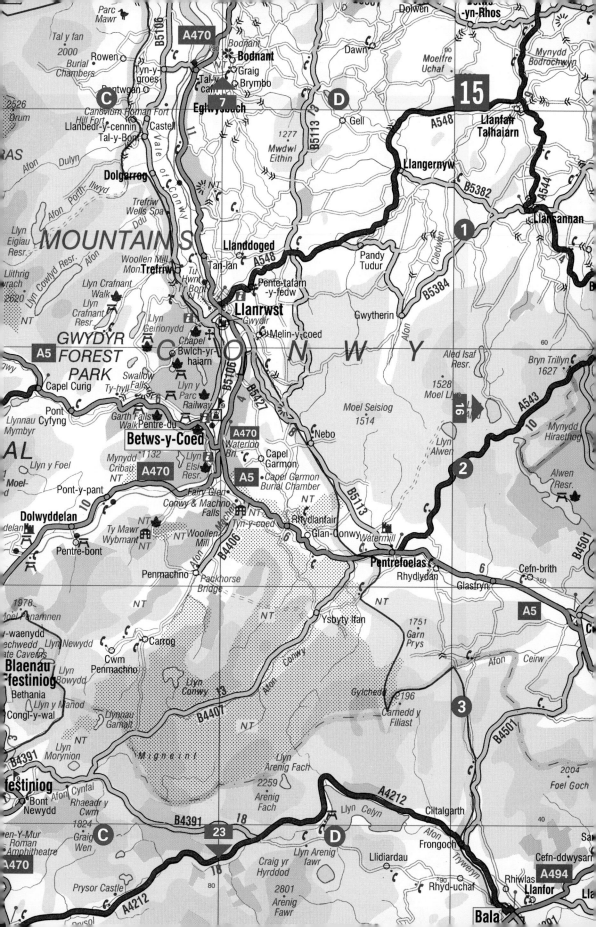

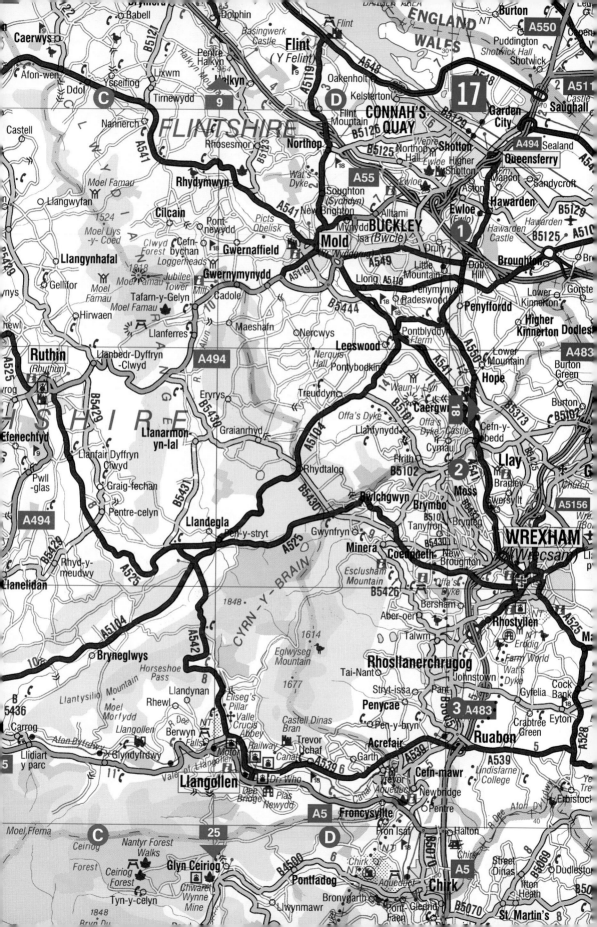

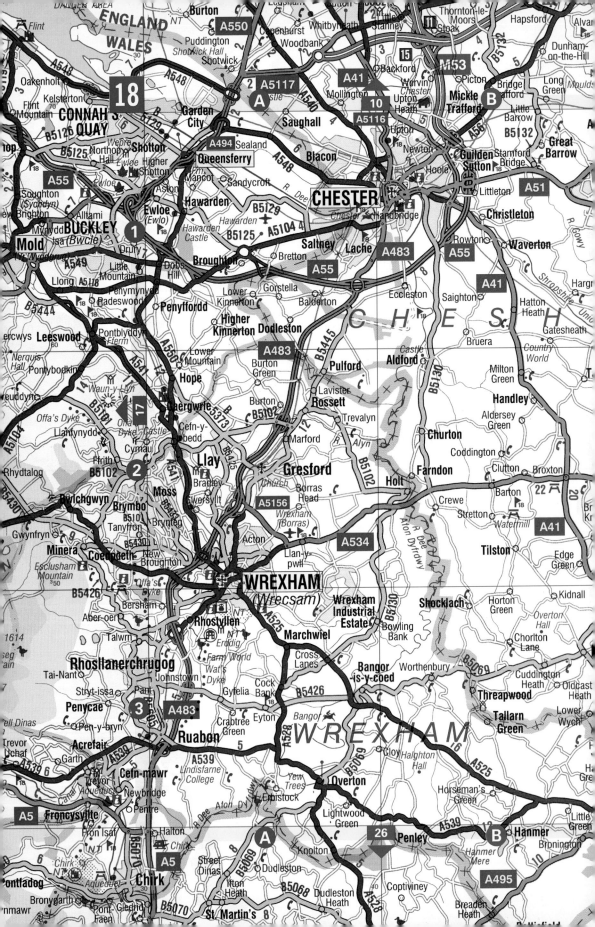

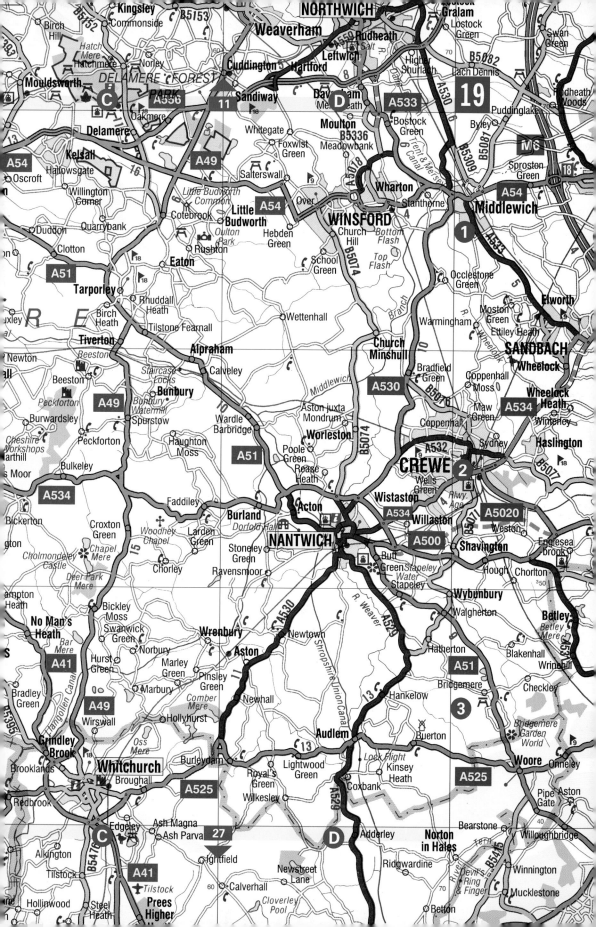

20

Carreg Ddu
Porth Dinllaer
Morf
Nefy

Groesffordd
Edern
B4412
Rhos-y-llan
Porth Ysglaig
Glanrhyd
Tudweiliog
Dinas
Rhos-ddu
Llaniestyn
Penllech
Fort Garn-fadryn
Bryn-mawr
Llangwnnadl
Pen-y-graig
Sarn Meyllteyrn
Bryncroes
Botwnnog

Porth Colmon

NT

Penrhyn Mawr

Rhydllos

Porth Oer
Roshirwaun

Llawr Dref

NT
NT
NT

Braich Anelog
Anelog
Penycaerau
Rhiw
Plas-yn-Rhiw
Llanengan

NT

Aberdaron
Llanfaelrhys
Porth Neigwl or Hell's Mouth
Bwl

Braich y Pwll
Uwchmynydd
Aberdaron Bay
NT
NT
NT
NT

Trwy
Cila

Ynys Gwylan-fawr

NT

Pen y Cil

BARDSEY SOUND

St. Mary's Abbey

Bardsey Island
(Ynys Enlli)

C

(B

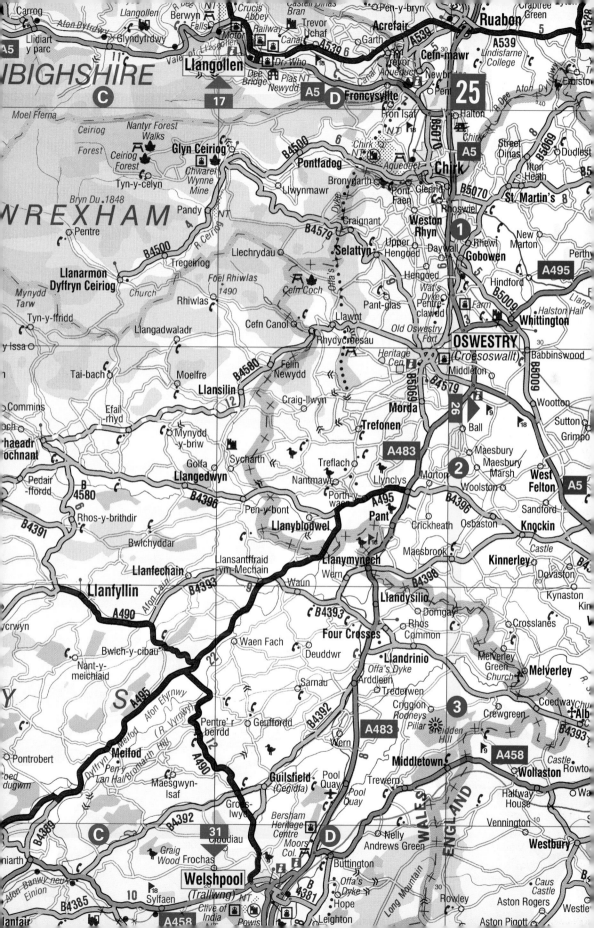

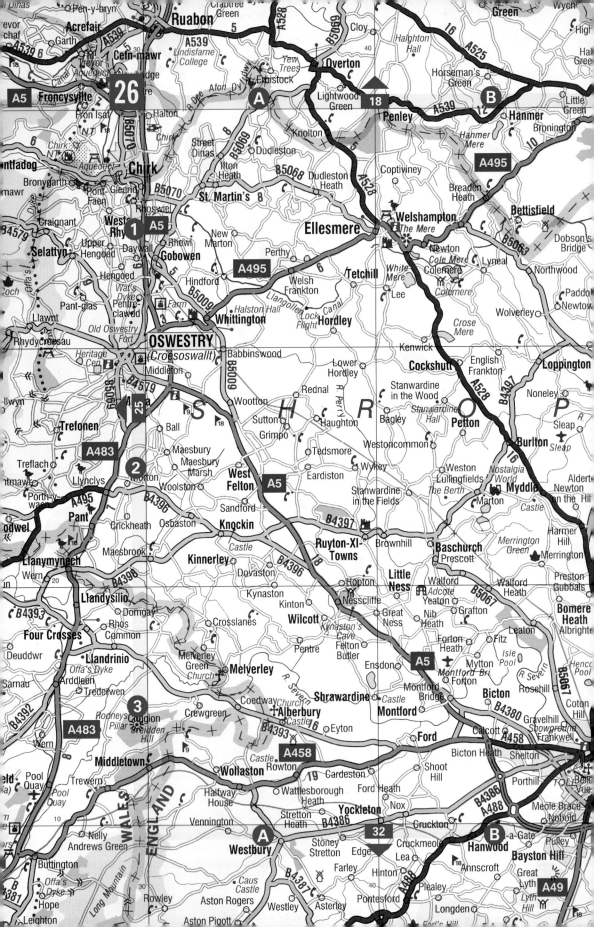

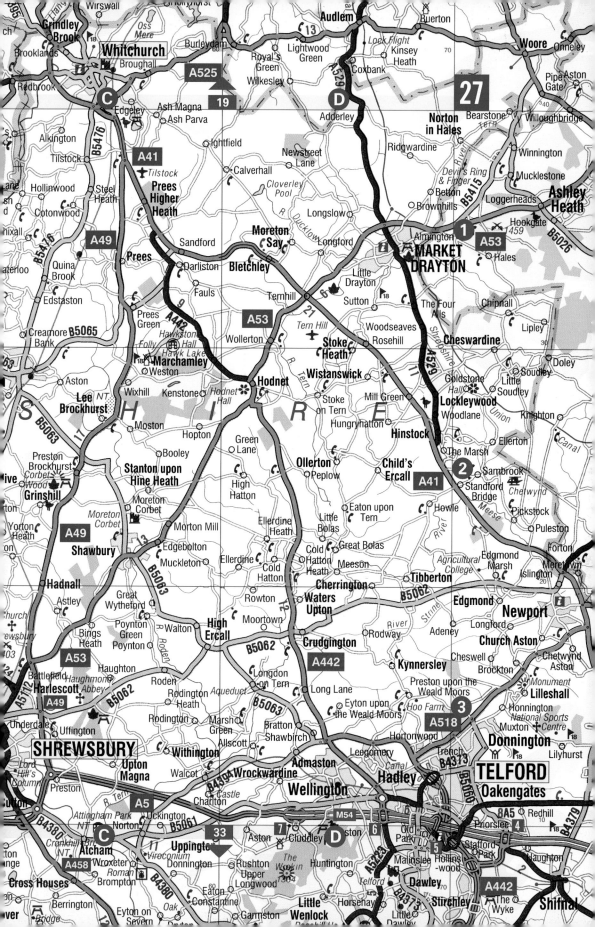

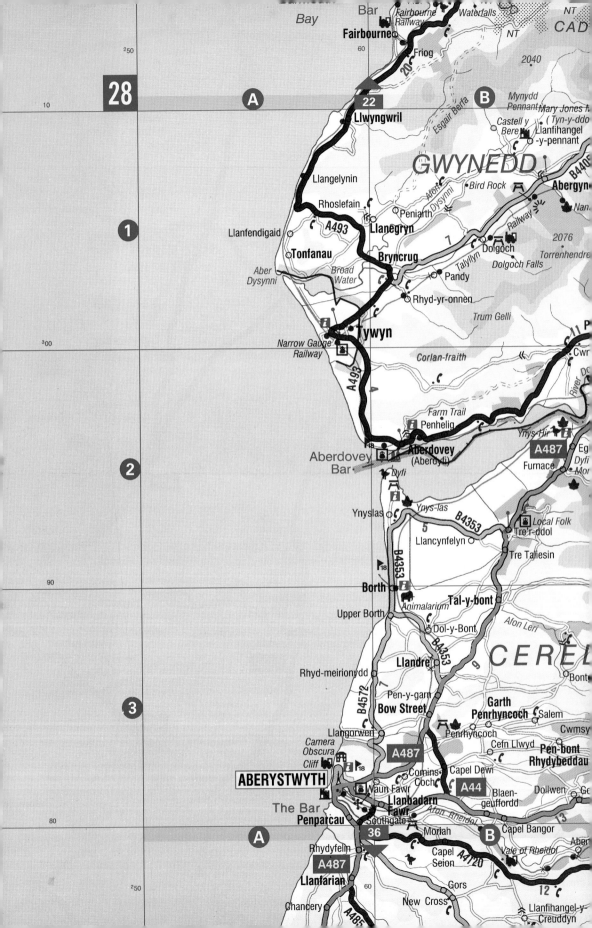

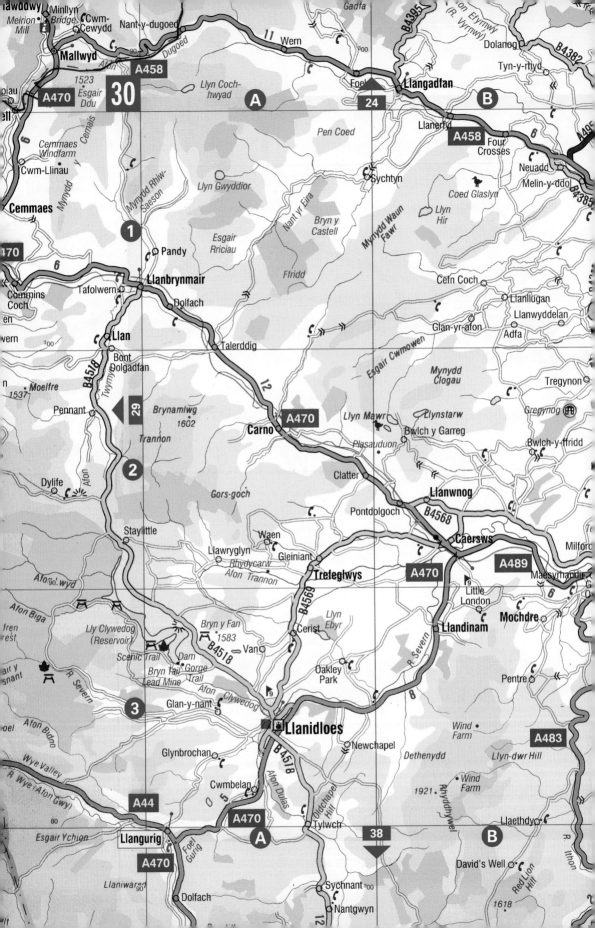

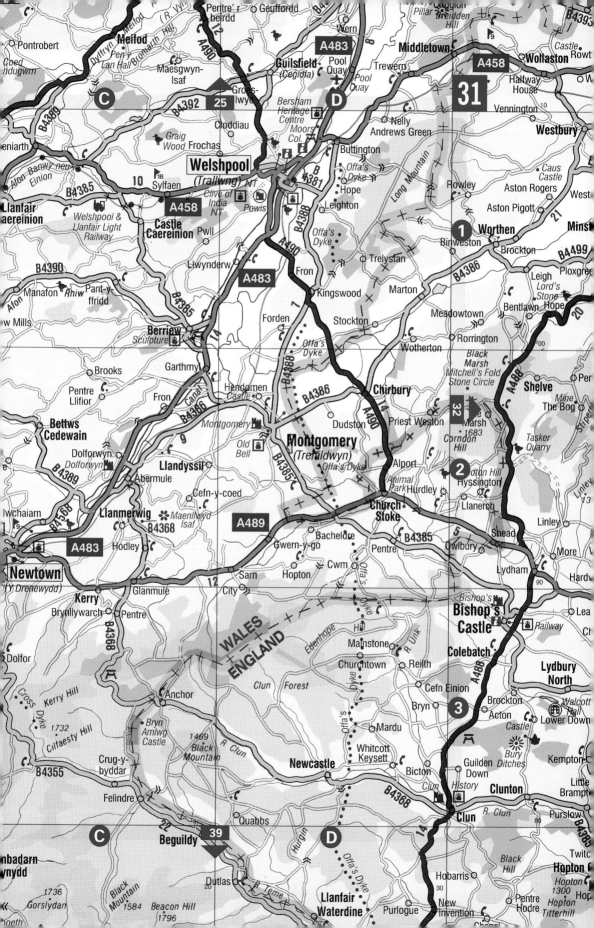

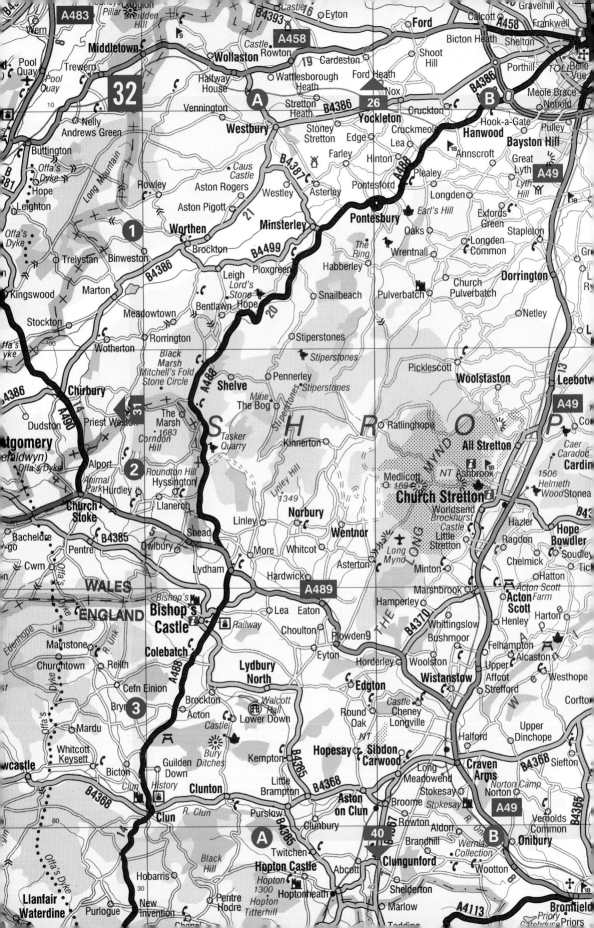

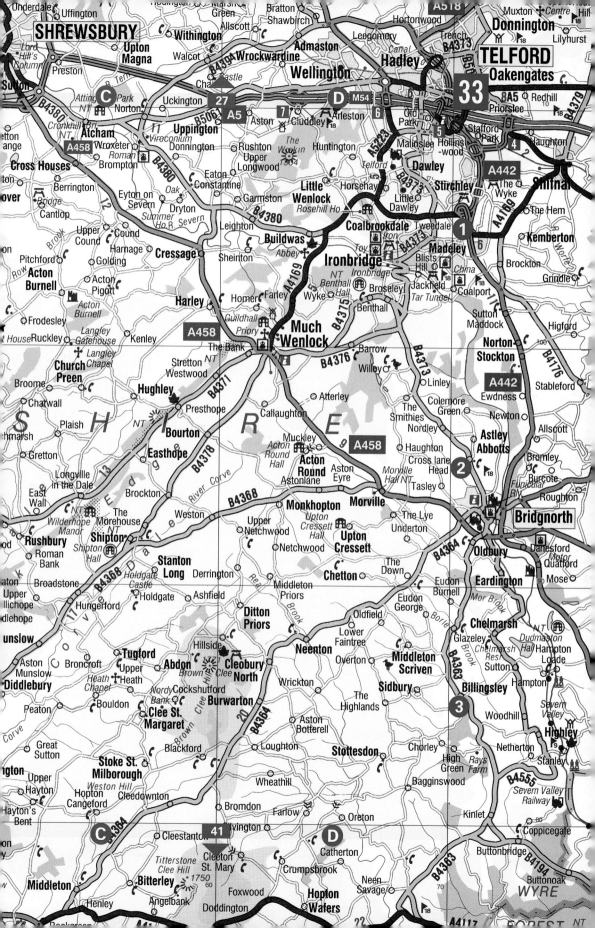

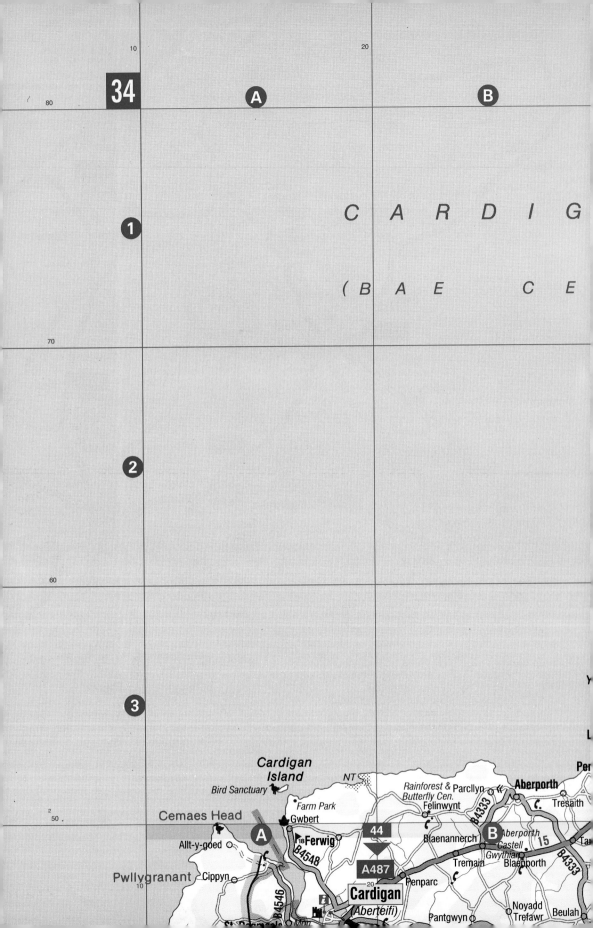

40 250 80

C D 35

1

B A Y

(E D I G I O N)

Carreg Ti-pw

Llanrhystud

70

18

B4337

36

Llansantffraed

Llan-non

A487

2

Rhos
Haminiog

Nebo

Cross
Inn

B4577

Pennant

Sea
Aquarium

Aberarth

Monachty

Aberaeron

Honey
Bee

Vineyard
Aberaeron

Cilcennin

60

Llanaeron

Ffos-y-ffin

A482

Llanerchaeron
NT

Bwl

New Quay
(Ceinewydd)

Llwyncelyn

Newbridge

A487

Gilfachreda

Oakford

Ciliau
Aeron

Afon Aeron

Llunda
fach

Maen-y-
groes

Bird &
Wildlife
Hospital

B4342

8

Llanarth

B4339

8

Trefilan

Cwmtudu

NT

Cross Inn

Geneva

Pen-cae

B4342

Ystrad
Aeron

Talsarn

Nanternis

Honey
Farm

Dihewyd

Felinfach

B4337

ochtyn

NT

Caerwedros

Mydroilyn

B4342

3

Llwyndafydd

Temple Bar

Blaen Celyn

Synod Inn or
Post-mawr

Ffynnon-
oer

og

Pontgarreg

A487

Noah's
Ark
Farm Park

Cribyn

A482

B4334

B4321

A486

Plwmp

B4338

Gorsgoch

250

Brynhoffnant

Pentregat

Talgarreg

Maestir

B4459

Lamp

Countryside
Collection

C

45

D

Aber

Cwrtnewydd

arthen

B4334

Capel
Cynon

Bwlch-y-fadfa

Castell
Howell

250

A475

Llanwnnen

Pentre-bach

Brithdir

Rhydlewis

Ffostrasol

40

Felin
Wnda

Pont-sian

12

Cwmsychpant

Mon.

Penrhiw-nal

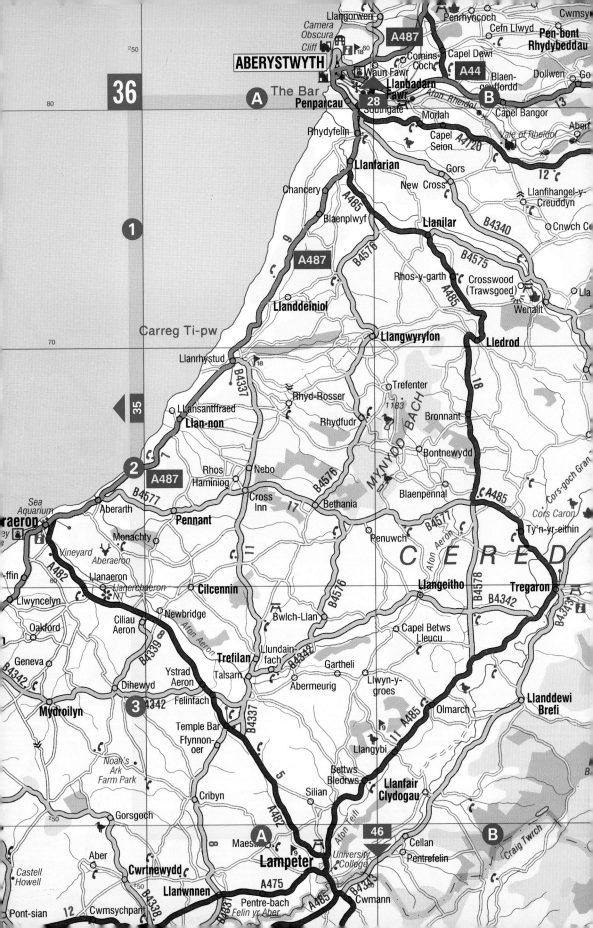

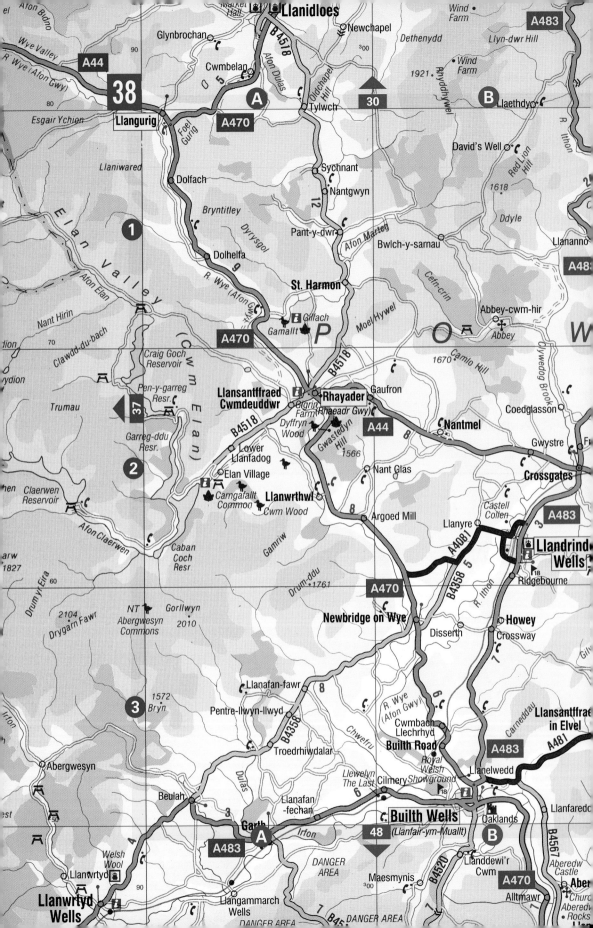

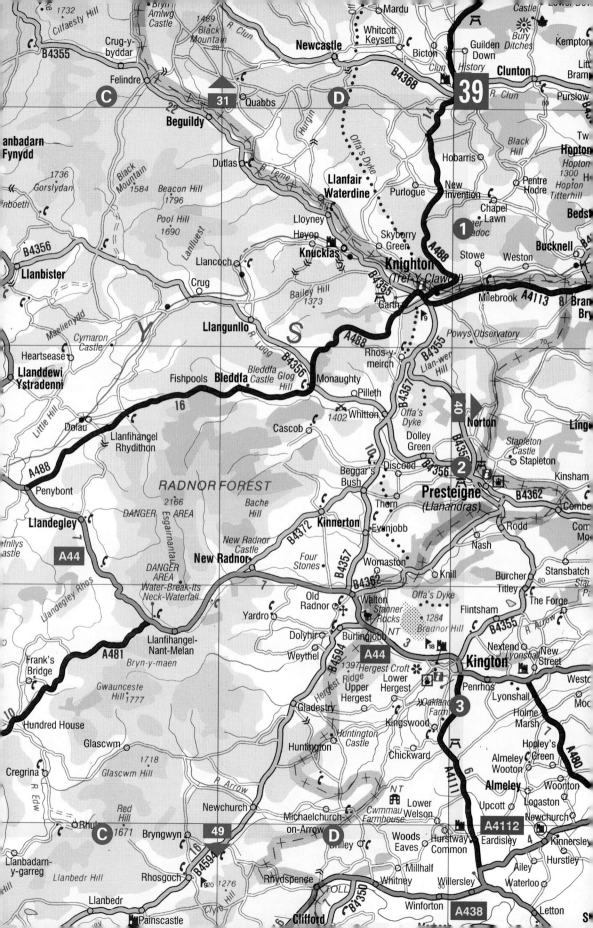

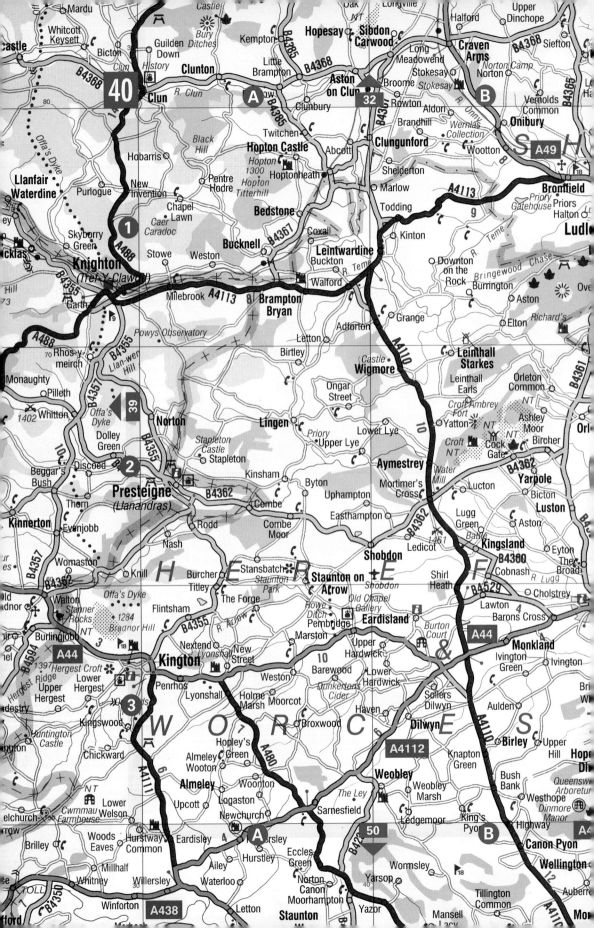

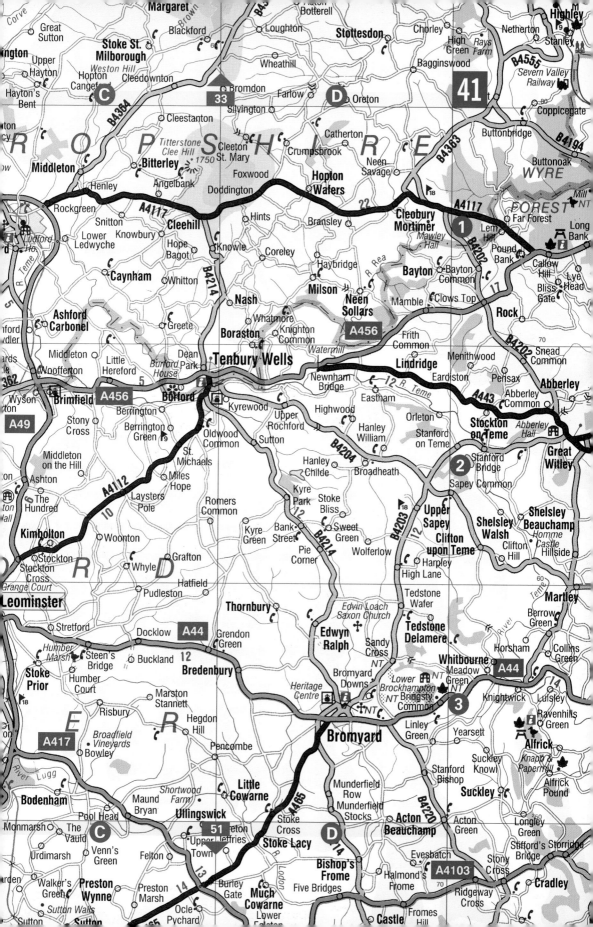

70   **A**   80   **B**

²50

1

40

STRUMBLE HEA

Pen Brush

Trefasser

Penbwchdy

2

Abercastle

Penclegyr

Porthgain   **Trefin**   **Mathry**

Blue
Lagoon

Carreg-gwylan-
fach   Abereiddy   **Llanrhian**   **Castle**

Croes-Goch   B4330

Penclegyr

ST. Penllechwen   NT   Tretio   Treffynnon   P E

DAVID'S   NT   Camhedryn
HEAD   Treleddyd-   R. Solva
fawr   Rhodiad
Y-Brenin
Farm   A487   Caerfarchell   Llandeloy

B4583   R. Alun   St.   Brawdy   Hayscast
Farm   David's   Woollen Mill
Whitesand Bay   **St. David's**   Whitchurch   Gigno
or Porth-mawr   (Tyddewi)
Rhosson

3   Ramsey
Island   NT   Cathedral &   NT   **Solva**   A487   Penycwm
Bishop's   NT
Palace   Castle   **Roch**
Chapel   **PEMBROKESHIRE   COAST**   Newgale   Wood   16

Green Scar   Simp
NATIONAL   PARK   Cr

Ynys Bery   20

70   **A**   80   **B**

S T .   B R I D E S   Rickets   Simpson
Head   Nolton   **Nolton**
Haven   Mot

B A Y   Druidston

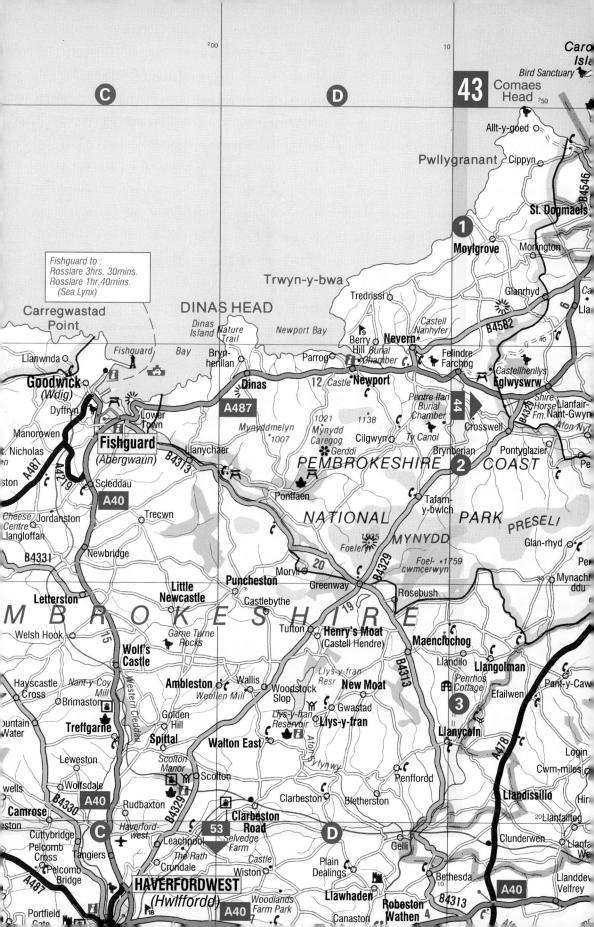

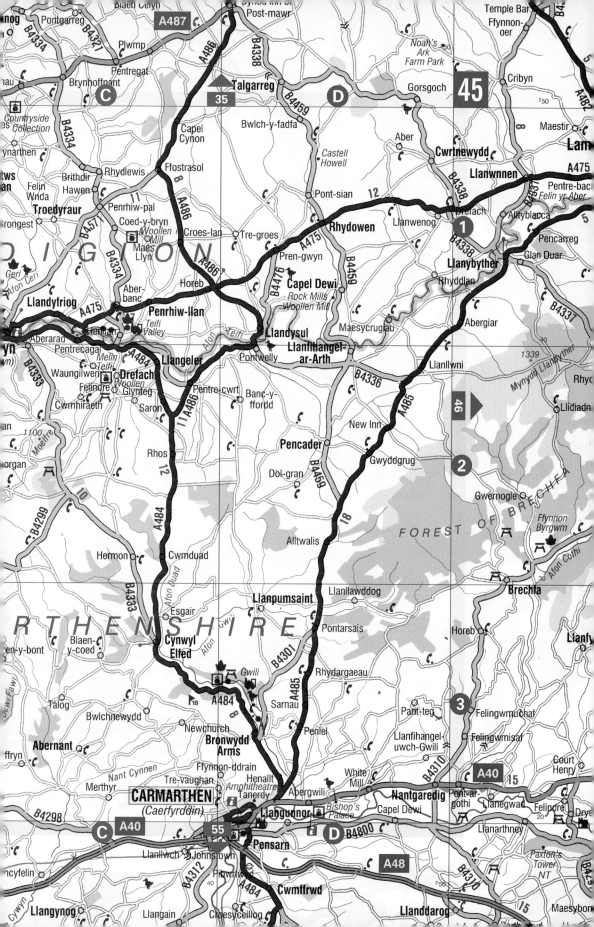

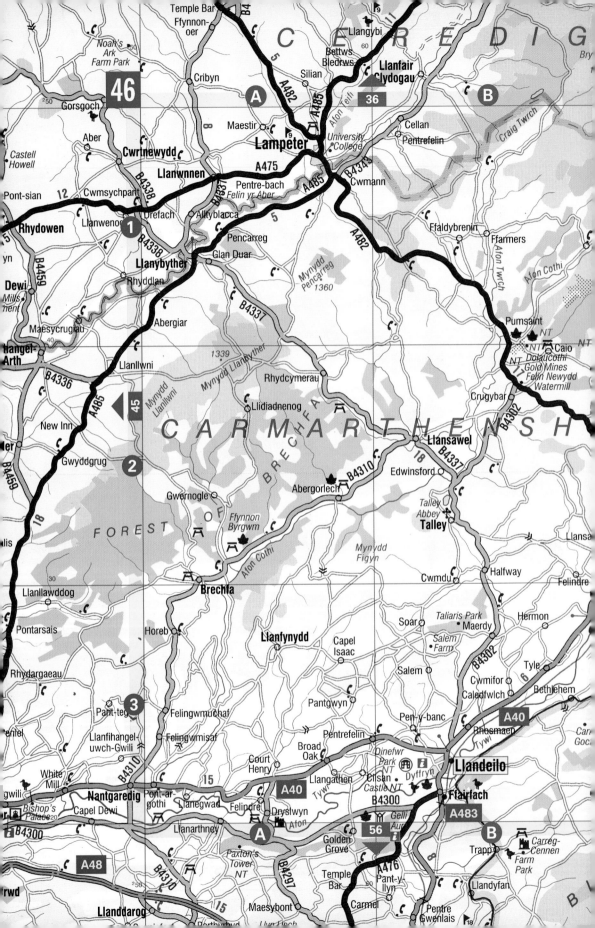

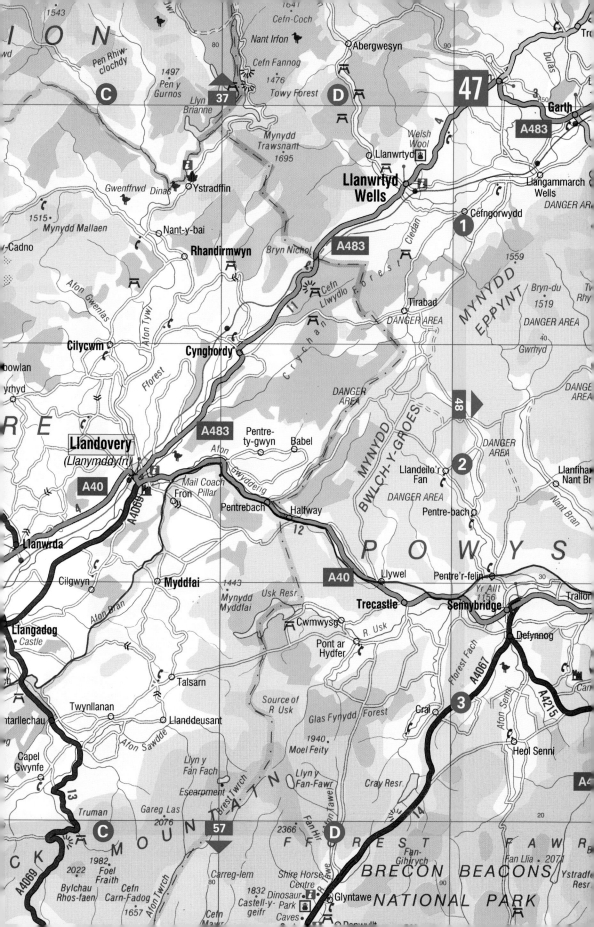

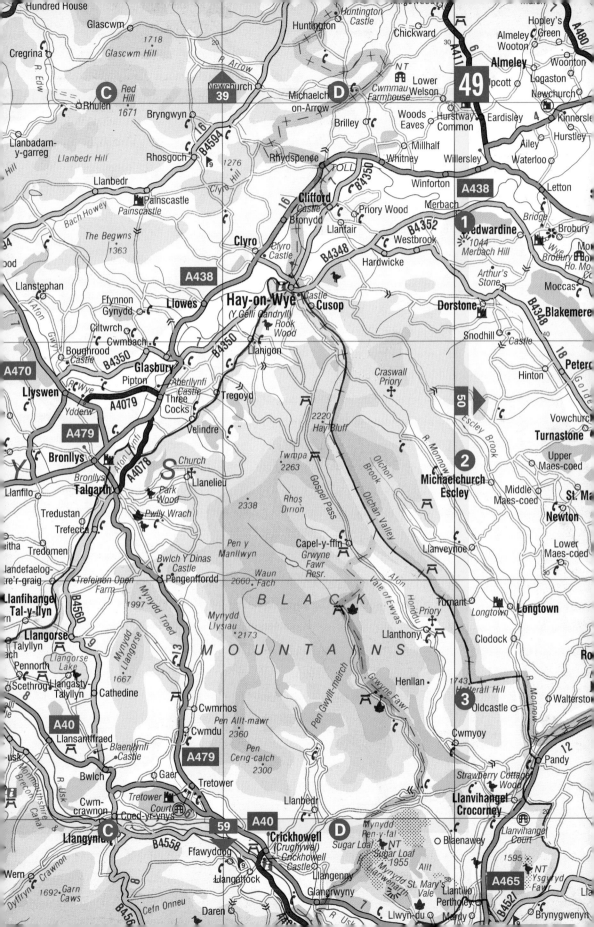

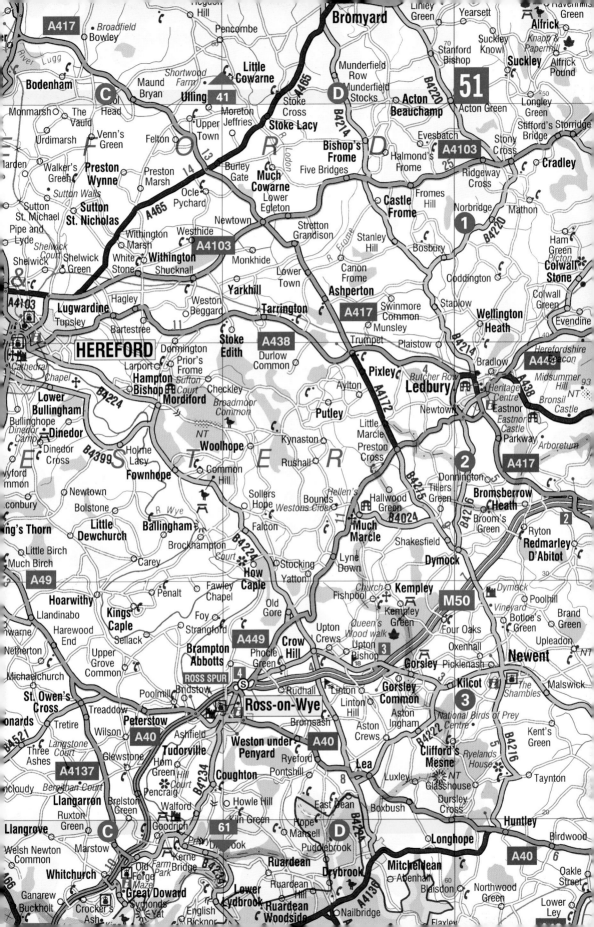

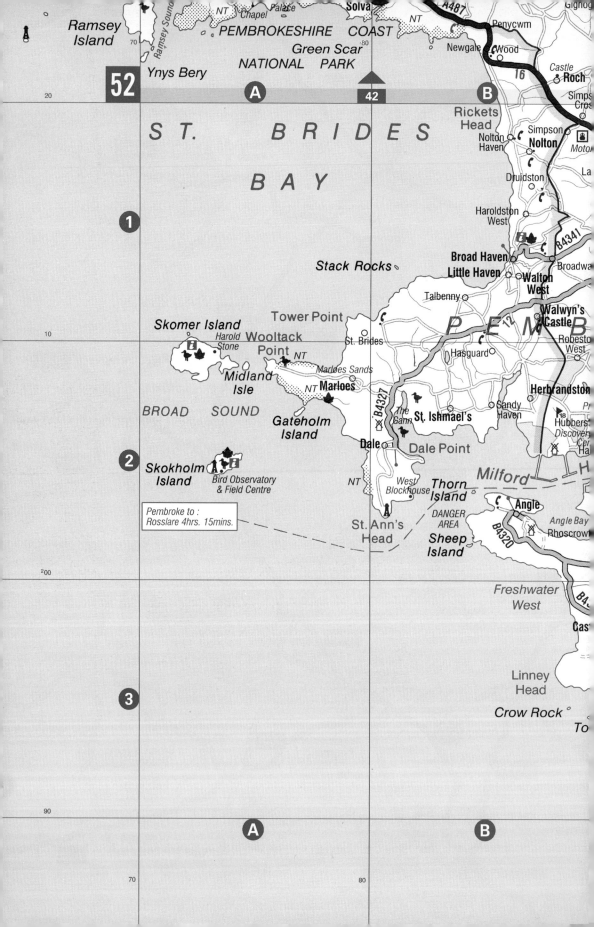

Ramsey Island 70

PEMBROKESHIRE COAST NATIONAL PARK

Chapel
Palace
Solva
NT
Green Scar '80
Ynys Bery

B487
Gignog
Penycwm
Newgale Wood
16
Castle Roch
Simps Cros

Rickets Head
Nolton Haven
Simpson
Nolton
Moto

20

S T.   B R I D E S

B A Y

Druidston

Haroldston West

B434

1

Stack Rocks

Broad Haven
Little Haven
Walton West
Broadwa

Talbenny

Walwyn's Castle

P E M B

Tower Point

St. Brides

Hasguard

Robesto West

10

Skomer Island
Harold Stone
Wooltack Point
NT

Marloes Sands

Herbrandston

Midland Isle

NT Marloes

St. Ishmael's

Sandy Haven

BROAD   SOUND

Gateholm Island

The Gann

Pr
Hubbers
Discover Cer
Ha

Dale

Dale Point

Milford

2

Skokholm Island
Bird Observatory & Field Centre

NT

West Blockhouse

Thorn Island

Angle
Angle Bay
Rhoscrow

Pembroke to :
Rosslare 4hrs. 15mins.

St. Ann's Head

DANGER AREA

Sheep Island

²00

Freshwater West

B4

3

Linney Head

Crow Rock
To

Cas

90

70
80

Llys-y-fran
Llanycefn
Login
Crosshands
Llanboidy
Gellywen
Caerlleon
Meidrim
Penfford
Bletherston
54
Llandissilio
Hiraeth
Henllan
44
Esgair
Plain
Dealings
Gelli
A
Llanfallteg
Amgoed
Cwmfelin
Boeth
Abbey
Llangynin
Afon Cynin
B
Groveland
Adventure
World
Bethesda
A40
Clunderwen
Llanfallteg
West
10
Pwlltrap
Llawhaden
Robeston
Wathen
B4313
Llanddewi
Velfrey
Whitland
A40
Backe
St. Cle
Canaston
Bridge
4
Narberth
(Arberth)
Afon Marlais
Lampeter Vale
Trevaughan
Llwyn-y-brain
Llanddowror
A477
A4066
Mill
Robeston
Back
Wilson
1
Lampeter
Velfrey
Crinow
B4328
6
Halfpenny
Furze
Narberth
Bridge
Castle
Cold
Blow
Llan-mill
Princes
Gate
Tavernspite
7
Red Roses
Llandawke
Oakwood
Canaston
Woods
Leisure
Park
B4315
Templeton
Ludchurch
B4314
4
Llansadurnen
Brook
PEMBROKESHIRE
A4115
Templeton
Llanteg
Marros
Llanmiloe
Bartletwy
6
Reynalton
Thomas
Chapel
A477
Pendine
(Pentywyn)
DANGER
Yerbeston
Loveston
Folly
Farm
Kilgetty
(Cilgeti)
Stepaside
Colby
NT
Summerhill
A4066
DANGER
AREA
Begelly
53
B4586
Cresselly
Jeffreyston
Steam
Sardis
Castle
Amroth
Cresswell
Quay
Broadmoor
Pentlepoir
B4316
Redberth
East
Williamston
Stammers
Saundersfoot
Carew
2
Broadfield
Monkstone
Point
Sageston
Manor House
Leisure Park
A478
New Hedges
Carew
Cheriton
St. Florence
Dinosaur
Experience
B4318
Aqu.
Tenby
CARMARTHEN
Palace
Manorbier
Newton
Gumfreston
(Dinbych-y-Pysgod)
11
Jameston
A4139
Penally
(Penalun)
NT
Manorbier
Lydstep
Giltar Point
Caldey Sound
DANGER
AREA
Old
Castle
Head
St. Margaret's
Island
Priory
Abbey
Caldey
Island
Chapel Point
3
90
A
B
10
20

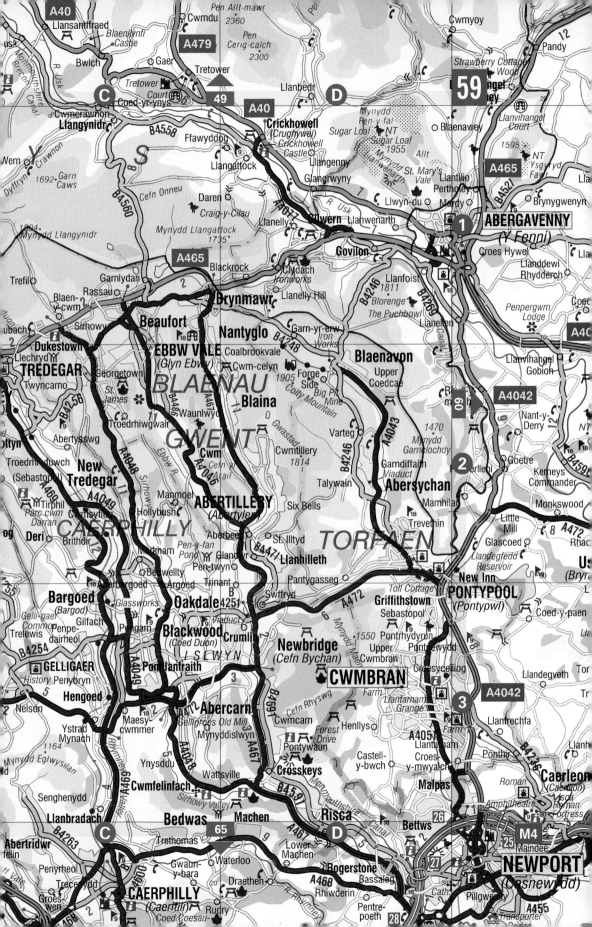

A40
Llansantffraed
Pen Allt-mawr
2360
Cwmdu
Cwmyoy
Pandy
12

Blaenllynfi
Castle
A479
Pen
Cerig-calch
2300
Strawberry Cottage
Wood

Bwlch
Gaer
Tretower
Llanbedr
angel
ey
59
Llanvihangel
Court

C
Tretower
Court
49
A40
D
NT
Ysgryyd
Fawr
1595

Coed-yr-ynys
6
Crickhowell
(Crughywel)
Llangenny
Mynydd
Pen-y-fal
NT
Sugar Loaf
Llantilio
Pertholey
A465

Llangynidr
B4558
Ffawyddog
Crickhowell
Castle
Sugar Loaf
1955
St. Mary's
Vale
Llwyn-du
Mardy
B4521
Brynygwenyn

Nern
Y
Crawnon
1692 Garn
Caws
Cefn Onneu
Llangattock
Glangrwyny
Allt
Llanwenarth
7
ABERGAVENNY
(Y Fenni)

B4560
Daren
Craig-y-Cilau
Llanelly
R Usk
Gilwern
Llanwenarth
1
Croes Hywel
Lla

Mynydd Llangynidr
Mynydd Llangattock
1735
A4077
Govilon
Llanfoist
A4269
Llanddewi
Rhydderch

Trefil
A465
Blackrock
Clydach
Ironworks
B4246
1811
Llanellen
Canal
Coe
A40

Garnlydan
2
Llanelly Hill
Blorenge
The Punchbowl
Penpergwm
Lodge

Blaen-
y-cwm
Rassau
Brynmawr
Garn-yr-erw
Iron
Works
B4248
Langefni

Dukestown
Sirhowy
Beaufort
18
Nantyglo
Blaenavon
Upper
Coedcae
Llanvihangel
Gobion
A4042

TREDEGAR
Georgetown
EBBW VALE
(Glyn Ebwy)
Coalbrookvale
Cwm-celyn
Big Pit
Mine
60
Nant-y-
Derry

Twyncarno
St.
James
BLAENAU
Forge
Side
Coity Mountain
1905
Garndiffaith
Viaduct
Goetre
Kemeys
Commander

Abertysswg
GWENT
Blaina
Waunlwyd
Cwmtillery
1814
Varteg
B4246
Mynydd
Garnclochdy
1470
Monkswood

Troedrhiwfuwch
(Sebastopol)
New
Tredegar
Cwm
Cefn Coed
Talywain
Abersychan
A4043
Perlleni
Goetre
A472

Deri
Tirphil
Parc cwm
Darran
Manmoel
ABERTILLERY
(Abertyleri)
Six Bells
Mamhilad
Trevethin
Little
Mill

CAERPHILLY
Brithdir
Markham
Hollybush
Aberbeeg
St. Illtyd
TORFAEN
Glascoed
Rhac

Pen-y-fan
Pond
Pen-twyn
B4471
Llanhilleth
Llandegfedd
Reservoir

Bedwellty
Glandwr
Trinant
Pantygasseg
New Inn
A472

Bargoed
(Bargod)
Aberbargoed
Argoed
Swffryd
Toll Cottage
PONTYPOOL
(Pontypwl)
Coed-y-paen

Glassworks
Oakdale
B4251
ISLWYN
Griffithstown
Sebastopol
Ponthir

Gilfach
Pengam
Blackwood
(Coed Duon)
Crumlin
Newbridge
(Cefn Bychan)
Pontrhydyrun
Pontnewydd

GELLIGAER
Pontllanfraith
Viaduct
1550
Upper
Cwmbran
A4042

Penybryn
A4049
Abercarn
CWMBRAN
Llantarnam
Grange
3
Llandegveth

Hengoed
Maesy-
cwmmer
Gelligroes Old Mill
Mynyddislwyn
Cwmcarn
Forest
Drive
Henllys
Croesyceiliog
A4051

Nelson
Ystrad
Mynach
1164
Ynysddu
Wattsville
Pontywaun
Castell-
y-bwch
A405
Llantarnam
Croes-
y-mwyalch
B4236
Llanfrechfa

Llanbradach
Cwmfelinfach
Sirhowy Valley
Crosskeys
B4591
Malpas
Roman
Caerleon
(Caerllion)

Abertridwr
felin
B4263
Bedwas
Machen
Risca
Bettws
26
27
25
M4
Amphitheatre
Roman
Fortress

C
65
Trethomas
D
Canal
18
Maindee

Penyrheol
Gwaun-
y-bara
Waterloo
Lower
Machen
A467
Rogerstone
Bassaleg
Transporter
NEWPORT
(Casnewydd)

CAERPHILLY
(Caerffili)
Draethen
A468
Rhiwderin
Pentre-
poeth
28
A455

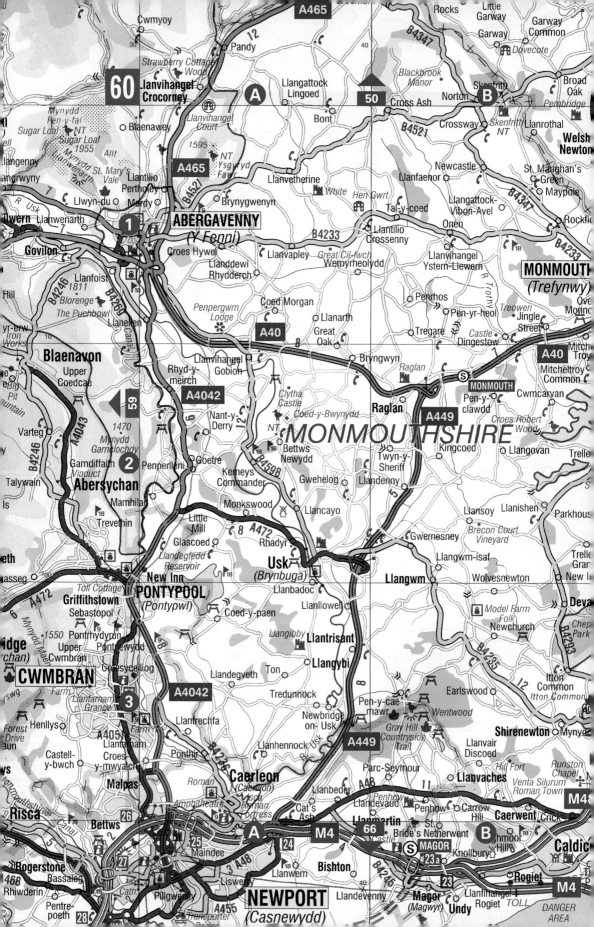

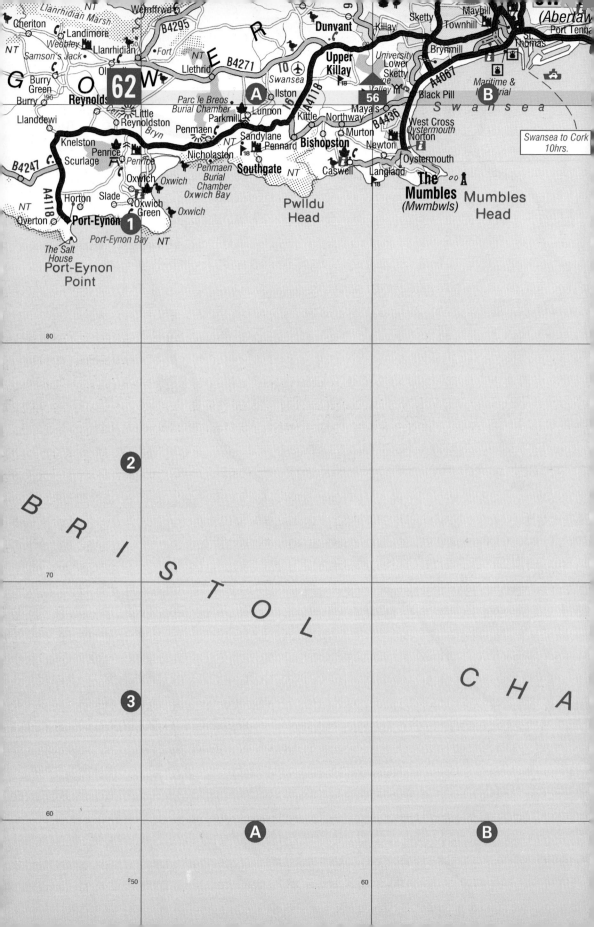

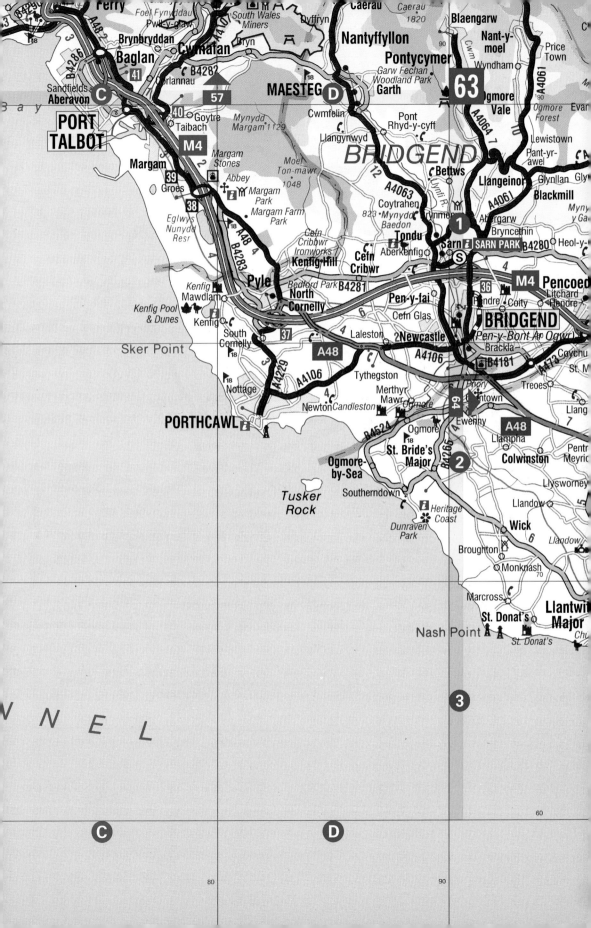

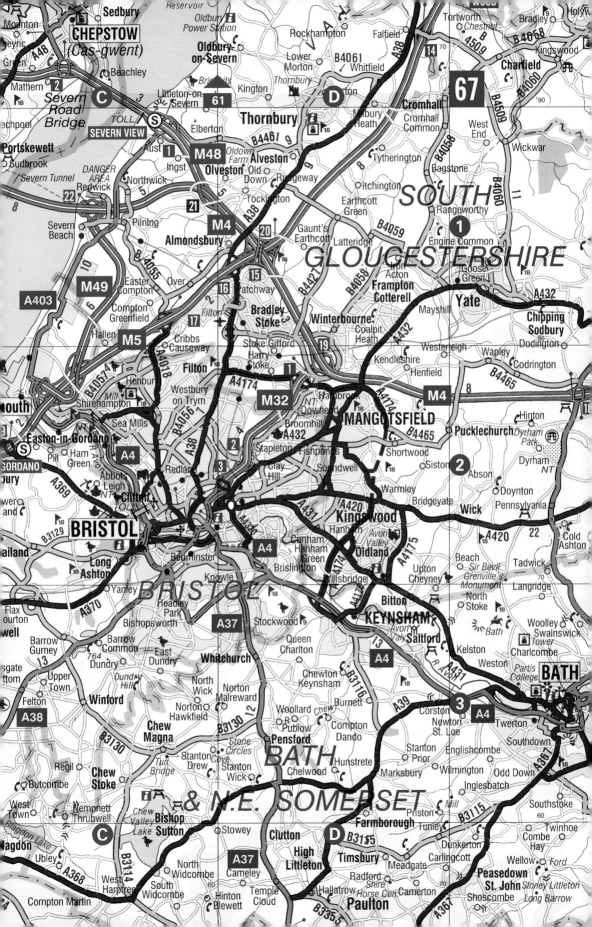

Index to Cities, Towns, Villages, Hamlets and Locations.

(1) A strict alphabetical order is used e.g. Ashperton follows Ash Parva but precedes Ashton.

(2) The map reference given refers to the actual map square in which the town spot or built-up area is located and not to the place name.

(3) Where two or more places of the same name occur in the same County or Unitary Authority, the nearest large town is also given; e.g. Allscott. *Shrp* —2D 33 (nr. Bridgnorth) indicates that Allscott is located in square 2D on page 33 and is situated near Bridgnorth in the County of Shropshire.

COUNTIES AND UNITARY AUTHORITIES with the abbreviations used in this index.

Bath & N E Somerset : *Bath*
Blaenau Gwent : *Blae*
Bridgend : *Bri*
Bristol : *Bris*
Caerphilly : *Cphy*
Cardiff : *Card*
Carmarthenshire : *Carm*
Ceredigion : *Cdgn*

Cheshire : *Ches*
Conwy : *Cnwy*
Denbighshire : *Den*
Flintshire : *Flin*
Gloucestershire : *Glos*
Greater Manchester : *G.Mn*
Gwynedd : *Gwyn*
Hereford & Worcester : *H&W*

Isle of Anglesey : *IOA*
Lancashire : *Lanc*
Merseyside : *Mers*
Merthyr Tydfil : *Mert*
Monmouthshire : *Mon*
Neath Port Talbot : *Neat*
Newport : *Newp*
North Somerset : *N.Sm*

Pembrokeshire : *Pemb*
Perth & Kinross : *Per*
Powys : *Powy*
Rhondda Cynon Taff : *Rhon*
Shropshire : *Shrp*
Somerset : *Som*
South Gloucestershire : *S.Glo*
Staffordshire : *Staf*

Swansea, the City &
    County of : *Swan*
Torfaen : *Torf*
Vale of Glamorgan, The : *V.Gl*
Wrexham : *Wrex*

INDEX TO STREETS

Abberley. *H&W* —2D 41
Abberley Common. *H&W*
    —2D 41
Abbey-cwm-hir. *Powy*
    —1B 38
Abbey Dore. *H&W* —2A 50
Abbots Leigh. *N.Sm* —2C 67
Abcott. *Shrp* —1A 40
Abdon. *Shrp* —3C 33
Abenhall. *Glos* —1D 61
Aber. *Cdgn* —1D 45
Aberaeron. *Cdgn* —2D 35
Aberaman. *Rhon* —2B 58
Aberangell. *Powy* —3D 23
Aberarad. *Carm* —2C 45
Aberarth. *Cdgn* —2D 35
Aberavon. *Neat* —3C 57
Aber-banc. *Cdgn* —1C 45
Aberbargoed. *Cphy* —3C 59
Aberbeeg. *Blae* —2D 59
Aberbowlan. *Carm* —2B 46
Aberbran. *Powy* —3A 48
Abercanaid. *Mert* —2B 58
Abercarn. *Cphy* —3D 59
Abercastle. *Pemb* —2B 42
Abercegir. *Powy* —1D 29
Abercraf. *Powy* —1D 57
Abercregan. *Neat* —3D 57
Abercwmboi. *Rhon* —3B 58
Abercych. *Pemb* —1B 44
Abercynon. *Rhon* —3B 58
Aber-Cywarch. *Gwyn* —3D 23
Aberdar. *Rhon* —2A 58
Aberdare. *Rhon* —2A 58
Aberdaron. *Gwyn* —2A 20
Aberdaugleddau. *Pemb*
    —2C 53
Aberdesach. *Gwyn* —2D 13
Aberdovey. *Gwyn* —2B 28
Aberdulais. *Neat* —3C 57
Aberdyfi. *Gwyn* —2B 28
Aberedw. *Powy* —1B 48
Abereiddy. *Pemb* —2A 42
Abererch. *Gwyn* —1C 21
Aberfan. *Mert* —2B 58
Aberffraw. *IOA* —1C 13
Aberffrwd. *Cdgn* —1B 36
Abergarw. *Bri* —1A 64
Abergarwed. *Neat* —2D 57
Abergavenny. *Mon* —1A 60
Abergele. *Cnwy* —3A 8
Abergiar. *Carm* —1A 46
Abergorlech. *Carm* —2A 46
Abergwaun. *Pemb* —2C 43
Abergwesyn. *Powy* —3D 37
Abergwili. *Carm* —3D 45
Abergwynfi. *Neat* —3D 57
Abergwyngregyn. *Gwyn*
    —3B 6
Abergynolwyn. *Gwyn* —1B 28
Aberhonddu. *Powy* —3B 48
Aberhosan. *Powy* —2D 29
Aberkenfig. *Bri* —1D 63

Aberllefenni. *Cdgn* —1C 29
Abermaw. *Gwyn* —3B 22
Abermeurig. *Cdgn* —3A 36
Abermule. *Powy* —2C 31
Abernant. *Carm* —3C 45
Abernant. *Rhon* —2B 58
Aber-oer. *Wrex* —3D 17
Aberpennar. *Rhon* —3B 58
Aberporth. *Cdgn* —3B 34
Abersoch. *Gwyn* —2C 21
Abersychan. *Torf* —2D 59
Abertawe. *Swan* —3B 56
Aberteifi. *Cdgn* —1A 44
Aberthin. *V.Gl* —2B 64
Abertillery. *Blae* —2D 59
Abertridwr. *Cphy* —1C 65
Abertridwr. *Powy* —3B 24
Abertyleri. *Blae* —2D 59
Abertysswg. *Cphy* —2C 59
Aber Village. *Powy* —3C 49
Aberyscir. *Powy* —3B 48
Aberystwyth. *Cdgn* —3A 28
Abram. *G.Mn* —1D 11
Abson. *S.Glo* —2D 67
Aconbury. *H&W* —2C 51
Acrefair. *Wrex* —3D 17
Acton. *Ches* —2D 19
Acton. *Shrp* —3A 32
Acton. *Wrex* —2A 18
Acton Beauchamp. *H&W*
    —3D 41
Acton Bridge. *Ches* —3D 11
Acton Burnell. *Shrp* —1C 33
Acton Green. *H&W* —3D 41
Acton Pigott. *Shrp* —1C 33
Acton Round. *Shrp* —2D 33
Acton Scott. *Shrp* —3B 32
Adderley. *Shrp* —1D 27
Adeney. *Shrp* —3D 27
Adfa. *Powy* —1B 30
Adforton. *H&W* —1B 40
Admaston. *Shrp* —3D 27
Adpar. *Cdgn* —1C 45
Afon-wen. *Flin* —3C 9
Aigburth. *Mers* —2A 10
Ailey. *H&W* —1A 50
Aintree. *Mers* —1A 10
Alberbury. *Shrp* —3A 26
Albert Town. *Pemb* —1C 53
Albrighton. *Shrp* —3B 26
Alcaston. *Shrp* —3B 32
Aldersey Green. *Ches* —2B 18
Alderton. *Shrp* —2B 26
Aldford. *Ches* —2B 18
Aldon. *Shrp* —1B 40
Alfrick. *H&W* —3D 41
Alfrick Pound. *H&W* —3D 41
Alkington. *Shrp* —1C 27
Allaston. *Glos* —2D 61
Allensmore. *H&W* —2B 50
Allerton. *Mers* —2B 10
Allscott. *Shrp* —2D 33
    (nr. Bridgnorth)

Allscott. *Shrp* —3D 27
    (nr. Wellington)
All Stretton. *Shrp* —2B 32
Allt. *Carm* —2A 56
Alltami. *Flin* —1D 17
Alltmawr. *Powy* —1B 48
Alltwalis. *Carm* —2D 45
Alltwen. *Neat* —2C 57
Alltyblacca. *Cdgn* —1A 46
Allt-y-goed. *Pemb* —1A 44
Almeley. *H&W* —3A 40
Almeley Wooton. *H&W*
    —3A 40
Almington. *Staf* —1D 27
Almondsbury. *S.Glo* —1D 67
Alport. *Powy* —2D 31
Alpraham. *Ches* —2C 19
Alvanley. *Ches* —3B 10
Alveley. *Shrp* —3D 33
Alveston. *S.Glo* —1D 67
Alvington. *Glos* —2D 61
Ambleston. *Pemb* —3C 43
Amlwch. *IOA* —1D 5
Amlwch Port. *IOA* —1D 5
Ammanford. *Carm* —1B 56
Amroth. *Pemb* —2A 54
Anchor. *Shrp* —3C 31
Anderton. *Ches* —3D 11
Anelog. *Gwyn* —2A 20
Anfield. *Mers* —1A 10
Angelbank. *Shrp* —1C 41
Angle. *Pemb* —2B 52
Annscroft. *Shrp* —1B 32
Antrobus. *Ches* —3D 11
Apley. *Shrp* —2C 11
Appleton Thorn. *Ches* —2D 11
Arberth. *Pemb* —1A 54
Arddleen. *Powy* —3D 25
Argoed. *Cphy* —3C 59
Argoed Mill. *Powy* —2A 38
Arleston. *Shrp* —3D 27
Arley. *Ches* —2D 11
Arlingham. *Glos* —1D 61
Arthog. *Gwyn* —3B 22
Ashbrook. *Shrp* —2B 32
Ashfield. *H&W* —3C 51
Ashfield. *Shrp* —3C 33
Ashford Bowdler. *Shrp*
    —1C 41
Ashford Carbonel. *Shrp*
    —1C 41
Ashley Heath. *Staf* —1D 27
Ashley Moor. *H&W* —2B 40
Ash Magna. *Shrp* —1C 27
Ash Parva. *Shrp* —1C 27
Ashperton. *H&W* —1D 51
Ashton. *Ches* —1C 19
Ashton. *H&W* —2C 41
Ashton-in-Makerfield. *G.Mn*
    —1C 11
Asterley. *Shrp* —1A 32
Asterton. *Shrp* —2A 32
Astley. *G.Mn* —1D 11

Astley. *Shrp* —3C 27
Astley Abbotts. *Shrp* —2D 33
Aston. *Ches* —3C 11
    (nr. Frodsham)
Aston. *Ches* —3D 19
    (nr. Nantwich)
Aston. *Flin* —1A 18
Aston. *H&W* —2B 40
    (nr. Leominster)
Aston. *H&W* —1B 40
    (nr. Ludlow)
Aston. *Shrp* —1D 33
    (nr. Wellington)
Aston. *Shrp* —2C 27
    (nr. Wem)
Aston. *Staf* —3D 19
Aston Botterell. *Shrp* —3D 33
Aston Crews. *H&W* —3D 51
Aston Eyre. *Shrp* —2D 33
Aston Ingham. *H&W* —3D 51
Aston juxta Mondrum. *Ches*
    —2D 19
Astonlane. *Shrp* —2D 33
Aston Munslow. *Shrp* —3C 33
Aston on Clun. *Shrp* —3A 32
Aston Pigott. *Shrp* —1A 32
Aston Rogers. *Shrp* —1A 32
Atcham. *Shrp* —1C 33
Atherton. *G.Mn* —1D 11
Atterley. *Shrp* —2D 33
Auberrow. *H&W* —1B 50
Audlem. *Ches* —3D 19
Aulden. *H&W* —3B 40
Aust. *S.Glo* —1C 67
Avonmouth. *Bris* —2C 67
Awre. *Glos* —2D 61
Aylburton. *Glos* —2D 61
Aylburton Common. *Glos*
    —2D 61
Aylton. *H&W* —2D 51
Aymestrey. *H&W* —2B 40

Babbinswood. *Shrp* —2A 26
Babel. *Carm* —2D 47
Babell. *Flin* —3C 9
Bachau. *IOA* —2D 5
Bacheldre. *Powy* —2D 31
Bachymbyd Fawr. *Den*
    —1B 16
Backe. *Carm* —1B 54
Backford. *Ches* —3B 10
Backwell. *N.Sm* —3B 66
Bacton. *H&W* —2A 50
Bae Cinmel. *Cnwy* —2A 8
Bae Colwyn. *Cnwy* —3D 7
Bae Penrhyn. *Cnwy* —2D 7
Bagginswood. *Shrp* —3D 33
Bagillt. *Flin* —3D 9
Baglan. *Neat* —3C 57
Bagley. *Shrp* —2B 26
Bagstone. *S.Glo* —1D 67
Bagwy Llydiart. *H&W* —3B 50

Bala. *Gwyn* —1A 24
Balderton. *Ches* —1A 18
Ball. *Shrp* —2A 26
Ballingham. *H&W* —2C 51
Bancffosfelen. *Carm* —1D 55
Bancycapel. *Carm* —1D 55
Bancyfelin. *Carm* —1C 55
Banc-y-ffordd. *Carm* —2D 45
Bangor. *Gwyn* —3A 6
Bangor-is-y-coed. *Wrex*
    —3A 18
Bank Street. *H&W* —2D 41
Bank, The. *Shrp* —2D 33
Banwell. *N.Sm* —3A 66
Barbridge. *Ches* —2D 19
Barewood. *H&W* —3A 40
Bargod. *Cphy* —3C 59
Bargoed. *Cphy* —3C 59
Barmouth. *Gwyn* —3B 22
Barnsley. *Shrp* —2D 33
Barnston. *Mers* —2D 9
Barnton. *Ches* —3D 11
Barons Cross. *H&W* —3B 40
Barri. *V.Gl* —3C 65
Barrow. *Shrp* —1D 33
Barrow Common. *N.Sm*
    —3C 67
Barrow Gurney. *N.Sm* —3C 67
Barrow Nook. *Lanc* —1B 10
Barrow's Green. *Ches* —2C 11
Barry. *V.Gl* —3C 65
Barry Island. *V.Gl* —3C 65
Bartestree. *H&W* —1C 51
Barton. *Ches* —2B 18
Barton. *N.Sm* —3A 66
Baschurch. *Shrp* —2B 26
Bassaleg. *Newp* —1D 65
Bate Heath. *Ches* —3D 11
Bath. *Bath* —3D 67
Battle. *Powy* —2B 48
Battlefield. *Shrp* —3C 27
Bayston Hill. *Shrp* —1B 32
Bayton. *H&W* —1D 41
Bayton Common. *H&W*
    —1D 41
Beach. *S.Glo* —2D 67
Beachley. *Glos* —3C 61
Bearstone. *Shrp* —1D 27
Beaufort. *Blae* —1C 59
Beaumaris. *IOA* —3B 6
Bebington. *Mers* —2A 10
Beddau. *Rhon* —1B 64
Beddgelert. *Gwyn* —3A 14
Bedford. *G.Mn* —1D 11
Bedlinog. *Mert* —2B 58
Bedminster. *Bris* —2C 67
Bedstone. *Shrp* —1A 40
Bedwas. *Cphy* —1C 65
Bedwellty. *Cphy* —2C 59
Beeston. *Ches* —2C 19
Began. *Card* —1D 65
Begelly. *Pemb* —2A 54
Beggar's Bush. *Powy* —2D 39

Beguildy. *Powy* —1C **39**
Belgrano. *Cnwy* —3A **8**
Belle Vue. *Shrp* —3B **26**
Benllech. *IOA* —2A **6**
Benthall. *Shrp* —1D **33**
Bentlawn. *Shrp* —1A **32**
Berkeley. *Glos* —3D **61**
Berriew. *Powy* —1C **31**
Berrington. *H&W* —2C **41**
Berrington. *Shrp* —1C **33**
Berrington Green. *H&W*
    —2C **41**
Berrow Green. *H&W* —3D **41**
Berry Hill. *Glos* —1C **61**
Berry Hill. *Pemb* —1D **43**
Bersham. *Wrex* —3A **18**
Berthengam. *Flin* —3C **9**
Berwyn. *Den* —3C **17**
Bethania. *Cdgn* —2A **36**
Bethania. *Gwyn* —3C **15**
   (nr. Blaenau Ffestiniog)
Bethania. *Gwyn* —2B **14**
   (nr. Caernarfon)
Bethel. *Gwyn* —1A **24**
   (nr. Bala)
Bethel. *Gwyn* —1A **14**
   (nr. Caernarfon)
Bethel. *IOA* —3C **5**
Bethesda. *Gwyn* —1B **14**
Bethesda. *Pemb* —1D **53**
Bethlehem. *Carm* —3B **46**
Betley. *Staf* —3D **19**
Bettisfield. *Wrex* —1B **26**
Betton. *Shrp* —1D **27**
Betton Strange. *Shrp* —1C **33**
Bettws. *Bri* —1D **63**
Bettws. *Newp* —3D **59**
Bettws Bledrws. *Cdgn* —3A **36**
Bettws Cedewain. *Powy*
    —2C **31**
Bettws Evan. *Cdgn* —1C **45**
Bettws Gwerfil Goch. *Den*
    —3B **16**
Bettws Newydd. *Mon* —2A **60**
Betws. *Carm* —1B **56**
Betws Garmon. *Gwyn* —2A **14**
Betws-y-Coed. *Cnwy* —2C **15**
Betws-yn-Rhos. *Cnwy* —3A **8**
Beulah. *Cdgn* —1B **44**
Beulah. *Powy* —3A **38**
Bevington. *Glos* —3D **61**
Bickershaw. *G.Mn* —1D **11**
Bickerton. *Ches* —2C **19**
Bickley Moss. *Ches* —3C **19**
Bicton. *H&W* —2B **40**
Bicton. *Shrp* —3D **31**
   (nr. Bishop's Castle)
Bicton. *Shrp* —3B **26**
   (nr. Shrewsbury)
Bicton Heath. *Shrp* —3B **26**
Bidston. *Mers* —2A **10**
Billinge. *Mers* —1C **11**
Billingsley. *Shrp* —3D **33**
Bilson Green. *Glos* —1D **61**
Bings Heath. *Shrp* —3C **27**
Binweston. *Shrp* —1A **32**
Bircher. *H&W* —2B **40**
Birchgrove. *Card* —2C **65**
Birchgrove. *Swan* —3C **57**
Birch Heath. *Ches* —1C **19**
Birch Hill. *Ches* —3C **11**
Birdwood. *Glos* —1D **61**
Birkenhead. *Mers* —2A **10**
Birley. *H&W* —3B **40**
Birtley. *H&W* —2A **40**
Bishop's Castle. *Shrp* —3A **32**
Bishop's Frome. *H&W*
    —1D **51**
Bishopston. *Swan* —4A **62**
Bishopstone. *H&W* —1B **50**
Bishop Sutton. *Bath* —3C **67**
Bishopsworth. *Bris* —3C **67**

Bishton. *Newp* —1A **66**
Bitterley. *Shrp* —1C **41**
Bitton. *S.Glo* —3D **67**
Blackbrook. *Mers* —1C **11**
Blackford. *Shrp* —3C **33**
Blackmill. *Bri* —1A **64**
Blackmoor. *G.Mn* —1D **11**
Black Pill. *Swan* —3B **56**
Blackrock. *Mon* —1D **59**
Black Tar. *Pemb* —2C **53**
Blacktown. *Newp* —1D **65**
Blackwood. *Cphy* —3C **59**
Blacon. *Ches* —1A **18**
Blaenannerch. *Cdgn* —1B **44**
Blaenau Dolwyddelan. *Cnwy*
    —2B **14**
Blaenau Ffestiniog. *Gwyn*
    —3C **15**
Blaenavon. *Torf* —2D **59**
Blaenawey. *Mon* —1D **59**
Blaen Celyn. *Cdgn* —3C **35**
Blaen Clydach. *Rhon* —2A **58**
Blaenffos. *Pemb* —2A **44**
Blaengarw. *Bri* —3A **58**
Blaen-geuffordd. *Cdgn*
    —3B **28**
Blaengwrach. *Neat* —2D **57**
Blaengwynfi. *Neat* —3D **57**
Blaenllechau. *Rhon* —3B **18**
Blaenpennal. *Cdgn* —2B **36**
Blaenplwyf. *Cdgn* —1A **36**
Blaenporth. *Cdgn* —1B **44**
Blaenrhondda. *Rhon* —3A **58**
Blaenwaun. *Carm* —3B **44**
Blaen-y-coed. *Carm* —3C **45**
Blaen-y-cwm. *Blae* —1C **59**
Blaenycwm. *Rhon* —3A **58**
Blagdon. *N.Sm* —3C **67**
Blaina. *Blae* —2D **59**
Blaisdon. *Glos* —1D **61**
Blakemere. *H&W* —1A **50**
Blakeney. *Glos* —2D **61**
Blakenhall. *Ches* —3D **19**
Bleadon. *N.Sm* —3A **66**
Bleddfa. *Powy* —2D **39**
Bletchley. *Shrp* —1D **27**
Bletherston. *Pemb* —3D **43**
Bliss Gate. *H&W* —1D **41**
Blists Hill. *Shrp* —1D **33**
Blue Anchor. *Swan* —3A **56**
Bodedern. *IOA* —2C **5**
Bodelwyddan. *Den* —3B **8**
Bodenham. *H&W* —3C **41**
Bodewryd. *IOA* —1C **5**
Bodfari. *Den* —3B **8**
Bodffordd. *IOA* —3D **5**
Bodfuan. *Gwyn* —1C **21**
Bodnant. *Cnwy* —3D **7**
Bodorgan. *IOA* —1C **13**
Bog, The. *Shrp* —2A **32**
Bold Heath. *Mers* —2C **11**
Bolstone. *H&W* —2C **51**
Bomere Heath. *Shrp* —3B **26**
Boncath. *Pemb* —2B **44**
Bont. *Mon* —1A **60**
Bontddu. *Gwyn* —3B **22**
Bont Dolgadfan. *Powy*
    —1D **29**
Bontgoch. *Cdgn* —3B **28**
Bontnewydd. *Cdgn* —2B **36**
Bont-newydd. *Cnwy* —3B **8**
Bontnewydd. *Gwyn* —1D **13**
   (nr. Caernarfon)
Bont Newydd. *Gwyn* —3C **15**
   (nr. Ffestiniog)
Bontuchel. *Den* —2B **16**
Bonvilston. *V.Gl* —2B **64**
Bon-y-maen. *Swan* —3B **56**
Booley. *Shrp* —2C **27**
Boothstown. *G.Mn* —1D **11**
Bootle. *Mers* —1A **10**
Boraston. *Shrp* —1D **41**

Boreton. *Shrp* —1C **33**
Borras Head. *Wrex* —2A **18**
Borth. *Cdgn* —3B **28**
Borth-y-Gest. *Gwyn* —1A **22**
Bosbury. *H&W* —1D **51**
Bosherston. *Pemb* —3C **53**
Bostock Green. *Ches* —1D **19**
Botloe's Green. *Glos* —3D **51**
Botwnnog. *Gwyn* —1B **20**
Boughrood. *Powy* —2C **49**
Boughspring. *Glos* —3C **61**
Bouldon. *Shrp* —3C **33**
Boulston. *Pemb* —1C **53**
Bounds. *H&W* —2D **51**
Bourton. *N.Sm* —3A **66**
Bourton. *Shrp* —2C **33**
Boverton. *V.Gl* —3A **64**
Bowley. *H&W* —3C **41**
Bowling Bank. *Wrex* —3B **18**
Bow Street. *Cdgn* —3B **28**
Boxbush. *Glos* —3D **51**
Brackla. *Bri* —2A **64**
Bradfield Green. *Ches* —2D **19**
Bradley. *Ches* —3C **11**
Bradley. *Glos* —3D **61**
Bradley. *Wrex* —2A **18**
Bradley Green. *Ches* —3C **19**
Bradley Stoke. *S.Glo* —1D **67**
Bradlow. *H&W* —2D **51**
Braichmelyn. *Gwyn* —1B **14**
Brampton Abbotts. *H&W*
    —3D **51**
Brampton Bryan. *H&W*
    —1A **40**
Brand Green. *Glos* —3D **51**
Brandhill. *Shrp* —1B **40**
Bransley. *Shrp* —1D **41**
Bratton. *Shrp* —3D **27**
Breaden Heath. *Shrp* —1B **26**
Breadstone. *Glos* —2D **61**
Bream. *Glos* —2D **61**
Bream's Meend. *Glos* —2D **61**
Brechfa. *Carm* —2A **46**
Brecon. *Powy* —3B **48**
Bredenbury. *H&W* —3D **41**
Bredwardine. *H&W* —1A **50**
Breinton. *H&W* —2B **50**
Breinton Common. *H&W*
    —2B **50**
Brelston Green. *H&W* —3C **51**
Bretton. *Flin* —1A **18**
Bridell. *Pemb* —1A **44**
Bridgemere. *Ches* —3D **19**
Bridgend. *Bri* —1A **64**
Bridge Sollers. *H&W* —1B **50**
Bridge Trafford. *Ches* —3B **10**
Bridgeyate. *S.Glo* —2D **67**
Bridgnorth. *Shrp* —2D **33**
Bridstow. *H&W* —3C **51**
Brierley. *Glos* —1D **61**
Brierley. *H&W* —3B **40**
Brilley. *H&W* —1D **49**
Brimaston. *Pemb* —3C **43**
Brimfield. *H&W* —2C **41**
Brimstage. *Mers* —2A **10**
Brinsty Common. *H&W*
    —3D **41**
Brislington. *S.Glo* —2D **67**
Bristol. *Bris* —2C **67**
Bristol (Lulsgate) Airport.
    N.Sm —3C **67**
Brithdir. *Cphy* —2C **59**
Brithdir. *Cdgn* —1C **45**
Brithdir. *Gwyn* —3C **23**
Briton Ferry. *Neat* —3C **57**
Broadfield. *Pemb* —2A **54**
Broad Haven. *Pemb* —1B **52**
Broadheath. *H&W* —2D **41**
Broadlay. *Carm* —2C **55**
Broadmoor. *Pemb* —2D **53**
Broad Oak. *Carm* —3A **46**
Broadoak. *Glos* —1D **61**

Broad Oak. *H&W* —3B **50**
Broadstone. *Shrp* —3C **33**
Broad, The. *H&W* —2B **40**
Broadway. *Carm* —2C **55**
   (nr. Kidwelly)
Broadway. *Carm* —1B **54**
   (nr. Laugharne)
Broadway. *Pemb* —1B **52**
Broadwell. *Glos* —1C **61**
Brobury. *H&W* —1A **50**
Brockhampton. *H&W* —2C **51**
Brockley. *N.Sm* —3B **66**
Brockton. *Shrp* —3A **32**
   (nr. Bishop's Castle)
Brockton. *Shrp* —1D **33**
   (nr. Madeley)
Brockton. *Shrp* —2C **33**
   (nr. Much Wenlock)
Brockton. *Shrp* —3D **27**
   (nr. Newport)
Brockton. *Shrp* —1A **32**
   (nr. Pontesbury)
Brockweir. *Glos* —2C **61**
Bromborough. *Mers* —2A **10**
Bromdon. *Shrp* —3D **33**
Bromfield. *Shrp* —1B **40**
Bromley. *Shrp* —2D **33**
Brompton. *Shrp* —1C **33**
Bromsash. *H&W* —3D **51**
Bromsberrow Heath. *Glos*
    —2D **51**
Bromyard. *H&W* —3D **41**
Bromyard Downs. *H&W*
    —3D **41**
Bronaber. *Gwyn* —1C **23**
Broncroft. *Shrp* —3C **33**
Brongest. *Cdgn* —1C **45**
Brongwyn. *Cdgn* —1B **44**
Bronington. *Wrex* —1B **26**
Bronllys. *Powy* —2C **49**
Bronnant. *Cdgn* —2B **36**
Bronwydd Arms. *Carm*
    —3D **45**
Bronydd. *Powy* —1D **49**
Bronygarth. *Shrp* —1D **25**
Brook. *Carm* —2B **54**
Brookend. *Glos* —2D **61**
Brookhurst. *Mers* —2A **10**
Brooklands. *Shrp* —3C **19**
Brooks. *Powy* —2C **31**
Broome. *Shrp* —2C **33**
   (nr. Cardington)
Broome. *Shrp* —3B **32**
   (nr. Craven Arms)
Broomedge. *Ches* —2D **11**
Broomhill. *Bris* —2D **67**
Broom's Green. *Glos* —2D **51**
Broseley. *Shrp* —1D **33**
Broughall. *Shrp* —3C **19**
Broughton. *Flin* —1A **18**
Broughton. *V.Gl* —2A **64**
Brownhill. *Shrp* —2B **26**
Brownhills. *Shrp* —1D **27**
Brown Knowl. *Ches* —2B **18**
Broxton. *Ches* —2B **18**
Broxwood. *H&W* —3A **40**
Bruera. *Ches* —1B **18**
Brymbo. *Cnwy* —3D **7**
Brymbo. *Wrex* —3D **17**
Bryn. *Carm* —2A **56**
Bryn. *G.Mn* —1C **11**
Bryn. *Neat* —3D **57**
Bryn. *Shrp* —3D **31**
Brynamman. *Carm* —1C **57**
Brynberian. *Pemb* —2A **44**
Brynbryddan. *Neat* —3C **57**
Bryncae. *Rhon* —1A **64**
Bryncethin. *Bri* —1A **64**
Bryncir. *Gwyn* —3D **13**
Bryn-coch. *Neat* —3C **57**
Bryncroes. *Gwyn* —1B **20**
Bryncrug. *Gwyn* —1B **28**

Bryn Du. *IOA* —3C **5**
Bryn Eden. *Gwyn* —2C **23**
Bryneglwys. *Den* —3C **17**
Bryn Eglwys. *Gwyn* —1B **14**
Brynford. *Flin* —3C **9**
Bryn Gates. *G.Mn* —1C **11**
Bryn Golau. *Rhon* —1B **64**
Bryngwran. *IOA* —3C **5**
Bryngwyn. *Mon* —2A **60**
Bryngwyn. *Powy* —1C **49**
Bryn-henllan. *Pemb* —2D **43**
Brynhoffnant. *Cdgn* —3C **35**
Bryn-llwyn. *Flin* —2B **8**
Brynllywarch. *Powy* —3C **31**
Brynmawr. *Blae* —1C **59**
Bryn-mawr. *Gwyn* —1B **20**
Brynmenyn. *Bri* —1A **64**
Brynmill. *Swan* —3B **56**
Brynna. *Rhon* —1A **64**
Brynrefail. *Gwyn* —1A **14**
Brynrefail. *IOA* —2D **5**
Brynsadler. *Rhon* —1B **64**
Bryn-Saith Marchog. *Den*
    —2B **16**
Brynsiencyn. *IOA* —1D **13**
Brynteg. *IOA* —2D **5**
Brynteg. *Wrex* —2A **18**
Brynygwenyn. *Mon* —1A **60**
Bryn-y-maen. *Cnwy* —3D **7**
Buckholt. *H&W* —1C **61**
Buckland. *H&W* —3C **41**
Buckley. *Flin* —1D **17**
Buckley Hill. *Mers* —1A **10**
Bucklow Hill. *Ches* —2D **11**
Bucknell. *Shrp* —1A **40**
Buckton. *H&W* —1A **40**
Buerton. *Ches* —3D **19**
Buildwas. *Shrp* —1D **33**
Builth Road. *Powy* —3B **38**
Builth Wells. *Powy* —3B **38**
Bulkeley. *Ches* —2C **19**
Bull Bay. *IOA* —1D **5**
Bullinghope. *H&W* —2C **51**
Bunbury. *Ches* —2C **19**
Burcher. *H&W* —2A **40**
Burcote. *Shrp* —2D **33**
Burford. *Shrp* —2C **41**
Burghill. *H&W* —1B **50**
Burland. *Ches* —2D **19**
Burley Gate. *H&W* —1C **51**
Burlingjobb. *Powy* —3D **39**
Burlton. *Shrp* —2B **26**
Burnett. *Bath* —3D **67**
Burnleydam. *Wrex* —3D **19**
Burrington. *H&W* —1B **40**
Burrington. *N.Sm* —3B **66**
Burry. *Swan* —3D **55**
Burry Green. *Swan* —3D **55**
Burry Port. *Carm* —2D **55**
Burton. *Ches* —1C **19**
   (nr. Kelsall)
Burton. *Ches* —3A **10**
   (nr. Neston)
Burton. *Pemb* —2C **53**
Burton. *Wrex* —2A **18**
Burton Green. *Wrex* —2A **18**
Burtonwood. *Ches* —1C **11**
Burwardsley. *Ches* —2C **19**
Burwarton. *Shrp* —3D **33**
Burwen. *IOA* —1D **5**
Bush Bank. *H&W* —3B **40**
Bushmoor. *Shrp* —3B **32**
Butcombe. *N.Sm* —3C **67**
Bute Town. *Cphy* —2C **59**
Butt Green. *Ches* —2D **19**
Buttington. *Powy* —1D **31**
Buttonbridge. *Shrp* —1D **41**
Buttonoak. *Shrp* —1D **41**
Bwcle. *Flin* —1D **17**
Bwlch. *Powy* —3C **49**
Bwlchderwin. *Gwyn* —3D **13**
Bwlchgwyn. *Wrex* —2D **17**

Bwlch-Llan. *Cdgn* —3A **36**
Bwlchnewydd. *Carm* —3C **45**
Bwlch-y-cibau. *Powy* —2C **25**
Bwlchyddar. *Powy* —2C **25**
Bwlch-y-fadfa. *Cdgn* —1D **45**
Bwlch-y-ffridd. *Powy* —2B **30**
Bwlch y Garreg. *Powy* —2B **30**
Bwlch-y-groes. *Pemb* —2B **44**
Bwlch-yr-haiarn. *Cnwy*
　　　　　—2C **15**
Bwlch-y-sarnau. *Powy*
　　　　　—1B **38**
Byford. *H&W* —1A **50**
Bylchau. *Cnwy* —1A **16**
Byley. *Ches* —1D **19**
Bynea. *Carm* —3A **56**
Byton. *H&W* —2A **40**

Cadishead. *G.Mn* —1D **11**
Cadole. *Flin* —1D **17**
Cadoxton-Juxta-Neath. *Neat*
　　　　　—3C **57**
Cadwst. *Den* —1B **24**
Caeathro. *Gwyn* —1A **14**
Caehopkin. *Powy* —1D **57**
Caerau. *Bri* —3D **57**
Caerau. *Card* —2C **65**
Cae'r-bont. *Powy* —1D **57**
Cae'r bryn. *Carm* —1A **56**
Caerdeon. *Gwyn* —3B **22**
Caerdydd. *Card* —2C **65**
Caerfarchell. *Pemb* —3A **42**
Caerffili. *Cphy* —1C **65**
Caerfyrddin. *Carm* —1D **55**
Caergeiliog. *IOA* —3C **5**
Caergwrle. *Flin* —2A **18**
Caergybi. *IOA* —2B **4**
Caerleon. *Newp* —2A **66**
Caerlleon. *Carm* —3B **44**
Caerllion. *Newp* —3A **60**
Caernarfon. *Gwyn* —1D **13**
Caerphilly. *Cphy* —1C **65**
Caersws. *Powy* —2B **30**
Caerwedros. *Cdgn* —3C **35**
Caerwent. *Mon* —3B **60**
Caerwys. *Flin* —3C **9**
Caim. *IOA* —2B **6**
Caio. *Carm* —2B **46**
Calcott. *Shrp* —3B **26**
Caldicot. *Mon* —1B **66**
Caldy. *Mers* —2D **9**
Caledfwlch. *Carm* —3B **46**
Callaughton. *Shrp* —2D **33**
Callow. *H&W* —2B **50**
Callow Hill. *H&W* —1D **41**
Calveley. *Ches* —2C **19**
Calverhall. *Shrp* —1D **27**
Cam. *Glos* —3D **61**
Cambridge. *Glos* —2D **61**
Cameley. *Bath* —3D **67**
Camerton. *Bath* —3D **67**
Camrose. *Pemb* —1C **53**
Canaston Bridge. *Pemb*
　　　　　—1D **53**
Canon Bridge. *H&W* —1B **50**
Canon Frome. *H&W* —1D **51**
Canon Pyon. *H&W* —1B **50**
Cantlop. *Shrp* —1C **33**
Canton. *Card* —2C **65**
Capel Bangor. *Cdgn* —3B **28**
Capel Betws Lleucu. *Cdgn*
　　　　　—3B **36**
Capel Coch. *IOA* —2D **5**
Capel Curig. *Cnwy* —2C **15**
Capel Cynon. *Cdgn* —1C **45**
Capel Dewi. *Carm* —3D **45**
Capel Dewi. *Cdgn* —3B **28**
　(nr. Aberystwyth)
Capel Dewi. *Cdgn* —1D **45**
　(nr. Llandyssul)

Capel Garmon. *Cnwy* —2D **15**
Capel Gwyn. *IOA* —3C **5**
Capel Gwynfe. *Carm* —3C **47**
Capel Hendre. *Carm* —1A **56**
Capel Isaac. *Carm* —3A **46**
Capel Iwan. *Carm* —2B **44**
Capel Llanilterne. *Card*
　　　　　—2B **64**
Capel-Mawr. *IOA* —3D **5**
Capel Seion. *Carm* —1A **56**
Capel Seion. *Cdgn* —3B **36**
Capel Uchaf. *Gwyn* —3D **13**
Capel-y-ffin. *Powy* —2D **49**
Capenhurst. *Ches* —3A **10**
Cardeston. *Shrp* —3A **26**
Cardiff. *Card* —2C **65**
Cardiff Airport. *V.Gl* —3B **64**
Cardigan. *Cdgn* —1A **44**
Cardington. *Shrp* —2C **33**
Carew. *Pemb* —2D **53**
Carew Cheriton. *Pemb*
　　　　　—2D **53**
Carew Newton. *Pemb* —2D **53**
Carey. *H&W* —2C **51**
Carlingcott. *Bath* —3D **67**
Carmarthen. *Carm* —1D **55**
Carmel. *Carm* —1A **56**
Carmel. *Flin* —3C **9**
Carmel. *Gwyn* —2D **13**
Carmel. *IOA* —2C **5**
Carnhedryn. *Pemb* —3A **42**
Carno. *Powy* —2A **30**
Carreglefn. *IOA* —2C **5**
Carrington. *G.Mn* —1D **11**
Carrog. *Cnwy* —3C **15**
Carrog. *Den* —3C **17**
Carrow Hill. *Mon* —3B **60**
Carway. *Carm* —2D **55**
Cascob. *Powy* —2D **39**
Cas-gwent. *Mon* —3C **61**
Casnewydd. *Newp* —1A **66**
Castell. *Cnwy* —1C **15**
Castell. *Den* —1C **17**
Castell Hendre. *Pemb* —3D **43**
Castell-nedd. *Neat* —3C **57**
Castell Newydd Emlyn. *Carm*
　　　　　—1C **45**
Castell-y-bwch. *Torf* —3D **59**
Castlebythe. *Pemb* —3D **43**
Castle Caereinion. *Powy*
　　　　　—1C **31**
Castle Frome. *H&W* —1D **51**
Castlemartin. *Pemb* —3C **53**
Castlemorris. *Pemb* —2C **43**
Castleton. *Newp* —1D **65**
Caswell. *Swan* —1A **62**
Catbrook. *Mon* —2C **61**
Cathedine. *Powy* —3C **49**
Catherton. *Shrp* —1D **41**
Cat's Ash. *Newp* —3A **60**
Caynham. *Shrp* —1C **41**
Cefn Berain. *Cnwy* —1A **16**
Cefn-brith. *Cnwy* —2A **16**
Cefn-bryn-brain. *Carm*
　　　　　—1C **57**
Cefn Bychan. *Cphy* —3D **59**
Cefn-bychan. *Flin* —1C **17**
Cefncaeau. *Carm* —3A **56**
Cefn Canol. *Powy* —1D **25**
Cefn Coch. *Powy* —1B **30**
　(nr. Llanfair Caereinion)
Cefn-coch. *Powy* —2C **25**
　(nr. Llanrhaeadr)
Cefn-coed-y-cymmer. *Mert*
　　　　　—2B **58**
Cefn Cribwr. *Bri* —1D **63**
Cefn-ddwysarn. *Gwyn*
　　　　　—1A **24**
Cefn Einion. *Shrp* —3D **31**
Cefneithin. *Carm* —1A **56**
Cefn Glas. *Bri* —1D **63**
Cefngorwydd. *Powy* —1A **48**

Cefn Llwyd. *Cdgn* —3B **28**
Cefn-mawr. *Wrex* —3D **17**
Cefn-y-bedd. *Wrex* —2A **18**
Cefn-y-coed. *Powy* —2C **31**
Cefn-y-pant. *Carm* —3A **44**
Cegidfa. *Powy* —3D **25**
Ceinewydd. *Cdgn* —3C **35**
Cellan. *Cdgn* —1B **46**
Cemaes. *IOA* —1C **5**
Cemmaes. *Powy* —1D **29**
Cemmaes Road. *Powy*
　　　　　—1D **29**
Cenarth. *Carm* —1B **44**
Cenin. *Gwyn* —3D **13**
Cerist. *Gwyn* —3A **30**
Cerrigceinwen. *IOA* —3D **5**
Cerrigydrudion. *Cnwy* —3A **16**
Ceunant. *Gwyn* —1A **14**
Chadwick Green. *Mers*
　　　　　—1C **11**
Chancery. *Cdgn* —1A **36**
Chapel Hill. *Mon* —2C **61**
Chapel Lawn. *Shrp* —1A **40**
Charfield. *S.Glo* —3D **61**
Charlcombe. *Bath* —3D **67**
Charlton. *Shrp* —3C **27**
Chatwall. *Shrp* —2C **33**
Chaxhill. *Glos* —1D **61**
Checkley. *Ches* —3D **19**
Checkley. *H&W* —2C **51**
Chelmarsh. *Shrp* —3D **33**
Chelmick. *Shrp* —2B **32**
Chelvey. *N.Sm* —3B **66**
Chelwood. *Bath* —3D **67**
Cheney Longville. *Shrp*
　　　　　—3B **32**
Chepstow. *Mon* —3C **61**
Cheriton. *Pemb* —3C **53**
Cheriton. *Swan* —3D **55**
Cherrington. *Shrp* —2D **27**
Chester. *Ches* —1B **18**
Cheswardine. *Shrp* —2D **27**
Cheswell. *Shrp* —3D **27**
Chetton. *Shrp* —2D **33**
Chetwynd Aston. *Shrp*
　　　　　—3D **27**
Chew Magna. *Bath* —3C **67**
Chew Stoke. *Bath* —3C **67**
Chewton Keynsham. *Bath*
　　　　　—3D **67**
Chickward. *H&W* —3D **39**
Childer Thornton. *Ches*
　　　　　—3A **10**
Child's Ercall. *Shrp* —2D **27**
Childwall. *Mers* —2B **10**
Chipnall. *Shrp* —1D **27**
Chipping Sodbury. *S.Glo*
　　　　　—1D **67**
Chirbury. *Shrp* —2D **31**
Chirk. *Wrex* —1D **25**
Cholstrey. *H&W* —3B **40**
Chorley. *Ches* —2C **19**
Chorley. *Shrp* —3D **33**
Chorlton. *Ches* —2D **19**
Chorlton Lane. *Ches* —3B **18**
Choulton. *Shrp* —3A **32**
Christchurch. *Glos* —1C **61**
Christleton. *Ches* —1B **18**
Christon. *N.Sm* —3A **66**
Church Aston. *Shrp* —3D **27**
Church End. *Glos* —2D **61**
Church Hill. *Ches* —1D **19**
Churchill. *N.Sm* —3B **66**
Church Minshull. *Ches*
　　　　　—1D **19**
Church Preen. *Shrp* —2C **33**
Church Pulverbatch. *Shrp*
　　　　　—1B **32**
Church Stoke. *Powy* —2D **31**
Church Stretton. *Shrp*
　　　　　—2B **33**
Churchtown. *Shrp* —3D **31**

Church Village. *Rhon* —1B **64**
Churton. *Ches* —2B **18**
Chwilog. *Gwyn* —1D **21**
Chwitffordd. *Flin* —3C **9**
Cilan Uchaf. *Gwyn* —2B **20**
Cilcain. *Flin* —1C **17**
Cilcennin. *Cdgn* —3A **36**
Cilfrew. *Neat* —2C **57**
Cilfynydd. *Rhon* —3B **58**
Cilgerran. *Pemb* —1A **44**
Cilgeti. *Pemb* —2A **54**
Cilgwyn. *Carm* —3C **47**
Cilgwyn. *Pemb* —2D **43**
Ciliau Aeron. *Cdgn* —3D **35**
Cilmaengwyn. *Neat* —2C **57**
Cilmery. *Powy* —3B **38**
Cilrhedyn. *Pemb* —2B **44**
Cilsan. *Carm* —3A **46**
Ciltalgarth. *Gwyn* —3D **15**
Ciltwrch. *Powy* —1C **49**
Cilybebyll. *Neat* —2C **57**
Cilycwm. *Carm* —2C **47**
Cimla. *Neat* —3C **57**
Cinderford. *Glos* —1D **61**
Cippyn. *Pemb* —1A **44**
City. *Powy* —2D **31**
City. *V.Gl* —2A **64**
City Dulas. *IOA* —2D **5**
Clapton-in-Gordano. *N.Sm*
　　　　　—2B **66**
Clarbeston. *Pemb* —3D **43**
Clarbeston Road. *Pemb*
　　　　　—3D **43**
Clatter. *Powy* —2A **30**
Claughton. *Mers* —2A **10**
Claverham. *N.Sm* —3B **66**
Clawdd-coch. *V.Gl* —2B **64**
Clawdd-newydd. *Den* —2B **16**
Clay Hill. *Bris* —2D **67**
Clearwell. *Glos* —2C **61**
Cleedownton. *Shrp* —3C **33**
Cleehill. *Shrp* —1C **41**
Clee St Margaret. *Shrp*
　　　　　—3C **33**
Cleestanton. *Shrp* —1C **41**
Cleeton St Mary. *Shrp*
　　　　　—1D **41**
Cleeve. *N.Sm* —3B **66**
Clehonger. *H&W* —2B **50**
Cleobury Mortimer. *Shrp*
　　　　　—1D **41**
Cleobury North. *Shrp* —3D **33**
Clevedon. *N.Sm* —2B **66**
Clifford's Mesne. *Glos*
　　　　　—3D **51**
Clifton. *Bris* —2C **67**
Clifton Hill. *H&W* —2D **41**
Clifton-upon-Teme. *H&W*
　　　　　—2D **41**
Clipiau. *Gwyn* —3D **23**
Clive. *Shrp* —2C **27**
Clocaenog. *Den* —2B **16**
Clock Face. *Mers* —1C **11**
Cloddiau. *Powy* —1D **31**
Clodock. *H&W* —3A **50**
Clotton. *Ches* —1C **19**
Clows Top. *H&W* —1D **41**
Cloy. *Wrex* —3A **18**
Cluddley. *Shrp* —1D **33**
Clun. *Shrp* —3A **32**
Clunbury. *Shrp* —3A **32**
Clunderwen. *Carm* —1A **54**
Clungunford. *Shrp* —1A **40**
Clunton. *Shrp* —3A **32**
Clutton. *Bath* —3D **67**
Clutton. *Ches* —2B **18**
Clwt-y-bont. *Gwyn* —1A **14**
Clwydfagwyr. *Mert* —2B **58**
Clydach. *Mon* —1D **59**
Clydach. *Swan* —2B **56**
Clydach Vale. *Rhon* —3A **58**
Clydey. *Pemb* —2B **44**

Clyne. *Neat* —2D **57**
Clynnog-fawr. *Gwyn* —3D **13**
Clyro. *Powy* —1D **49**
Cnwcau. *Pemb* —1B **44**
Cnwch Coch. *Cdgn* —1B **36**
Coalbrookdale. *Shrp* —1D **33**
Coalbrookvale. *Blae* —2D **59**
Coalpit Heath. *S.Glo* —1D **67**
Coalport. *Shrp* —1D **33**
Coalway. *Glos* —1C **61**
Cobhall. *H&W* —2B **50**
Cobnash. *H&W* —2B **40**
Cock Bank. *Wrex* —3A **18**
Cock Gate. *H&W* —2B **40**
Cockshutford. *Shrp* —3C **33**
Cockshutt. *Shrp* —2B **26**
Cockyard. *H&W* —2B **50**
Coddington. *Ches* —2B **18**
Coddington. *H&W* —1D **51**
Codrington. *S.Glo* —1D **67**
Coed Duon. *Cphy* —3C **59**
Coedely. *Rhon* —1B **64**
Coedglasson. *Powy* —2B **38**
Coedkernew. *Newp* —1D **65**
Coed Morgan. *Mon* —1A **60**
Coedpoeth. *Wrex* —2D **17**
Coedway. *Powy* —3A **26**
Coed-y-bryn. *Cdgn* —1C **45**
Coed-y-paen. *Mon* —3A **60**
Coed-yr-ynys. *Powy* —3C **49**
Coed Ystumgwern. *Gwyn*
　　　　　—2A **22**
Coelbren. *Powy* —1D **57**
Cogan. *V.Gl* —2C **65**
Coity. *Bri* —1A **64**
Cold Ashton. *S.Glo* —2D **67**
Cold Blow. *Pemb* —1A **54**
Coldharbour. *Glos* —2C **61**
Cold Hatton. *Shrp* —2D **27**
Cold Hatton Heath. *Shrp*
　　　　　—2D **27**
Coldwell. *H&W* —2B **50**
Colebatch. *Shrp* —3A **32**
Coleford. *Glos* —1C **61**
Colemere. *Shrp* —1B **26**
Colemore Green. *Shrp*
　　　　　—2D **33**
Collins Green. *Ches* —1C **11**
Collins Green. *H&W* —3D **41**
Colwall Green. *H&W* —1D **51**
Colwall Stone. *H&W* —1D **51**
Colwinston. *V.Gl* —2A **64**
Colwyn Bay. *Cnwy* —3D **7**
Combe. *H&W* —2A **40**
Combe Hey. *Bath* —3D **67**
Combe Moor. *H&W* —2A **40**
Comberbach. *Ches* —3D **11**
Comberton. *H&W* —2B **40**
Comins Coch. *Cdgn* —3B **28**
Comley. *Shrp* —2B **32**
Commins. *Powy* —2C **25**
Commins Coch. *Powy*
　　　　　—1D **29**
Common Hill. *H&W* —2C **51**
Commonside. *Ches* —3C **11**
Compton Dando. *Bath*
　　　　　—3D **67**
Compton Greenfield. *S.Glo*
　　　　　—1C **67**
Compton Martin. *Bath*
　　　　　—3C **67**
Condover. *Shrp* —1B **32**
Congl-y-wal. *Gwyn* —3C **15**
Congresbury. *N.Sm* —3B **66**
Conham. *S.Glo* —2D **67**
Connah's Quay. *Flin* —1D **17**
Conwy. *Cnwy* —3C **7**
Coppenhall. *Ches* —2D **19**
Coppenhall Moss. *Ches*
　　　　　—2D **19**
Coppicegate. *Shrp* —3D **33**
Coptiviney. *Shrp* —1B **26**

Coreley. *Shrp* —1D **41**
Corfton. *Shrp* —3B **32**
Corlannau. *Neat* —3C **57**
Corntown. *V.Gl* —2A **64**
Corris. *Gwyn* —1C **29**
Corris Uchaf. *Gwyn* —1C **29**
Corston. *Bath* —3D **67**
Corwen. *Den* —3B **16**
Cosheston. *Pemb* —2D **53**
Cosmeston. *V.Gl* —3C **65**
Cotebrook. *Ches* —1C **19**
Cotland. *Mon* —2C **61**
Coton Hill. *Shrp* —3B **26**
Cotonwood. *Shrp* —1C **27**
Coughton. *H&W* —3C **51**
Cound. *Shrp* —1C **33**
Court Henry. *Carm* —3A **46**
Cowbridge. *V.Gl* —2A **64**
Cowslip Green. *N.Sm* —3B **66**
Coxall. *H&W* —1A **40**
Coxbank. *Ches* —3D **19**
Coychurch. *V.Gl* —2A **64**
Coytrahen. *Bri* —1D **63**
Crabtree Green. *Wrex* —3A **18**
Crackleybank. *Shrp* —3D **27**
Cradley. *H&W* —1D **51**
Cradoc. *Powy* —2B **48**
Crai. *Powy* —3D **47**
Craig-cefn-parc. *Swan*
—2B **56**
Craig-llwyn. *Shrp* —2D **25**
Craignant. *Shrp* —1D **25**
Craig-y-Duke. *Neat* —2C **57**
Craig-y-nos. *Powy* —1D **57**
Cranage. *Ches* —1D **19**
Crank. *Mers* —1C **11**
Craven Arms. *Shrp* —3B **32**
Crawford. *Lanc* —1B **10**
Creamore Bank. *Shrp* —1C **27**
Credenhill. *H&W* —1B **50**
Cregrina. *Powy* —3C **39**
Creigiau. *Card* —1B **64**
Cressage. *Shrp* —1C **33**
Cresselly. *Pemb* —2D **53**
Cresswell Quay. *Pemb*
—2D **53**
Crewe. *Ches* —2B **18**
(nr. Farndon)
Crewe. *Ches* —2D **19**
(nr. Nantwich)
Crewgreen. *Powy* —3A **26**
Cribbs Causeway. *S.Glo*
—2C **67**
Cribyn. *Cdgn* —3A **36**
Criccieth. *Gwyn* —1D **21**
Crick. *Mon* —3B **60**
Crickadarn. *Powy* —1B **48**
Crickheath. *Shrp* —2D **25**
Crickhowell. *Powy* —1D **59**
Criggion. *Powy* —3D **25**
Crinow. *Pemb* —1A **54**
Crocker's Ash. *H&W* —1C **61**
Croeserw. *Neat* —3D **57**
Croes-Goch. *Pemb* —2B **42**
Croes Hywel. *Mon* —1A **60**
Croes-lan. *Cdgn* —1C **45**
Croesor. *Gwyn* —3B **14**
Croesowallt. *Shrp* —2D **9**
Croesyceiliog. *Carm* —1D **55**
Croesyceiliog. *Torf* —3A **60**
Croes-y-mwyalch. *Newp*
—3A **60**
Croeswaun. *Gwyn* —2A **14**
Croft. *Ches* —1D **11**
Crofty. *Swan* —3A **56**
Cromhall. *S.Glo* —3D **61**
Cromhall Common. *S.Glo*
—1D **67**
Cronton. *Mers* —2B **10**
Crosby. *Mers* —1A **10**
Cross Ash. *Mon* —1B **60**
Cross Foxes. *Gwyn* —3C **23**

Crossgates. *Powy* —2B **38**
Cross Hands. *Carm* —1A **56**
(nr. Ammanford)
Crosshands. *Carm* —3A **44**
(nr. Whitland)
Cross Hill. *Glos* —3C **61**
Cross Houses. *Shrp* —1C **33**
Cross Inn. *Cdgn* —2A **36**
(nr. Aberaeron)
Cross Inn. *Cdgn* —3C **35**
(nr. New Quay)
Cross Inn. *Rhon* —1B **64**
Crosskeys. *Cphy* —3D **59**
Cross Lane Head. *Shrp*
—2D **33**
Crosslanes. *Shrp* —3A **26**
Cross Lanes. *Wrex* —3A **18**
Cross Oak. *Powy* —3C **49**
Crossway. *Mon* —1B **60**
Crossway. *Powy* —3B **38**
Crossway Green. *Mon*
—3C **61**
Crosswell. *Pemb* —2A **44**
Crosswood. *Cdgn* —1B **36**
Crow Hill. *H&W* —3D **51**
Crowton. *Ches* —3C **11**
Croxton Green. *Ches* —2C **19**
Cruckmeole. *Shrp* —1B **32**
Cruckton. *Shrp* —3B **26**
Crudgington. *Shrp* —3D **27**
Crug. *Powy* —1C **39**
Crughywel. *Powy* —1D **59**
Crugybar. *Carm* —2B **46**
Crug-y-byddar. *Powy* —3C **31**
Crumlin. *Cphy* —3D **59**
Crumpsbrook. *Shrp* —1D **41**
Crundale. *Pemb* —1C **53**
Crwbin. *Carm* —1D **55**
Crymych. *Pemb* —2A **44**
Crynant. *Neat* —2C **57**
Cublington. *H&W* —2A **50**
Cuddington. *Ches* —3D **11**
Cuddington Heath. *Ches*
—3B **18**
Cuerdley Cross. *Ches* —2C **11**
Culcheth. *Ches* —1D **11**
Culmington. *Shrp* —3B **32**
Cusop. *H&W* —1D **49**
Cutiau. *Gwyn* —3B **22**
Cuttybridge. *Pemb* —1C **53**
Cwm. *Blae* —2C **59**
Cwm. *Den* —3B **8**
Cwm. *Powy* —2D **31**
Cwmafan. *Neat* —3C **57**
Cwmaman. *Rhon* —3A **58**
Cwmann. *Carm* —1A **46**
Cwmbach. *Carm* —3B **44**
Cwmbach. *Powy* —2C **49**
Cwmbach. *Rhon* —2B **58**
Cwmbach Llechryd. *Powy*
—3B **38**
Cwmbelan. *Powy* —3A **30**
Cwmbran. *Torf* —3D **59**
Cwmbrwyno. *Cdgn* —3C **29**
Cwm Capel. *Carm* —2D **55**
Cwmcarn. *Cphy* —3D **59**
Cwmcarvan. *Mon* —2B **60**
Cwm-celyn. *Blae* —2D **59**
Cwmcerdinen. *Swan* —2B **56**
Cwm-Cewydd. *Gwyn* —3D **23**
Cwmcoy. *Cdgn* —1B **44**
Cwmcrawnon. *Powy* —1C **59**
Cwmcych. *Pemb* —2B **44**
Cwmdare. *Rhon* —2A **58**
Cwmdu. *Carm* —2B **46**
Cwmdu. *Powy* —3C **49**
Cwmduad. *Carm* —2C **45**
Cwm Dulais. *Swan* —2B **56**
Cwmerfyn. *Cdgn* —2D **29**
Cwmfelin. *Bri* —1D **63**
Cwmfelin Boeth. *Carm*
—1A **54**

Cwmfelinfach. *Cphy* —3C **59**
Cwmfelin Mynach. *Carm*
—3B **44**
Cwmffrwd. *Carm* —1D **55**
Cwmgiedd. *Powy* —1C **57**
Cwmgors. *Neat* —1C **57**
Cwmgwili. *Carm* —1A **56**
Cwmgwrach. *Neat* —2D **57**
Cwmhiraeth. *Carm* —2C **45**
Cwmifor. *Carm* —3B **46**
Cwmisfael. *Carm* —1D **55**
Cwm-Llinau. *Powy* —1D **29**
Cwmllynfell. *Neat* —1C **57**
Cwm-mawr. *Carm* —1A **56**
Cwm-miles. *Carm* —3A **44**
Cwmorgan. *Carm* —2B **44**
Cwmparc. *Rhon* —3A **58**
Cwm Penmachno. *Cnwy*
—3C **15**
Cwmpennar. *Rhon* —2B **58**
Cwm Plysgog. *Pemb* —1A **44**
Cwmrhos. *Powy* —3C **49**
Cwmsychpant. *Cdgn* —1D **45**
Cwmsyfiog. *Cphy* —2C **59**
Cwmsymlog. *Cdgn* —3B **28**
Cwmtillery. *Blae* —2D **59**
Cwm-twrch Isaf. *Powy*
—2C **57**
Cwm-twrch Uchaf. *Powy*
—1C **57**
Cwmwysg. *Powy* —3D **47**
Cwm-y-glo. *Gwyn* —1A **14**
Cwmyoy. *Mon* —3A **50**
Cwmystwyth. *Cdgn* —1C **37**
Cwrt. *Gwyn* —2B **28**
Cwrtnewydd. *Cdgn* —1D **45**
Cwrt-y-Cadno. *Carm* —1B **46**
Cydweli. *Carm* —2D **55**
Cyffylliog. *Den* —2B **16**
Cymau. *Flin* —2D **17**
Cymmer. *Neat* —3D **57**
Cymmer. *Rhon* —3B **58**
Cyncoed. *Card* —1C **65**
Cynghordy. *Carm* —2D **47**
Cynghordy. *Swan* —2B **56**
Cynheidre. *Carm* —2D **55**
Cynonville. *Neat* —3D **57**
Cynwyd. *Den* —3B **16**
Cynwyl Elfed. *Carm* —3C **45**
Cywarch. *Gwyn* —3D **23**

Dafen. *Carm* —2A **56**
Dale. *Pemb* —2B **52**
Danesford. *Shrp* —2D **33**
Daren. *Powy* —1D **59**
Daresbury. *Ches* —2C **11**
Darliston. *Shrp* —1C **27**
Darowen. *Powy* —1D **29**
Davenham. *Ches* —3D **11**
David's Well. *Powy* —1B **38**
Dawley. *Shrp* —1D **33**
Dawn. *Cnwy* —3D **7**
Daywall. *Shrp* —1D **25**
Ddol. *Flin* —3C **9**
Ddol Cownwy. *Powy* —3B **24**
Dean Park. *Shrp* —2C **41**
Defynnog. *Powy* —3A **48**
Deganwy. *Cnwy* —3C **7**
Deiniolen. *Gwyn* —1A **14**
Delamere. *Ches* —1C **19**
Denbigh. *Den* —1B **16**
Denio. *Gwyn* —1C **21**
Deri. *Cphy* —2C **59**
Derrington. *Shrp* —2D **33**
Derwen. *Den* —2B **16**
Derwenlas. *Powy* —2C **29**
Deuddwr. *Powy* —3D **25**
Devauden. *Mon* —3B **60**
Devil's Bridge. *Cdgn* —1C **37**
Dewshall Court. *H&W* —2B **50**
Diddlebury. *Shrp* —3C **33**

Didley. *H&W* —2B **50**
Dihewyd. *Cdgn* —3D **35**
Dilwyn. *H&W* —3B **40**
Dinas. *Carm* —2B **44**
Dinas. *Gwyn* —1B **20**
Dinas. *Pemb* —2D **43**
Dinas Dinlle. *Gwyn* —2D **13**
Dinas Mawddwy. *Gwyn*
—3D **23**
Dinas Powys. *V.Gl* —2C **65**
Dinbych. *Den* —1B **16**
Dinbych-y-Pysgod. *Pemb*
—2A **54**
Dinedor. *H&W* —2C **51**
Dinedor Cross. *H&W* —2C **51**
Dingestow. *Mon* —1B **60**
Dingle. *Mers* —2A **10**
Dinmael. *Cnwy* —3B **16**
Dinorwic. *Gwyn* —1A **14**
Discoed. *Powy* —2D **39**
Disserth. *Powy* —3B **38**
Ditton. *Ches* —2B **10**
Ditton Priors. *Shrp* —3D **33**
Dixton. *Mon* —1C **61**
Dobs Hill. *Flin* —1A **18**
Dobson's Bridge. *Shrp*
—1B **26**
Docklow. *H&W* —3C **41**
Doc Penfro. *Pemb* —2C **53**
Doddenham. *H&W* —3D **41**
Doddington. *Shrp* —1D **41**
Dodington. *S.Glo* —2D **67**
Dodleston. *Ches* —1A **18**
Dolanog. *Powy* —3B **24**
Dolau. *Powy* —2C **39**
Dolau. *Rhon* —1B **64**
Dolbenmaen. *Gwyn* —3A **14**
Doley. *Shrp* —2D **27**
Dolfach. *Powy* —1A **30**
(nr. Llanbrynmair)
Dolfach. *Powy* —1A **38**
(nr. Llanidloes)
Dolfor. *Powy* —3C **31**
Dolforwyn. *Powy* —2C **31**
Dolgarrog. *Cnwy* —1C **15**
Dolgellau. *Gwyn* —3C **23**
Dolgoch. *Gwyn* —1B **28**
Dol-gran. *Carm* —2D **45**
Dolhelfa. *Powy* —1A **38**
Dolley Green. *Powy* —2D **39**
Dollwen. *Cdgn* —3B **28**
Dolphin. *Flin* —3C **9**
Dolwen. *Cnwy* —3D **7**
Dolwyddelan. *Cnwy* —2C **15**
Dol-y-Bont. *Cdgn* —3B **28**
Dolyhir. *Powy* —3D **39**
Domgay. *Powy* —3D **25**
Donnington. *H&W* —2D **51**
Donnington. *Shrp* —1C **33**
(nr. Shrewsbury)
Donnington. *Shrp* —3D **27**
(nr. Telford)
Dormington. *H&W* —1C **51**
Dorrington. *Shrp* —1B **32**
Dorstone. *H&W* —1A **50**
Dovaston. *Shrp* —2A **26**
Dowlais. *Mert* —2B **58**
Downall Green. *G.Mn* —1C **11**
Downend. *S.Glo* —2D **67**
Down, The. *Shrp* —2D **33**
Downton on the Rock. *H&W*
—1B **40**
Doynton. *S.Glo* —2D **67**
Draethen. *Cphy* —1D **65**
Dreenhill. *Pemb* —1C **53**
Drefach. *Carm* —1A **56**
(nr. Meidrim)
Drefach. *Carm* —2C **45**
(nr. Newcastle Emlyn)
Drefach. *Carm* —3B **44**
(nr. Tumble)
Drefach. *Cdgn* —1A **46**

Drope. *V.Gl* —2C **65**
Druid. *Den* —3B **16**
Druidston. *Pemb* —1B **52**
Drury. *Flin* —1D **17**
Drybrook. *Glos* —1D **61**
Drybrook. *H&W* —1C **61**
Dryslwyn. *Carm* —3A **46**
Dryton. *Shrp* —1C **33**
Duckington. *Ches* —2B **18**
Duddon. *Ches* —1C **19**
Dudleston. *Shrp* —1A **26**
Dudleston Heath. *Shrp*
—1A **26**
Dudston. *Shrp* —2D **31**
Dudwells. *Pemb* —3C **43**
Duffryn. *Neat* —3D **57**
Dukestown. *Blae* —1C **59**
Dulas. *IOA* —2D **5**
Dundry. *N.Sm* —3C **67**
Dunham-on-the-Hill. *Ches*
—3B **10**
Dunham Town. *G.Mn* —2D **11**
Dunham Woodhouses. *G.Mn*
—2D **11**
Dunkerton. *Bath* —3D **67**
Dunvant. *Swan* —3A **56**
Durlow Common. *H&W*
—2D **51**
Dursley. *Glos* —3D **61**
Dursley Cross. *Glos* —1D **61**
Dutlas. *Powy* —1D **39**
Dutton. *Ches* —3C **11**
Dwygyfylchi. *Cnwy* —3C **7**
Dwyran. *IOA* —1D **13**
Dyffryn. *Bri* —3D **57**
Dyffryn. *Carm* —3C **45**
Dyffryn. *IOA* —3B **4**
Dyffryn. *Pemb* —2C **43**
Dyffryn. *V.Gl* —2B **64**
Dyffryn Ardudwy. *Gwyn*
—2A **22**
Dyffryn Castell. *Cdgn* —3C **29**
Dyffryn Ceidrych. *Carm*
—3C **47**
Dyffryn Cellwen. *Neat*
—2D **57**
Dylife. *Powy* —2D **29**
Dymock. *Glos* —2D **51**
Dyrham. *S.Glo* —2D **67**
Dyserth. *Den* —3B **8**

Eardington. *Shrp* —2D **33**
Eardisland. *H&W* —3B **40**
Eardisley. *H&W* —1A **50**
Eardiston. *H&W* —2D **41**
Eardiston. *Shrp* —2A **26**
Earlestown. *Mers* —1C **11**
Earlswood. *Mon* —3B **60**
Earthcott Green. *S.Glo*
—1D **67**
East Aberthaw. *V.Gl* —3B **64**
East Clevedon. *N.Sm* —2B **66**
East Dean. *Glos* —3D **51**
East Dundry. *N.Sm* —3C **67**
East End. *N.Sm* —3B **66**
Easter Compton. *S.Glo*
—1C **67**
Eastham. *H&W* —2D **41**
Eastham. *Mers* —2A **10**
Eastham Ferry. *Mers* —2A **10**
Easthampton. *H&W* —2B **40**
Easthope. *Shrp* —2C **33**
Eastnor. *H&W* —2D **51**
Easton-in-Gordano. *N.Sm*
—2C **67**
East Wall. *Shrp* —2C **33**
East Williamston. *Pemb*
—2D **53**
Eaton. *Ches* —1C **19**
Eaton. *Shrp* —3A **32**
(nr. Bishop's Castle)

Eaton. *Shrp* —2C **33**
(nr. Church Stretton)
Eaton Bishop. *H&W* —2B **50**
Eaton Constantine. *Shrp*
—1C **33**
Eaton upon Tern. *Shrp*
—2D **27**
Ebbw Vale. *Blae* —2C **59**
Ebnal. *Ches* —3B **18**
Eccles Green. *H&W* —1A **50**
Eccleston. *Ches* —1B **18**
Eccleston. *Mers* —1B **10**
Edern. *Gwyn* —1B **20**
Edge. *Shrp* —1A **32**
Edgebolton. *Shrp* —2C **27**
Edge End. *Glos* —1C **61**
Edge Green. *Ches* —2B **18**
Edgeley. *Shrp* —3C **19**
Edgmond. *Shrp* —3D **27**
Edgmond Marsh. *Shrp*
—2D **27**
Edgton. *Shrp* —3A **32**
Edstaston. *Shrp* —1C **27**
Edwardsville. *Mert* —3B **58**
Edwinsford. *Carm* —2B **46**
Edwyn Ralph. *H&W* —3D **41**
Efail-fach. *Neat* —3C **57**
Efail Isaf. *Rhon* —1B **64**
Efailnewydd. *Gwyn* —1C **21**
Efail-rhyd. *Powy* —2C **25**
Efailwen. *Carm* —3A **44**
Efenechtyd. *Den* —2C **17**
Eglwysbach. *Cnwy* —3D **7**
Eglwys Brewis. *V.Gl* —3B **64**
Eglwys Fach. *Cdgn* —2B **28**
Eglwyswrw. *Pemb* —2A **44**
Egremont. *Mers* —1A **10**
Eisingrug. *Gwyn* —1B **22**
Elan Village. *Powy* —2A **38**
Elberton. *S.Glo* —1D **67**
Ellerdine. *Shrp* —2D **27**
Ellerdine Heath. *Shrp* —2D **27**
Ellerton. *Shrp* —2D **27**
Ellesmere. *Shrp* —1B **26**
Ellesmere Port. *Ches* —3B **10**
Ellwood. *Glos* —2C **61**
Elton. *Ches* —3B **10**
Elton. *Glos* —1D **61**
Elton. *H&W* —1B **40**
Elton Green. *Ches* —3B **10**
Elworth. *Ches* —1D **19**
Ely. *Card* —2C **65**
Enchmarsh. *Shrp* —2C **33**
Engine Common. *S.Glo*
—1D **67**
Engleseabrook. *Ches* —2D **19**
English Bicknor. *Glos* —1C **61**
Englishcombe. *Bath* —3D **67**
English Frankton. *Shrp*
—2B **26**
Ensdon. *Shrp* —3B **26**
Erbistock. *Wrex* —3A **18**
Erwood. *Powy* —1B **48**
Eryrys. *Den* —2D **17**
Esgair. *Carm* —3C **45**
(nr. Carmarthen)
Esgair. *Carm* —1B **54**
(nr. St Clears)
Esgairgeiliog. *Powy* —1C **29**
Etloe. *Glos* —2D **61**
Ettiley Heath. *Ches* —1D **19**
Eudon Burnell. *Shrp* —3D **33**
Eudon George. *Shrp* —3D **33**
Evanstown. *Bri* —1A **64**
Evendine. *H&W* —1D **51**
Evenjobb. *Powy* —2D **39**
Everton. *Mers* —1A **10**
Evesbatch. *H&W* —1D **51**
Ewdness. *Shrp* —2D **33**
Ewenny. *V.Gl* —2A **64**
Ewlo. *Flin* —1A **18**
Ewloe. *Flin* —1A **18**

Ewyas Harold. *H&W* —3A **50**
Exfords Green. *Shrp* —1B **32**
Eye. *H&W* —2B **40**
Eyton. *H&W* —2B **40**
Eyton. *Shrp* —3A **32**
(nr. Bishop's Castle)
Eyton. *Shrp* —3A **26**
(nr. Shrewsbury)
Eyton. *Wrex* —3A **18**
Eyton on Severn. *Shrp*
—1C **33**
Eyton upon the Weald Moors.
Shrp —3D **27**

Faddiley. *Ches* —2C **19**
Fagwyr. *Swan* —2B **56**
Failand. *N.Sm* —2C **67**
Fairbourne. *Gwyn* —3B **22**
Fairwater. *Card* —2C **65**
Falcon. *H&W* —2D **51**
Falfield. *S.Glo* —3D **61**
Far Forest. *H&W* —1D **41**
Farleigh. *N.Sm* —3B **66**
Farley. *N.Sm* —3B **66**
Farley. *Shrp* —1A **32**
(nr. Shrewsbury)
Farley. *Shrp* —1D **33**
(nr. Telford)
Farlow. *Shrp* —3D **33**
Farmborough. *Bath* —3D **67**
Far Moor. *G.Mn* —1C **11**
Farndon. *Ches* —2B **18**
Farnworth. *Ches* —2C **11**
Fauls. *Shrp* —1C **27**
Fawley Chapel. *H&W* —3C **51**
Fazakerley. *Mers* —1A **10**
Fearnhead. *Ches* —1D **11**
Felhampton. *Shrp* —3B **32**
Felindre. *Carm* —3A **46**
(nr. Llandeilo)
Felindre. *Carm* —2B **46**
(nr. Llandovery)
Felindre. *Carm* —2C **45**
(nr. Newcastle Emlyn)
Felindre. *Powy* —3C **31**
Felindre. *Swan* —2B **56**
Felindre Farchog. *Pemb*
—2A **44**
Felinfach. *Cdgn* —3A **36**
Felinfach. *Powy* —2B **48**
Felinfoel. *Carm* —2A **56**
Felingwmisaf. *Carm* —3A **46**
Felingwmuchaf. *Carm* —3A **46**
Felin Newydd. *Powy* —2D **25**
Felin Wnda. *Cdgn* —1C **45**
Felinwynt. *Cdgn* —3B **34**
Felton. *H&W* —1C **51**
Felton. *N.Sm* —3C **67**
Felton Butler. *Shrp* —3A **26**
Fenn's Bank. *Wrex* —1C **27**
Ferndale. *Rhon* —3A **58**
Ferryside. *Carm* —1C **55**
Ferwig. *Cdgn* —1A **44**
Ffairfach. *Carm* —3B **46**
Ffair Rhos. *Cdgn* —2C **37**
Ffaldybrenin. *Carm* —1B **46**
Ffarmers. *Carm* —1B **46**
Ffawyddog. *Powy* —1D **59**
Ffestiniog. *Gwyn* —3C **15**
Fforest. *Carm* —2A **56**
Fforest-fach. *Swan* —3B **56**
Fforest Goch. *Neat* —2C **57**
Ffostrasol. *Cdgn* —1C **45**
Ffos-y-ffin. *Cdgn* —2D **35**
Ffrith. *Flin* —2D **17**
Ffrwdgrech. *Powy* —3B **48**
Ffynnon-ddrain. *Carm*
—3D **45**
Ffynnongroyw. *Flin* —2C **9**
Ffynnon Gynydd. *Powy*
—1C **49**

Ffynnonoer. *Cdgn* —3A **36**
Filton. *Bris* —2D **67**
Fishguard. *Pemb* —2C **43**
Fishponds. *Bris* —2D **67**
Fishpool. *Glos* —3D **51**
Fishpools. *Powy* —2C **39**
Fitz. *Shrp* —3B **26**
Five Bridges. *H&W* —1D **51**
Five Roads. *Carm* —2D **55**
Flax Bourton. *N.Sm* —3C **67**
Flaxley. *Glos* —1D **61**
Flemingston. *V.Gl* —2B **64**
Flint. *Flin* —3D **9**
Flint Mountain. *Flin* —3D **9**
Flintsham. *H&W* —3A **40**
Flixton. *G.Mn* —1D **11**
Fochriw. *Cphy* —2C **59**
Foel. *Powy* —3A **24**
Ford. *Shrp* —3B **26**
Forden. *Powy* —1D **31**
Ford Heath. *Shrp* —3B **26**
Forge. *Powy* —2C **29**
Forge Side. *Torf* —2D **59**
Forge, The. *H&W* —3A **40**
Forthay. *Glos* —3D **61**
Forton. *Shrp* —3B **26**
Forton. *Staf* —2D **27**
Forton Heath. *Shrp* —3B **26**
Four Alls, The. *Shrp* —1D **27**
Four Crosses. *Powy* —1B **30**
(nr. Llanerfyl)
Four Crosses. *Powy* —3D **25**
(nr. Llanymynech)
Four Mile Bridge. *IOA* —3B **4**
Four Oaks. *Glos* —3D **51**
Four Roads. *Carm* —2D **55**
Fowley Common. *Ches*
—1D **11**
Fownhope. *H&W* —2C **51**
Foxwist Green. *Ches* —1D **19**
Foxwood. *Shrp* —1D **41**
Foy. *H&W* —3C **51**
Frampton Cotterell. *S.Glo*
—1D **67**
Frampton on Severn. *Glos*
—2D **61**
Frandley. *Ches* —3D **11**
Frankby. *Mers* —2D **9**
Frank's Bridge. *Powy* —3C **39**
Frankwell. *Shrp* —3B **26**
Freshwater East. *Pemb*
—3D **53**
Fretherne. *Glos* —2D **61**
Freystrop. *Pemb* —1C **53**
Friog. *Gwyn* —3B **22**
Frith Common. *H&W* —2D **41**
Frochas. *Powy* —1C **31**
Frodesley. *Shrp* —1C **33**
Frodsham. *Ches* —3C **11**
Fromes Hill. *H&W* —1D **51**
Fron. *Carm* —2C **47**
Fron. *Gwyn* —2A **14**
(nr. Caernarfon)
Fron. *Gwyn* —1C **21**
(nr. Pwllheli)
Fron. *Powy* —2B **38**
(nr. Llandrindod Wells)
Fron. *Powy* —2C **31**
(nr. Newtown)
Fron. *Powy* —1D **31**
(nr. Welshpool)
Froncysyllte. *Den* —3D **17**
Frongoch. *Gwyn* —1A **24**
Fron Isaf. *Wrex* —3D **17**
Fronoleu. *Gwyn* —1C **23**
Fuller's Moor. *Ches* —2B **18**
Furnace. *Carm* —2A **56**
Furnace. *Cdgn* —2B **28**

Gaer. *Powy* —3C **49**
Gaerwen. *IOA* —3D **5**

Gallt Melyd. *Den* —2B **8**
Ganarew. *H&W* —1C **61**
Ganllwyd. *Gwyn* —2C **23**
Garden City. *Flin* —1A **18**
Garden Village. *Swan* —3A **56**
Garmston. *Shrp* —1D **33**
Garnant. *Carm* —1B **56**
Garndiffaith. *Torf* —2D **59**
Garndolbenmaen. *Gwyn*
—3D **13**
Garnfadryn. *Gwyn* —1B **20**
Garnlydan. *Blae* —1C **59**
Garnswllt. *Swan* —2B **56**
Garn-yr-erw. *Torf* —1D **59**
Garreg. *Gwyn* —3B **14**
Garston. *Mers* —2B **10**
Garswood. *Mers* —1C **11**
Garth. *Bri* —3D **57**
Garth. *Den* —3D **17**
Garth. *Gwyn* —1A **22**
Garth. *Powy* —1A **48**
(nr. Builth Wells)
Garth. *Powy* —1D **39**
(nr. Knighton)
Garthbrengy. *Powy* —2B **48**
Gartheli. *Cdgn* —3A **36**
Garthmyl. *Powy* —2C **31**
Garth Owen. *Powy* —2C **31**
Garth Penrhyncoch. *Cdgn*
—3B **28**
Garway. *H&W* —3B **50**
Garway Common. *H&W*
—3B **50**
Garway Hill. *H&W* —3B **50**
Gateacre. *Mers* —2B **10**
Gatesheath. *Ches* —1B **18**
Gaufron. *Powy* —2A **38**
Gaunt's Earthcott. *S.Glo*
—1D **67**
Gayton. *Mers* —2D **9**
Gell. *Cnwy* —1D **15**
Gelli. *Pemb* —1D **53**
Gelli. *Rhon* —3A **58**
Gellifor. *Den* —1C **17**
Gelligaer. *Cphy* —3C **59**
Gellilydan. *Gwyn* —1B **22**
Gellinudd. *Neat* —2C **57**
Gellywen. *Carm* —3B **44**
Geneva. *Cdgn* —3D **35**
Georgetown. *Blae* —2C **59**
Gerlan. *Gwyn* —1B **14**
Geuffordd. *Powy* —3D **25**
Gignog. *Pemb* —3B **42**
Gileston. *V.Gl* —3B **64**
Gilfach. *Cphy* —3C **59**
Gilfach Goch. *Rhon* —1A **64**
Gilfachreda. *Cdgn* —3D **35**
Gillar's Green. *Mers* —1B **10**
Gilwern. *Mon* —1D **59**
Gladestry. *Powy* —3D **39**
Glais. *Swan* —2C **57**
Glanaman. *Carm* —1B **56**
Glan-Conwy. *Cnwy* —2D **15**
Glan Duar. *Carm* —1A **46**
Glandwr. *Blae* —2D **59**
Glandwr. *Pemb* —3A **44**
Glan-Dwyfach. *Gwyn* —3D **13**
Glandyfi. *Cdgn* —2B **28**
Glangrwyney. *Powy* —1D **59**
Glanmule. *Powy* —2C **31**
Glanrhyd. *Gwyn* —1B **20**
Glan-rhyd. *Neat* —2C **57**
Glanrhyd. *Pemb* —1A **44**
(nr. Cardigan)
Glan-rhyd. *Pemb* —2A **44**
(nr. Crymmych)
Glan-y-don. *Flin* —3C **9**
Glan-y-nant. *Powy* —3A **30**
Glan-yr-afon. *Gwyn* —3B **16**
Glan-yr-afon. *IOA* —2B **6**
Glan-yr-afon. *Powy* —1B **30**
Glan-y-wern. *Gwyn* —1B **22**

Glasbury. *Powy* —2C **49**
Glascoed. *Den* —3A **8**
Glascoed. *Mon* —2A **60**
Glascwm. *Powy* —3C **39**
Glasfryn. *Cnwy* —2A **16**
Glasinfryn. *Gwyn* —1A **14**
Glaspwll. *Powy* —2C **29**
Glasshouse. *Glos* —3D **51**
Glazebrook. *Ches* —1D **11**
Glazebury. *Ches* —1D **11**
Glazeley. *Shrp* —3D **33**
Gledrid. *Shrp* —1D **25**
Gleiniant. *Powy* —2A **30**
Glewstone. *H&W* —3C **51**
Glyn. *Cnwy* —3D **7**
Glynarthen. *Cdgn* —1C **45**
Glynbrochan. *Powy* —3A **30**
Glyn Ceiriog. *Wrex* —1D **25**
Glyncoch. *Rhon* —3B **58**
Glyncorrwg. *Neat* —3D **57**
Glyndyfrdwy. *Den* —3C **17**
Glyn Ebwy. *Blae* —2C **59**
Glynllan. *Bri* —1A **64**
Glyn-neath. *Neat* —2D **57**
Glynogwr. *Bri* —1A **64**
Glyntaff. *Rhon* —1B **64**
Glyntawe. *Powy* —1D **57**
Glynteg. *Carm* —2C **45**
Gobowen. *Shrp* —1A **26**
Godre'r-graig. *Neat* —2C **57**
Goetre. *Mon* —2A **60**
Goginan. *Cdgn* —3B **28**
Golan. *Gwyn* —3A **14**
Golborne. *G.Mn* —1D **11**
Goldcliff. *Newp* —1A **66**
Golden Grove. *Carm* —1A **56**
Golden Hill. *Pemb* —3C **43**
Golding. *Shrp* —1C **33**
Goldstone. *Shrp* —2D **27**
Golfa. *Powy* —2C **25**
Goodrich. *H&W* —1C **61**
Goodwick. *Pemb* —2C **43**
Goose Green. *S.Glo* —1D **67**
Gors. *Cdgn* —1B **36**
Gorsedd. *Flin* —3C **9**
Gorseinon. *Swan* —3A **56**
Gorsgoch. *Cdgn* —2D **35**
Gorslas. *Carm* —1A **56**
Gorsley. *Glos* —3D **51**
Gorsley Common. *H&W*
—3D **51**
Gorstella. *Ches* —1A **18**
Gorsty Common. *H&W*
—2B **50**
Gossington. *Glos* —2D **61**
Govilon. *Mon* —1D **59**
Gowerton. *Swan* —3A **56**
Goytre. *Neat* —1C **63**
Grafton. *H&W* —2B **50**
(nr. Hereford)
Grafton. *H&W* —2C **41**
(nr. Leominster)
Grafton. *Shrp* —3B **26**
Graianrhyd. *Den* —2D **17**
Graig. *Carm* —2D **55**
Graig. *Cnwy* —3D **7**
Graig. *Den* —3B **8**
Graig-fechan. *Den* —2C **17**
Graig Penllyn. *V.Gl* —2A **64**
Grange. *H&W* —1B **40**
Grange. *Mers* —2D **9**
Grangetown. *Card* —2C **65**
Granston. *Pemb* —2B **42**
Grappenhall. *Ches* —2D **11**
Grassendale. *Mers* —2A **10**
Gravelhill. *Shrp* —3B **26**
Greasby. *Mers* —2D **9**
Great Barrow. *Ches* —1B **18**
Great Bolas. *Shrp* —2D **27**
Great Budworth. *Ches*
—3D **11**
Great Crosby. *Mers* —1A **10**

Great Doward. H&W —1C **61**
Great Lyth. Shrp —1B **32**
Great Ness. Shrp —3B **26**
Great Oak. Mon —2A **60**
Great Ryton. Shrp —1B **32**
Great Sankey. Ches —2C **11**
Great Sutton. Ches —3A **10**
Great Sutton. Shrp —3C **33**
Great Witley. H&W —2D **41**
Great Wytheford. Shrp
—3C **27**
Greenfield. Flin —3C **9**
Green Lane. Shrp —2D **27**
Greenway. Pemb —3D **43**
Greenway. V.Gl —2B **64**
Greete. Shrp —1C **41**
Grendon Green. H&W —3C **41**
Gresford. Wrex —2A **18**
Gretton. Shrp —2C **33**
Griffithstown. Torf —3D **59**
Grimpo. Shrp —2A **26**
Grindle. Shrp —1D **33**
Grindley Brook. Shrp —3C **19**
Grinshill. Shrp —2C **27**
Groes. Cnwy —1B **16**
Groes. Neat —1C **63**
Groes-faen. Rhon —1B **64**
Groesffordd. Gwyn —1B **20**
Groesffordd. Powy —3B **48**
Groeslon. Gwyn —2D **13**
Groes-lwyd. Powy —3D **25**
Groes-wen. Cphy —1C **65**
Gronant. Flin —2B **8**
Grosmont. Mon —3B **50**
Grovesend. Swan —2A **56**
Guilden Down. Shrp —3A **32**
Guilden Sutton. Ches —1B **18**
Guilsfield. Powy —3D **25**
Gumfreston. Pemb —2A **54**
Gurnos. Powy —2C **57**
Gwaelod-y-garth. Card
—1C **65**
Gwaenynog Bach. Den
—1B **16**
Gwaenysgor. Flin —2B **8**
Gwalchmai. IOA —3C **5**
Gwastad. Pemb —3D **43**
Gwaun-Cae-Gurwen. Neat
—1C **57**
Gwbert. Cdgn —3A **34**
Gwehelog. Mon —2A **60**
Gwenddwr. Powy —1B **48**
Gwernaffield. Flin —1D **17**
Gwernesney. Mon —2B **60**
Gwernogle. Carm —2A **46**
Gwern-y-go. Powy —2D **31**
Gwernymynydd. Flin —1D **17**
Gwersyllt. Wrex —2A **18**
Gwespyr. Flin —2C **9**
Gwredog. IOA —2D **5**
Gwyddelwern. Den —3B **16**
Gwyddgrug. Carm —2D **45**
Gwynfryn. Wrex —2D **17**
Gwystre. Powy —2B **38**
Gwytherin. Cnwy —1D **15**
Gyfelia. Wrex —3A **18**
Gyffin. Cnwy —3C **7**

Habberley. Shrp —1A **32**
Hadley. Shrp —3D **27**
Hadnall. Shrp —2C **27**
Hagley. H&W —1C **51**
Hakin. Pemb —2B **52**
Hale. Ches —2B **10**
Hales. Staf —1D **27**
Halewood. Mers —2B **10**
Halford. Shrp —3B **32**
Halfpenny Furze. Carm
—1B **54**

Halfway. Carm —2B **46**
Halfway. Powy —2D **47**
Halfway House. Shrp —3A **26**
Halkyn. Flin —3D **9**
Hallatrow. Bath —3D **67**
Hallen. S.Glo —1C **67**
Hall Green. Wrex —3B **18**
Hallowsgate. Ches —1C **19**
Hallwood Green. Glos —2D **51**
Halmond's Frome. H&W
—1D **51**
Halmore. Glos —2D **61**
Halton. Ches —2C **11**
Halton. Wrex —1A **26**
Ham. Glos —3D **61**
Hambrook. S.Glo —2D **67**
Ham Green. H&W —1D **51**
Ham Green. N.Sm —2C **67**
Hamperley. Shrp —3B **32**
Hampton. Shrp —3D **33**
Hampton Bishop. H&W
—2C **51**
Hampton Heath. Ches —3C **19**
Hampton Loade. Shrp
—3D **33**
Handbridge. Ches —1B **18**
Handley. Ches —2B **18**
Hanham. S.Glo —2D **67**
Hanham Green. S.Glo
—2D **67**
Hankelow. Ches —3D **19**
Hanley Childe. H&W —2D **41**
Hanley William. H&W —2D **41**
Hanmer. Wrex —1B **26**
Hanwood. Shrp —1B **32**
Hapsford. Ches —3B **10**
Hardwick. Shrp —2A **32**
Hardwicke. H&W —1D **49**
Haresfinch. Mers —1C **11**
Harewood End. H&W —3C **51**
Hargrave. Ches —1B **18**
Harlech. Gwyn —1A **22**
Harlescott. Shrp —3C **27**
Harley. Shrp —1C **33**
Harmer Hill. Shrp —2B **26**
Harnage. Shrp —1C **33**
Haroldston West. Pemb
—1B **52**
Harpley. H&W —2D **41**
Harry Stoke. S.Glo —2D **67**
Hartford. Ches —3D **11**
Harthill. Ches —2C **19**
Harton. Shrp —3B **32**
Hasguard. Pemb —2B **52**
Haslington. Ches —2D **19**
Haston. Shrp —2C **27**
Hatchmere. Ches —3C **11**
Hatfield. H&W —3C **41**
Hatherton. Ches —3D **19**
Hatton. Ches —2C **11**
Hatton. Shrp —2B **32**
Hatton Heath. Ches —1B **18**
Haughton. Shrp —2D **33**
(nr. Bridgnorth)
Haughton. Shrp —2A **26**
(nr. Oswestry)
Haughton. Shrp —1D **33**
(nr. Shifnal)
Haughton. Shrp —3C **27**
(nr. Shrewsbury)
Haughton Moss. Ches
—2C **19**
Haven. H&W —3B **40**
Haverfordwest. Pemb —1C **53**
Hawarden. Flin —1A **18**
Hawen. Cdgn —1C **45**
Haybridge. Shrp —1D **41**
Haydock. Mers —1C **11**
Hay-on-Wye. Powy —1D **49**
Hayscastle. Pemb —3B **42**
Hayscastle Cross. Pemb
—3C **43**

Hayton's Bent. Shrp —3C **33**
Hazler. Shrp —2B **32**
Headley Park. Bris —3C **67**
Heartsease. Powy —2C **39**
Heatley. G.Mn —2D **11**
Hebden Green. Ches —1D **19**
Hebron. Carm —3A **44**
Hegdon Hill. H&W —3C **41**
Helsby. Shrp —3B **10**
Hem, The. Shrp —1D **33**
Henallt. Carm —3D **45**
Henbury. Bris —2C **67**
Hendomen. Powy —2D **31**
Hendre. Bri —1A **64**
Hendreforgan. Rhon —1A **64**
Hendy. Carm —2A **56**
Heneglwys. IOA —3D **5**
Henfeddau Fawr. Pemb
—2B **44**
Henfield. S.Glo —2D **67**
Hengoed. Cphy —3C **59**
Hengoed. Shrp —1D **25**
Heniarth. Powy —1C **31**
Henley. Shrp —3B **32**
(nr. Church Stretton)
Henley. Shrp —1C **41**
(nr. Ludlow)
Henllan. Cdgn —1C **45**
Henllan. Den —1B **16**
Henllan. Mon —3D **49**
Henllan Amgoed. Carm
—3A **44**
Henllys. Torf —3D **59**
Henryd. Cnwy —3C **7**
Henry's Moat. Pemb —3D **43**
Heol Senni. Powy —3A **48**
Heol-y-Cyw. Bri —1A **64**
Herbrandston. Pemb —2B **52**
Hereford. H&W —2C **51**
Hermon. Carm —3B **46**
(nr. Llandeilo)
Hermon. Carm —2C **45**
(nr. Newcastle Emlyn)
Hermon. IOA —1C **13**
Hermon. Pemb —2B **44**
Heswall. Mers —2D **9**
Hewelsfield. Glos —2C **61**
Hewish. N.Sm —3A **66**
Heyop. Powy —1D **39**
Higford. Shrp —1D **33**
High Ercall. Shrp —3C **27**
Higher End. G.Mn —1C **11**
Higher Kinnerton. Flin —1A **18**
Higher Shotton. Flin —1A **18**
Higher Shurlach. Ches
—3D **11**
Higher Walton. Ches —2D **11**
Higher Whitley. Ches —3D **11**
Higher Wincham. Ches
—3D **11**
Higher Wych. Ches —3B **18**
Highgate. Powy —2C **31**
High Green. Shrp —3D **33**
High Hatton. Shrp —2D **27**
Highlands, The. Shrp —3D **33**
High Lane. H&W —2D **41**
High Legh. Ches —2D **11**
Highley. Shrp —3D **33**
High Littleton. Bath —3D **67**
Highmoor Hill. Mon —1B **66**
Hightown. Mers —1D **9**
Highway. H&W —1B **50**
Highwood. H&W —2D **41**
Hill. S.Glo —3D **61**
Hillend. Swan —3D **55**
Hillersland. Glos —1C **61**
Hill Gate. H&W —3B **50**
Hillside. H&W —2D **41**
Hillside. Shrp —3D **33**
Hindford. Shrp —1A **26**
Hindley. G.Mn —1D **11**
Hindley Green. G.Mn —1D **11**

Hinstock. Shrp —2D **27**
Hinton. H&W —2A **50**
Hinton. Shrp —1B **32**
Hinton. S.Glo —2D **67**
Hinton Blewett. Bath —3C **67**
Hints. Shrp —1D **41**
Hiraeth. Carm —3A **44**
Hirnant. Powy —2B **24**
Hirwaen. Den —1C **17**
Hirwaun. Rhon —2A **58**
Hoarwithy. H&W —3C **51**
Hobarris. Shrp —1A **40**
Hodgeston. Pemb —3D **53**
Hodley. Powy —2C **31**
Hodnet. Shrp —2D **27**
Holdgate. Shrp —3C **33**
Hollinfare. Ches —1D **11**
Hollinswood. Shrp —1D **33**
Hollinwood. Shrp —1C **27**
Hollybush. Cphy —2C **59**
Hollyhurst. Ches —3D **19**
Holme Lacy. H&W —2C **51**
Holme Marsh. H&W —3A **40**
Holmer. H&W —1C **51**
Holmes Chapel. Ches —1D **19**
Holt. Wrex —2B **18**
Holyhead. IOA —2B **4**
Holywell. Flin —3C **9**
Holywell. Glos —3D **61**
Homer. Shrp —1D **33**
Homer Green. Mers —1A **10**
Hom Green. H&W —3C **51**
Honeyborough. Pemb —2C **53**
Honnington. Shrp —3D **27**
Hook. Pemb —1C **53**
Hook-a-Gate. Shrp —1B **32**
Hookgate. Staf —1D **27**
Hook Street. Glos —3D **61**
Hoole. Ches —1B **18**
Hooton. Ches —3A **10**
Hope. Flin —2A **18**
Hope. Powy —1D **31**
Hope. Shrp —1A **32**
Hope Bagot. Shrp —1C **41**
Hope Bowdler. Shrp —2B **32**
Hope Mansell. H&W —1D **61**
Hopesay. Shrp —3A **32**
Hope under Dinmore. H&W
—3C **41**
Hopley's Green. H&W —3A **40**
Hopton. Powy —2D **31**
Hopton. Shrp —2A **26**
(nr. Oswestry)
Hopton. Shrp —2C **27**
(nr. Wem)
Hopton Cangeford. Shrp
—3C **33**
Hopton Castle. Shrp —1A **40**
Hoptonheath. Shrp —1A **40**
Hopton Wafers. Shrp —1D **41**
Horderley. Shrp —3B **32**
Hordley. Shrp —1A **26**
Horeb. Carm —3A **46**
(nr. Brechfa)
Horeb. Carm —2D **55**
(nr. Llanelli)
Horeb. Cdgn —1C **45**
Horsecastle. N.Sm —3B **66**
Horsehay. Shrp —1D **33**
Horseman's Green. Wrex
—3B **18**
Horsham. H&W —3D **41**
Horton. Shrp —1B **26**
Horton. Swan —1A **62**
Horton Green. Ches —3B **18**
Hortonwood. Shrp —3D **27**
Hough. Ches —2D **19**
Hough Green. Ches —2B **10**
Houghton. Pemb —2C **53**
How Caple. H&W —2D **51**
Howey. Powy —3B **38**
Howle. Shrp —2D **27**

Howle Hill. H&W —3D **51**
Howley. Ches —2D **11**
Howton. H&W —3B **50**
Hoylake. Mers —2D **9**
Hubberston. Pemb —2B **52**
Hughley. Shrp —2C **33**
Humber Court. H&W —3C **41**
Hundleton. Pemb —2C **53**
Hundred House. Powy
—3C **39**
Hundred, The. H&W —2C **41**
Hungerford. Shrp —3C **33**
Hungryhatton. Shrp —2D **27**
Hunstrete. Bath —3D **67**
Huntington. H&W —3D **39**
Huntington. Shrp —1D **33**
Huntley. Glos —1D **61**
Hunt's Cross. Mers —2B **10**
Huntstrete. Bath —3D **67**
Hurdley. Powy —2D **31**
Hurst Green. Ches —3C **19**
Hurstley. H&W —1A **50**
Hurstway Common. H&W
—1D **49**
Hutton. N.Sm —3A **66**
Huxley. Ches —1C **19**
Huyton-with-Roby. Mers
—1B **10**
Hwlffordd. Pemb —1C **53**
Hyssington. Powy —2A **32**

Icelton. N.Sm —3A **66**
Idole. Carm —1D **55**
Ifton Heath. Shrp —1A **26**
Ightfield. Shrp —1C **27**
Ilston. Swan —3A **56**
Ince. Ches —3B **10**
Ince Blundell. Mers —1A **10**
Inglesbatch. Bath —3D **67**
Ingst. S.Glo —1C **67**
Irby. Mers —2D **9**
Irlam. G.Mn —1D **11**
Iron Acton. S.Glo —1D **67**
Ironbridge. Shrp —1D **33**
Islington. Shrp —2D **27**
Islwyn. Cphy —3D **59**
Itchington. S.Glo —1D **67**
Itton Common. Mon —3B **60**
Ivington. H&W —3B **40**
Ivington Green. H&W —3B **40**

Jackfield. Shrp —1D **33**
Jameston. Pemb —3D **53**
Jeffreyston. Pemb —2D **53**
Jersey Marine. Neat —3C **57**
Jingle Street. Mon —1B **60**
Johnston. Pemb —1C **53**
Johnstown. Carm —1C **55**
Johnstown. Wrex —3A **18**
Jordanston. Pemb —2C **43**

Keckwick. Ches —2C **11**
Keeston. Pemb —1C **53**
Kelsall. Ches —1C **19**
Kelsterton. Flin —3D **9**
Kelston. Bath —3D **67**
Kemberton. Shrp —1D **33**
Kemeys Commander. Mon
—2A **60**
Kempley. Glos —3D **51**
Kempley Green. Glos —3D **51**
Kempton. Shrp —3A **32**
Kenchester. H&W —1B **50**
Kendleshire. S.Glo —2D **67**
Kenfig. Bri —1D **63**
Kenfig Hill. Bri —1D **63**
Kenley. Shrp —1C **33**
Kenn. N.Sm —3B **66**
Kenstone. Shrp —2C **27**

Kentchurch. H&W —3B **50**
Kent's Green. Glos —3D **51**
Kenwick. Shrp —1B **26**
Kenyon. Ches —1D **11**
Kerne Bridge. H&W —1C **61**
Kerry. Powy —3C **31**
Kerry's Gate. H&W —2A **50**
Kewstoke. N.Sm —3A **66**
Keynsham. Bath —3D **67**
Kidnall. Ches —3B **18**
Kidwelly. Carm —2D **55**
Kilcot. Glos —3D **51**
Kilgetty. Pemb —2A **54**
Killay. Swan —3B **56**
Kiln Green. H&W —1C **61**
Kilpeck. H&W —2B **50**
Kimbolton. H&W —2C **41**
Kingcoed. Mon —2B **60**
King's Acre. H&W —1B **50**
Kings Caple. H&W —3C **51**
Kingsland. H&W —2B **40**
Kingsland. IOA —2B **4**
Kingsley. Ches —3C **11**
Kings Moss. Mers —1C **11**
King's Pyon. H&W —3B **40**
King's Thorn. H&W —2C **51**
Kingstone. H&W —2B **50**
Kingston Seymour. N.Sm
—3B **66**
Kingswood. Glos —3D **61**
Kingswood. H&W —3D **39**
Kingswood. Powy —1D **31**
Kingswood. S.Glo —2D **67**
Kington. H&W —3A **40**
Kington. S.Glo —3D **61**
Kinlet. Shrp —3D **33**
Kinmel Bay. Cnwy —2A **8**
Kinnerley. Shrp —2A **26**
Kinnersley. H&W —1A **50**
Kinnerton. Powy —2D **39**
Kinnerton. Shrp —2A **32**
Kinsey Heath. Ches —3D **19**
Kinsham. H&W —2A **40**
Kinton. H&W —1B **40**
Kinton. Shrp —3A **26**
Kirkby. Mers —1A **10**
Kirkby Industrial Estate. Mers
—1B **10**
Kirkdale. Mers —1A **10**
Kittle. Swan —1A **62**
Kivernoll. H&W —2B **50**
Knapton Green. H&W —3B **40**
Knelston. Swan —2B **56**
Knightcott. N.Sm —3A **66**
Knighton. Powy —1D **39**
Knighton. Staf —2D **27**
Knighton Common. H&W
—1D **41**
Knightwick. H&W —3D **41**
Knill. H&W —2D **39**
Knockin. Shrp —2A **26**
Knollbury. Mon —1B **66**
Knolton. Wrex —1A **26**
Knotty Ash. Mers —1B **10**
Knowbury. Shrp —1C **41**
Knowle. Bris —2D **67**
Knowle. Shrp —1C **41**
Knowsley. Mers —1B **10**
Knowsley Hall. Mers —1B **10**
Knucklas. Powy —1D **39**
Knutsford. Ches —3D **11**
Kymin. Mon —1C **61**
Kynaston. H&W —2D **51**
Kynaston. Shrp —2A **26**
Kynnersley. Shrp —3D **27**
Kyre Green. H&W —2D **41**
Kyre Park. H&W —2D **41**
Kyrewood. H&W —2D **41**

Lach Dennis. Ches —3D **11**
Lache. Ches —1A **18**

Lady Green. Mers —1A **10**
Laleston. Bri —1D **63**
Lambston. Pemb —1C **53**
Lampeter. Cdgn —1A **46**
Lampeter Velfrey. Pemb
—1A **54**
Lamphey. Pemb —2D **53**
Land Gate. G.Mn —1C **11**
Landimore. Swan —3D **55**
Landore. Swan —3B **56**
Landshipping. Pemb —1D **53**
Lane Head. G.Mn —1D **11**
Langland. Swan —1B **62**
Langridge. Bath —3D **67**
Larden Green. Ches —2C **19**
Larkhall. Bath —3D **67**
Larport. H&W —2C **51**
Latteridge. S.Glo —1D **67**
Laugharne. Carm —1C **55**
Lavister. Wrex —2A **18**
Lawrenny. Pemb —2D **53**
Lawton. H&W —3B **40**
Laysters Pole. H&W —2C **41**
Lea. H&W —3D **51**
Lea. Shrp —3A **32**
(nr. Bishop's Castle)
Lea. Shrp —1B **32**
(nr. Shrewsbury)
Leachpool. Pemb —1C **53**
Leasowe. Mers —1D **9**
Leaton. Shrp —3B **26**
Leckwith. V.Gl —2C **65**
Ledbury. H&W —2D **51**
Ledgemoor. H&W —3B **40**
Ledicot. H&W —2B **40**
Ledsham. Ches —3A **10**
Lee. Shrp —1B **26**
Leebotwood. Shrp —2B **32**
Lee Brockhurst. Shrp —2C **27**
Leechpool. Mon —1C **67**
Leegomery. Shrp —3D **27**
Leeswood. Flin —2D **17**
Leftwich. Ches —3D **11**
Leigh. G.Mn —1D **11**
Leigh. Shrp —1A **32**
Leighton. Powy —1D **31**
Leighton. Shrp —1D **33**
Leinthall Earls. H&W —2B **40**
Leinthall Starkes. H&W
—2B **40**
Leintwardine. H&W —1B **40**
Lem Hill. H&W —1D **41**
Leominster. H&W —3B **40**
Letterston. Pemb —3C **43**
Letton. H&W —1A **50**
(nr. Kington)
Letton. H&W —1A **40**
(nr. Leintwardine)
Leweston. Pemb —3C **43**
Lewistown. Bri —1A **64**
Libanus. Powy —3A **48**
Lightwood Green. Ches
—3D **19**
Lightwood Green. Wrex
—3A **18**
Lilleshall. Shrp —3D **27**
Lilyhurst. Shrp —3D **27**
Lindridge. H&W —2D **41**
Lingen. H&W —2A **40**
Lingoed. Mon —1A **60**
Linley. Shrp —2A **32**
(nr. Bishop's Castle)
Linley. Shrp —2D **33**
(nr. Bridgnorth)
Linley Green. H&W —3D **41**
Linton. H&W —3D **51**
Linton Hill. H&W —3D **51**
Lipley. Shrp —1D **27**
Liscard. Mers —1A **10**
Lisvane. Card —1C **65**
Liswerry. Newp —1A **66**
Litchard. Bri —1A **64**

Litherland. Mers —1A **10**
Little Barrow. Ches —1B **18**
Little Birch. H&W —2C **51**
Little Bolas. Shrp —2D **27**
Little Bollington. Ches —2D **11**
Little Brampton. Shrp —3A **32**
Little Budworth. Ches —1C **19**
Little Cowarne. H&W —3D **41**
Little Crosby. Mers —1A **10**
Little Dawley. Shrp —1D **33**
Littledean. Glos —1D **61**
Little Dewchurch. H&W
—2C **51**
Little Drayton. Shrp —1D **27**
Little Garway. H&W —3B **50**
Little Green. Wrex —3B **18**
Little Haven. Pemb —1B **52**
Little Hereford. H&W —2C **41**
Little Hulton. G.Mn —1D **11**
Little Leigh. Ches —3D **11**
Little London. Powy —3B **30**
Little Marcle. H&W —2D **51**
Little Mill. Mon —2A **60**
Little Mountain. Flin —1D **17**
Little Ness. Shrp —3B **26**
Little Neston. Ches —3A **10**
Little Newcastle. Pemb
—3C **43**
Little Reynoldston. Swan
—3D **55**
Little Ryton. Shrp —1B **32**
Little Sodbury. S.Glo —1D **67**
Little Soudley. Shrp —2D **27**
Little Stanney. Ches —3B **10**
Little Stretton. Shrp —2B **32**
Little Sutton. Ches —3A **10**
Littleton. Ches —1B **18**
Littleton-upon-Severn. S.Glo
—1C **67**
Little Wenlock. Shrp —1D **33**
Liverpool. Mers —1A **10**
Liverpool Airport. Mers
—2B **10**
Lixwm. Flin —3C **9**
Llaethdy. Powy —3B **30**
Llaingoch. IOA —2B **4**
Llampha. V.Gl —2A **64**
Llan. Powy —1D **29**
Llanaber. Gwyn —3B **22**
Llanaelhaearn. Gwyn —3C **13**
Llanaeron. Cdgn —3D **35**
Llanafan. Cdgn —1B **36**
Llanafan-fawr. Powy —3A **38**
Llanafan-fechan. Powy
—3A **38**
Llanallgo. IOA —2D **5**
Llanandras. Powy —2D **39**
Llananno. Powy —1B **38**
Llanarmon. Gwyn —1D **21**
Llanarmon Dyffryn Ceiriog.
Wrex —1C **25**
Llanarmon-yn-Ial. Den
—2C **17**
Llanarth. Cdgn —3D **35**
Llanarth. Mon —1A **60**
Llanarthney. Carm —3A **46**
Llanasa. Flin —2C **9**
Llanbabo. IOA —2C **5**
Llanbadarn Fawr. Cdgn
—3B **28**
Llanbadarn Fynydd. Powy
—1B **38**
Llanbadarn-y-garreg. Powy
—1C **49**
Llanbadoc. Mon —2A **60**
Llanbadrig. IOA —1C **5**
Llanbeder. Newp —3A **60**
Llanbedr. Gwyn —2A **22**
Llanbedr. Powy —3D **49**
(nr. Crickhowell)
Llanbedr. Powy —1C **49**
(nr. Hay-on-Wye)

Llanbedr-Dyffryn-Clwyd. Den
—2C **17**
Llanbedrgoch. IOA —2A **6**
Llanbedrog. Gwyn —1C **21**
Llanbedr-y-cennin. Cnwy
—1C **15**
Llanberis. Gwyn —1A **14**
Llanbethery. V.Gl —3B **64**
Llanbister. Powy —1C **39**
Llanblethian. V.Gl —2B **64**
Llanboidy. Carm —3B **44**
Llanbradach. Cphy —3C **59**
Llanbrynmair. Powy —1D **29**
Llancadle. V.Gl —3B **64**
Llancarfan. V.Gl —2B **64**
Llancayo. Mon —2A **60**
Llancloudy. H&W —3B **50**
Llancoch. Powy —1D **39**
Llancynfelyn. Cdgn —2B **28**
Llandaff. Card —2C **65**
Llandanwg. Gwyn —2A **22**
Llandarcy. Neat —3C **57**
Llandawke. Carm —1B **54**
Llanddaniel-Fab. IOA —3D **5**
Llanddarog. Carm —1A **56**
Llanddeiniol. Cdgn —1A **36**
Llanddeiniolen. Gwyn —1A **14**
Llandderfel. Gwyn —1A **24**
Llanddeusant. Carm —3C **47**
Llanddeusant. IOA —2C **5**
Llanddew. Powy —2B **48**
Llanddewi. Swan —3D **55**
Llanddewi Brefi. Cdgn
—3B **36**
Llanddewi'r Cwm. Powy
—1B **48**
Llanddewi Rhydderch. Mon
—1A **60**
Llanddewi Velfrey. Pemb
—1A **54**
Llanddewi Ystradenni. Powy
—2C **39**
Llanddoged. Cnwy —1D **15**
Llanddona. IOA —3A **6**
Llanddowror. Carm —1B **54**
Llanddulas. Cnwy —3A **8**
Llanddwywe. Gwyn —2A **22**
Llanddyfnan. IOA —3A **6**
Llandecwyn. Gwyn —1B **22**
Llandefaelog Fach. Powy
—2B **48**
Llandefaelog-tre'r-graig. Powy
—2C **49**
Llandefalle. Powy —2C **49**
Llandegai. Gwyn —3A **6**
Llandegfan. IOA —3A **6**
Llandegla. Den —2C **17**
Llandegley. Powy —2C **39**
Llandegveth. Mon —3A **60**
Llandeilo. Carm —3B **46**
Llandeilo Graban. Powy
—1B **48**
Llandeilo'r Fan. Powy —2D **47**
Llandeloy. Pemb —3B **42**
Llandenny. Mon —2B **60**
Llandevaud. Newp —3B **60**
Llandevenny. Newp —1B **66**
Llandilo. Pemb —3A **44**
Llandinabo. H&W —3C **51**
Llandinam. Powy —3B **30**
Llandissilio. Pemb —3A **44**
Llandogo. Mon —2C **61**
Llandough. V.Gl —2A **64**
(nr. Cowbridge)
Llandough. V.Gl —2C **65**
(nr. Penarth)
Llandovery. Carm —2C **47**
Llandow. V.Gl —2A **64**
Llandre. Cdgn —3B **28**
Llandrillo. Den —1B **24**
Llandrillo-yn-Rhos. Cnwy
—2D **7**

Llandrindod Wells. Powy
—2B **38**
Llandrinio. Powy —3D **25**
Llandsadwrn. Carm —2B **46**
Llandudno. Cnwy —2C **7**
Llandudno Junction. Cnwy
—3C **7**
Llandwrog. Gwyn —2D **13**
Llandybie. Carm —1B **56**
Llandyfaelog. Carm —1D **55**
Llandyfan. Carm —1B **56**
Llandyfriog. Cdgn —1C **45**
Llandyfrydog. IOA —2D **5**
Llandygwydd. Cdgn —1B **44**
Llandynan. Den —3C **17**
Llandyrnog. Den —1C **17**
Llandysilio. Powy —3D **25**
Llandyssil. Powy —2C **31**
Llandysul. Cdgn —1D **45**
Llanedeyrn. Card —1D **65**
Llaneglwys. Powy —2B **48**
Llanegryn. Gwyn —1B **28**
Llanegwad. Carm —3A **46**
Llaneilian. IOA —1D **5**
Llanelian-yn-Rhos. Cnwy
—3D **7**
Llanelidan. Den —2C **17**
Llanelieu. Powy —2C **49**
Llanellen. Mon —1A **60**
Llanelli. Carm —3A **56**
Llanelltyd. Gwyn —3C **23**
Llanelly. Mon —1D **59**
Llanelly Hill. Mon —1D **59**
Llanelwedd. Powy —3B **38**
Llanelwy. Den —3B **8**
Llanenddwyn. Gwyn —2A **22**
Llanengan. Gwyn —2B **20**
Llanerch. Powy —2A **32**
Llanerchymedd. IOA —2D **5**
Llanerfyl. Powy —1B **30**
Llaneuddog. IOA —2D **5**
Llanfachraeth. IOA —2C **5**
Llanfaelog. IOA —3C **5**
Llanfaelrhys. Gwyn —2B **20**
Llanfaenor. Mon —1B **60**
Llanfaes. IOA —3B **6**
Llanfaes. Powy —3B **48**
Llanfaethlu. IOA —2C **5**
Llanfaglan. Gwyn —1D **13**
Llanfair. Gwyn —2A **22**
Llanfair. H&W —1D **49**
Llanfair Caereinion. Powy
—1C **31**
Llanfair Clydogau. Cdgn
—3B **36**
Llanfair Dyffryn Clwyd. Den
—2C **17**
Llanfairfechan. Cnwy —3B **6**
Llanfair-Nant-Gwyn. Pemb
—2A **44**
Llanfair Pwllgwyngyll. IOA
—3A **6**
Llanfair Talhaiarn. Cnwy
—3A **8**
Llanfair Waterdine. Shrp
—1D **39**
Llanfair-ym-Muallt. Powy
—3B **38**
Llanfairyneubwll. IOA —3C **5**
Llanfairynghornwy. IOA
—1C **5**
Llanfallteg. Carm —1A **54**
Llanfallteg West. Carm
—1A **54**
Llanfaredd. Powy —3B **38**
Llanfarian. Cdgn —1A **36**
Llanfechain. Powy —2C **25**
Llanfechell. IOA —1C **5**
Llanfechreth. Gwyn —2C **23**
Llanfendigaid. Gwyn —1A **28**
Llanferres. Den —1C **17**
Llanfflewyn. IOA —2C **5**

74 Wales Regional Atlas

Llanfihangel Glyn Myfyr. *Cnwy* —3A **16**

Llanfihangel Nant Bran. *Powy* —2A **48**

Llanfihangel-Nant-Melan. *Powy* —3C **39**

Llanfihangel Rhydithon. *Powy* —2C **39**

Llanfihangel Rogiet. *Mon* —1B **66**

Llanfihangel Tal-y-llyn. *Powy* —3C **49**

Llanfihangel-uwch-Gwili. *Carm* —3D **45**

Llanfihangel-yng-ngwynfa. *Powy* —3B **24**

Llanfihangel yn Nhowyn. *IOA* —3C **5**

Llanfihangel-y-pennant. *Gwyn* (nr. Golan) —3A **14**

Llanfihangel-y-pennant. *Gwyn* (nr. Tywyn) —1B **28**

Llanfilo. *Powy* —2C **49**

Llanfinhangel-ar-Arth. *Carm* —2D **45**

Llanfinhangel-y-Creuddyn. *Cdgn* —1B **36**

Llanfinhangel-y-traethau. *Gwyn* —1A **22**

Llanfoist. *Mon* —1D **59**

Llanfor. *Gwyn* —1A **24**

Llanfrechfa. *Torf* —3A **60**

Llanfrothen. *Gwyn* —3B **14**

Llanfrynach. *Powy* —3B **48**

Llanfwrog. *Den* —2C **17**

Llanfwrog. *IOA* —2C **5**

Llanfyllin. *Powy* —3C **25**

Llanfynydd. *Carm* —3A **46**

Llanfynydd. *Flin* —2D **17**

Llanfyrnach. *Pemb* —2B **44**

Llangadfan. *Powy* —3B **24**

Llangadog. *Carm* —3C **47** (nr. Llandovery)

Llangadog. *Carm* —2D **55** (nr. Llanelli)

Llangadwaladr. *IOA* —1C **13**

Llangadwaladr. *Powy* —1C **25**

Llangaffo. *IOA* —1D **13**

Llangain. *Carm* —1C **55**

Llangammarch Wells. *Powy* —1A **48**

Llangan. *V.GI* —2A **64**

Llangarron. *H&W* —3C **51**

Llangasty-Talyllyn. *Powy* —3C **49**

Llangathen. *Carm* —3A **46**

Llangattock. *Powy* —1D **59**

Llangattock Lingoed. *Mon* —3A **50**

Llangattock-Vibon-Avel. *Mon* —1B **60**

Llangedwyn. *Powy* —2C **25**

Llangefni. *IOA* —3D **5**

Llangeinor. *Bri* —1A **64**

Llangeitho. *Cdgn* —3B **36**

Llangeler. *Carm* —2C **45**

Llangelynin. *Gwyn* —1A **28**

Llangendeirne. *Carm* —1D **55**

Llangennech. *Carm* —2A **56**

Llangenneth. *Swan* —3D **55**

Llangenny. *Powy* —1D **59**

Llangernyw. *Cnwy* —1D **15**

Llangian. *Gwyn* —2B **20**

Llangiwg. *Neat* —2C **57**

Llangloffan. *Pemb* —2C **43**

Llanglydwen. *Carm* —3A **44**

Llangoed. *IOA* —3B **6**

Llangoedmor. *Cdgn* —1B **44**

Llangollen. *Den* —3D **17**

Llangolman. *Pemb* —3A **44**

Llangorse. *Powy* —3C **49**

Llangorwen. *Cdgn* —3B **28**

Llangovan. *Mon* —2B **60**

Llangower. *Gwyn* —1A **24**

Llangranog. *Cdgn* —3C **35**

Llangristiolus. *IOA* —3D **5**

Llangrove. *H&W* —1C **61**

Llangua. *Mon* —3A **50**

Llangunllo. *Powy* —1D **39**

Llangunnor. *Carm* —3D **45**

Llangurig. *Powy* —1A **38**

Llangwm. *Cnwy* —3A **16**

Llangwm. *Mon* —2B **60**

Llangwm. *Pemb* —2C **53**

Llangwm-isaf. *Mon* —2B **60**

Llangwnnadl. *Gwyn* —1B **20**

Llangwyfan. *Den* —1C **17**

Llangwyfan-isaf. *IOA* —1C **13**

Llangwyllog. *IOA* —3D **5**

Llangwyryfon. *Cdgn* —1A **36**

Llangybi. *Cdgn* —3B **36**

Llangybi. *Gwyn* —3D **13**

Llangybi. *Mon* —3A **60**

Llangyfelach. *Swan* —3B **56**

Llangynhafal. *Den* —1C **17**

Llangynidr. *Powy* —1C **59**

Llangynin. *Carm* —1B **54**

Llangynog. *Carm* —1C **55**

Llangynog. *Powy* —2B **24**

Llangynwyd. *Bri* —1D **63**

Llanhamlach. *Powy* —3B **48**

Llanharan. *Rhon* —1B **64**

Llanharry. *Rhon* —1B **64**

Llanhennock. *Mon* —3A **60**

Llanhilleth. *Blae* —2D **59**

Llanidloes. *Powy* —3A **30**

Llaniestyn. *Gwyn* —1B **20**

Llanigon. *Powy* —1D **49**

Llanilar. *Cdgn* —1B **36**

Llanilid. *Rhon* —1A **64**

Llanishen. *Card* —1C **65**

Llanishen. *Mon* —2B **60**

Llanllawddog. *Carm* —3D **45**

Llanllechid. *Gwyn* —1B **14**

Llanllowell. *Mon* —3A **60**

Llanllugan. *Powy* —1B **30**

Llanllwch. *Carm* —1C **55**

Llanllwchaiarn. *Powy* —2C **31**

Llanllwni. *Carm* —2D **45**

Llanllyfni. *Gwyn* —2D **13**

Llanmadoc. *Swan* —3D **55**

Llanmaes. *V.GI* —3A **64**

Llanmartin. *Newp* —1A **66**

Llanmerwig. *Powy* —2C **31**

Llanmihangel. *V.GI* —2A **64**

Llan-mill. *Pemb* —1A **54**

Llanmiloe. *Carm* —2B **54**

Llanmorlais. *Swan* —3A **56**

Llannefydd. *Cnwy* —3A **8**

Llannon. *Carm* —2A **56**

Llan-non. *Cdgn* —2A **36**

Llannor. *Gwyn* —1C **21**

Llanpumsaint. *Carm* —3D **45**

Llanrhaeadr. *Den* —1B **16**

Llanrhaeadr-ym-Mochnant. *Powy* —2C **25**

Llanrhidian. *Swan* —3D **55**

Llanrhos. *Cnwy* —2C **7**

Llanrhyddlad. *IOA* —2C **5**

Llanrhystud. *Cdgn* —2A **36**

Llanrian. *Pemb* —2B **42**

Llanrothal. *H&W* —1B **60**

Llanrug. *Gwyn* —1A **14**

Llanrumney. *Card* —1D **65**

Llanrwst. *Cnwy* —1C **15**

Llansadurnen. *Carm* —1B **54**

Llansadwrn. *IOA* —3A **6**

Llansaint. *Carm* —2C **55**

Llansamlet. *Swan* —3B **56**

Llansanffraid Glan Conwy. *Cnwy* —3D **7**

Llansannan. *Cnwy* —1A **16**

Llansannor. *V.GI* —2A **64**

Llansantffraed. *Cdgn* —2D **35**

Llansantffraed. *Powy* —3C **49**

Llansantffraed Cwmdeuddwr. *Powy* —2A **38**

Llansantffraed in Elvel. *Powy* —3C **39**

Llansantffraid-ym-Mechain. *Powy* —2D **25**

Llansawel. *Carm* —2B **46**

Llansilin. *Powy* —2D **25**

Llansoy. *Mon* —2B **60**

Llanspyddid. *Powy* —3B **48**

Llanstadwell. *Pemb* —2C **53**

Llansteffan. *Carm* —1C **55**

Llanstephan. *Powy* —1C **49**

Llantarnam. *Torf* —3D **59**

Llanteg. *Pemb* —1A **54**

Llanthony. *Mon* —3D **49**

Llantilio Crossenny. *Mon* —1A **60**

Llantilio Pertholey. *Mon* —1A **60**

Llantood. *Pemb* —1A **44**

Llantrisant. *Mon* —3A **60**

Llantrisant. *Rhon* —1B **64**

Llantrithyd. *V.GI* —2B **64**

Llantwit Fardre. *Rhon* —1B **64**

Llantwit Major. *V.GI* —3A **64**

Llanuwchllyn. *Gwyn* —1D **23**

Llanvaches. *Newp* —3B **60**

Llanvair Discoed. *Mon* —3B **60**

Llanvapley. *Mon* —1A **60**

Llanvetherine. *Mon* —1A **60**

Llanveynoe. *H&W* —2A **50**

Llanvihangel Crucorney. *Mon* —3A **50**

Llanvihangel Gobion. *Mon* —2A **60**

Llanvihangel Ystern-Llewern. *Mon* —1B **60**

Llanwarne. *H&W* —3C **51**

Llanwddyn. *Powy* —3B **24**

Llanwenarth. *Mon* —1D **59**

Llanwenog. *Cdgn* —1D **45**

Llanwern. *Newp* —1A **66**

Llanwinio. *Carm* —3B **44**

Llanwnda. *Gwyn* —2D **13**

Llanwnda. *Pemb* —2C **43**

Llanwnnen. *Cdgn* —1A **46**

Llanwnog. *Powy* —2B **30**

Llanwrda. *Carm* —2C **47**

Llanwrin. *Powy* —1C **29**

Llanwrthwl. *Powy* —2A **38**

Llanwrtyd. *Powy* —1D **47**

Llanwrtyd Wells. *Powy* —1D **47**

Llanwyddelan. *Powy* —1B **30**

Llanyblodwel. *Shrp* —2D **25**

Llanybri. *Carm* —1C **55**

Llanybyther. *Carm* —1A **46**

Llanycefn. *Pemb* —3D **43**

Llanychaer. *Pemb* —2C **43**

Llanycil. *Gwyn* —1A **24**

Llanymawddwy. *Gwyn* —3A **24**

Llanymddyfri. *Carm* —2C **47**

Llanymynech. *Powy* —2D **25**

Llanynghenedl. *IOA* —2C **5**

Llanynys. *Den* —1C **17**

Llan-y-pwll. *Wrex* —2A **18**

Llanyre. *Powy* —2B **38**

Llanystumdwy. *Gwyn* —1D **21**

Llanywern. *Powy* —3C **49**

Llawhaden. *Pemb* —1D **53**

Llawndy. *Flin* —2C **9**

Llawnt. *Shrp* —1D **25**

Llawr Dref. *Gwyn* —2B **20**

Llawryglyn. *Powy* —2A **30**

Llay. *Wrex* —2A **18**

Llechfaen. *Powy* —3B **48**

Llechryd. *Cphy* —2C **59**

Llechryd. *Cdgn* —1B **44**

Llechrydau. *Powy* —1D **25**

Lledrod. *Cdgn* —1B **36**

Llethrid. *Swan* —3A **56**

Llidiadnenog. *Carm* —2A **46**

Llidiardau. *Gwyn* —1D **23**

Llidiart y Parc. *Den* —3C **17**

Llithfaen. *Gwyn* —3C **13**

Lloc. *Flin* —3C **9**

Llong. *Flin* —1D **17**

Llowes. *Powy* —1C **49**

Lloyney. *Powy* —1D **39**

Llundain-fach. *Cdgn* —3A **36**

Llwydcoed. *Rhon* —2A **58**

Llwyncelyn. *Cdgn* —3D **35**

Llwyncelyn. *Swan* —2B **56**

Llwyndaffydd. *Cdgn* —3C **35**

Llwynderw. *Powy* —1D **31**

Llwyn-du. *Mon* —1D **59**

Llwyngwril. *Gwyn* —1A **28**

Llwynhendy. *Carm* —3A **56**

Llwynmawr. *Wrex* —1D **25**

Llwyn-on Village. *Mert* —1B **58**

Llwyn-teg. *Carm* —2A **56**

Llwyn-y-brain. *Carm* —1A **54**

Llwyn-y-groes. *Cdgn* —3A **36**

Llwynypia. *Rhon* —3A **58**

Llynclys. *Shrp* —2D **25**

Llynfaes. *IOA* —3D **5**

Llysfaen. *Cnwy* —3D **7**

Llyswen. *Powy* —2C **49**

Llysworney. *V.GI* —2A **64**

Llys-y-fran. *Pemb* —3D **43**

Llywel. *Powy* —2D **47**

Llywernog. *Cdgn* —3C **29**

Locking. *N.Sm* —3A **66**

Lockleywood. *Shrp* —2D **27**

Logaston. *H&W* —3A **40**

Loggerheads. *Staf* —1D **27**

Login. *Carm* —3A **44**

Long Ashton. *N.Sm* —2C **67**

Long Bank. *H&W* —1D **41**

Longden. *Shrp* —1B **32**

Longden Common. *Shrp* —1B **32**

Longdon on Tern. *Shrp* —3D **27**

Longford. *Shrp* —1D **27** (nr. Market Drayton)

Longford. *Shrp* —3D **27** (nr. Newport)

Long Green. *Ches* —3B **10**

Longhope. *Glos* —1D **61**

Long Lane. *Shrp* —3D **27**

Longley Green. *H&W* —3D **41**

Long Meadowend. *Shrp* —3B **32**

Longnor. *Shrp* —1B **32**

Longshaw. *G.Mn* —1C **11**

Longslow. *Shrp* —1D **27**

Longtown. *H&W* —3A **50**

Longville in the Dale. *Shrp* —2C **33**

Loppington. *Shrp* —2B **26**

Lostock Gralam. *Ches* —3D **11**

Lostock Green. *Ches* —3D **11**

Loughor. *Swan* —3A **56**

Loughton. *Shrp* —3D **33**

Loveston. *Pemb* —2D **53**

Lowe. *Shrp* —1C **27**

Lower Brynamman. *Neat* —1C **57**

Lower Bullingham. *H&W* —2C **51**

Lower Cam. *Glos* —2D **61**

Lower Chapel. *Powy* —2B **48**

Lower Down. *Shrp* —3A **32**

Lower Egleton. *H&W* —1D **51**

Lower Failand. *N.Sm* —2C **67**

Lower Faintree. *Shrp* —3D **33**

Lower Hardwick. *H&W* —3B **40**

Lower Hayton. *Shrp* —3C **33**

Lower Hergest. *H&W* —3D **39**

Lower Hordley. *Shrp* —2A **26**

Lower Kinnerton. *Ches* —1A **18**

Lower Langford. *N.Sm* —3B **66**

Lower Ledwyche. *Shrp* —1C **41**

Lower Ley. *Glos* —1D **61**

Lower Llanfadog. *Powy* —2A **38**

Lower Lydbrook. *Glos* —1C **61**

Lower Lye. *H&W* —2B **40**

Lower Machen. *Newp* —1D **65**

Lower Maes-coed. *H&W* —2A **50**

Lower Meend. *Glos* —2C **61**

Lower Morton. *S.Glo* —3D **61**

Lower Mountain. *Flin* —2A **18**

Lower Penarth. *V.GI* —3C **65**

Lower Peover. *Ches* —3D **11**

Lower Sketty. *Swan* —3B **56**

Lower Soudley. *Glos* —1D **61**

Lower Town. *H&W* —1D **51**

Lower Town. *Pemb* —2C **43**

Lower Walton. *Ches* —2D **11**

Lower Welson. *H&W* —3D **39**

Lower Whitley. *Ches* —3D **11**

Lower Wych. *Ches* —3B **18**

Lowton. *G.Mn* —1D **11**

Lowton Common. *G.Mn* —1D **11**

Lucton. *H&W* —2B **40**

Ludchurch. *Pemb* —1A **54**

Ludford. *Shrp* —1C **41**

Ludlow. *Shrp* —1C **41**

Lugg Green. *H&W* —2B **40**

Lugwardine. *H&W* —1C **51**

Lulham. *H&W* —1B **50**

Lulsgate Bottom. *N.Sm* —3C **67**

Lulsley. *H&W* —3D **41**

Lunnon. *Swan* —1A **62**

Lunt. *Mers* —1A **10**

Luston. *H&W* —2B **40**

Luxley. *Glos* —3D **51**

Lydbury North. *Shrp* —3A **32**

Lydham. *Shrp* —2A **32**

Lydiate. *Mers* —1A **10**

Lydney. *Glos* —2D **61**

Lydstep. *Pemb* —3D **53**

Lye Head. *H&W* —1D **41**

Lye, The. *Shrp* —2D **33**

Lymm. *Ches* —2D **11**

Lyneal. *Shrp* —1B **26**

Lyne Down. *H&W* —2D **51**

Lyonshall. *H&W* —3A **40**

Machen. *Cphy* —1D **65**

Machroes. *Gwyn* —2C **21**

Machynlleth. *Powy* —1C **29**

Madeley. *Shrp* —1D **33**

Madley. *H&W* —2B **50**

Maenaddwyn. *IOA* —2C **5**

Maenclochog. *Pemb* —3D **43**

Maendy. *V.GI* —2B **64**

Maentwrog. *Gwyn* —3B **14**

Maen-y-groes. *Cdgn* —1A **44**

Maerdy. *Carm* —3B **46**

Maerdy. *Cnwy* —3B **16**

Maerdy. *Rhon* —3A **58**

Maesbrook. *Shrp* —2A **26**

Maesbury. *Shrp* —2A **26**

Maesbury Marsh. *Shrp* —2A **26**

Maes-glas. *Flin* —3C **9**

Maesgwyn-Isaf. *Powy* —3C **25**

Maeshafn. *Den* —1D **17**

Maes Llyn. *Cdgn* —1C **45**

Maesmynis. *Powy* —1B **48**
Maesteg. *Bri* —3D **57**
Maestir. *Cdgn* —1A **46**
Maesybont. *Carm* —1A **56**
Maesycrugiau. *Carm* —1D **45**
Maesycwmmer. *Cphy* —3C **59**
Maesyrhandir. *Powy* —2B **30**
Maghull. *Mers* —1A **10**
Magor. *Mon* —1B **66**
Magwyr. *Mon* —1B **66**
Maiden Wells. *Pemb* —3C **53**
Maindee. *Newp* —1A **66**
Mainstone. *Shrp* —3D **31**
Malinslee. *Shrp* —1D **33**
Malltraeth. *IOA* —1D **13**
Mallwyd. *Gwyn* —3D **23**
Malpas. *Ches* —3B **18**
Malpas. *Newp* —3D **59**
Malswick. *Glos* —3D **51**
Mamble. *H&W* —1D **41**
Mamhilad. *Mon* —2A **60**
Manafon. *Powy* —1C **31**
Mancot. *Flin* —1A **18**
Mangotsfield. *S.Glo* —2D **67**
Manley. *Ches* —3C **11**
Manmoel. *Cphy* —2C **59**
Manorbier. *Pemb* —3D **53**
Manorbier Newton. *Pemb*
—3D **53**
Manorowen. *Pemb* —2C **43**
Mansell Gamage. *H&W*
—1A **50**
Mansell Lacy. *H&W* —1B **50**
Marbury. *Ches* —3C **19**
Marchamley. *Shrp* —2C **27**
Marchwiel. *Wrex* —3A **18**
Marcross. *V.Gl* —3A **64**
Marden. *H&W* —1C **51**
Mardu. *Shrp* —3D **31**
Mardy. *Mon* —1A **60**
Marford. *Wrex* —2A **18**
Margam. *Neat* —1C **63**
Marian Cwm. *Den* —3B **8**
Mariandyrys. *IOA* —2B **6**
Marian-glas. *IOA* —2A **6**
Marian-y-de. *Gwyn* —1C **21**
Marion-y-mor. *Gwyn* —1C **21**
Market Drayton. *Shrp* —1D **27**
Markham. *Cphy* —2C **59**
Marksbury. *Bath* —3D **67**
Marley Green. *Ches* —3C **19**
Marloes. *Pemb* —2A **52**
Marlow. *H&W* —1B **40**
Marros. *Carm* —2B **54**
Marshbrook. *Shrp* —3B **32**
Marshfield. *Newp* —1D **65**
Marsh Green. *Shrp* —3D **27**
Marsh, The. *Powy* —2A **32**
Marsh, The. *Shrp* —2D **27**
Marston. *Ches* —3D **11**
Marston. *H&W* —3A **40**
Marston Stannett. *H&W*
—3C **41**
Marstow. *H&W* —1C **61**
Martletwy. *Pemb* —1D **53**
Martley. *H&W* —3D **41**
Marton. *Shrp* —2B **26**
(nr. Myddle)
Marton. *Shrp* —1D **31**
(nr. Worthen)
Mathern. *Mon* —3C **61**
Mathon. *H&W* —1D **51**
Mathry. *Pemb* —2B **42**
Maund Bryan. *H&W* —3C **41**
Mawdlam. *Bri* —1D **63**
Maw Green. *Ches* —2D **19**
Mayals. *Swan* —1B **62**
Mayhill. *Swan* —3B **56**
Maypole. *Mon* —1B **60**
Mayshill. *S.Glo* —1D **67**
Meadgate. *Bath* —3D **67**
Meadowbank. *Ches* —1D **19**

Meadow Green. *H&W* —3D **41**
Meadowtown. *Shrp* —1A **32**
Medlicott. *Shrp* —2B **32**
Meeson. *Shrp* —2D **27**
Meidrim. *Carm* —3B **44**
Meifod. *Powy* —3C **25**
Meinciau. *Carm* —1D **55**
Meliden. *Den* —2B **8**
Melinbyrhedyn. *Powy* —2D **29**
Melincourt. *Neat* —2D **57**
Melin-y-coed. *Cnwy* —1D **15**
Melin-y-ddol. *Powy* —1B **30**
Melin-y-wig. *Den* —3B **16**
Melling. *Mers* —1A **10**
Melling Mount. *Mers* —1B **10**
Melverley. *Shrp* —3A **26**
Melverley Green. *Shrp*
—3A **26**
Menai Bridge. *IOA* —3A **6**
Menithwood. *H&W* —2D **41**
Meole Brace. *Shrp* —3B **26**
Meols. *Mers* —2D **9**
Merbach. *H&W* —1A **50**
Mere. *Ches* —2D **11**
Mere Heath. *Ches* —3D **11**
Meretown. *Staf* —2D **27**
Merlin's Bridge. *Pemb*
—1C **53**
Merrington. *Shrp* —2B **26**
Merrion. *Pemb* —3C **53**
Merthyr. *Carm* —3C **45**
Merthyr Cynog. *Powy* —2A **48**
Merthyr Dyfan. *V.Gl* —3C **65**
Merthyr Mawr. *Bri* —2D **63**
Merthyr Tydfil. *Mert* —2B **58**
Merthyr Vale. *Mert* —2B **58**
Michaelchurch. *H&W* —3C **51**
Michaelchurch Escley. *H&W*
—2A **50**
Michaelchurch-on-Arrow.
Powy —3D **39**
Michaelston-le-Pit. *V.Gl*
—2C **65**
Michaelston-y-Vedw. *Newp*
—1D **65**
Mickle Trafford. *Ches* —1B **18**
Middlehope. *Shrp* —3B **32**
Middle Maes-coed. *H&W*
—2A **50**
Middleton. *H&W* —2C **41**
Middleton. *Shrp* —1C **41**
(nr. Ludlow)
Middleton. *Shrp* —2A **26**
(nr. Oswestry)
Middleton. *Swan* —3D **55**
Middleton on the Hill. *H&W*
—2C **41**
Middleton Priors. *Shrp*
—2D **33**
Middleton Scriven. *Shrp*
—3D **33**
Middletown. *Powy* —3A **26**
Middlewich. *Ches* —1D **19**
Milbury Heath. *S.Glo* —3D **61**
Milebrook. *Powy* —1A **40**
Miles Hope. *H&W* —2C **41**
Milford. *Powy* —2B **30**
Milford Haven. *Pemb* —2C **53**
Milkwall. *Glos* —2C **61**
Millend. *Glos* —3D **61**
Mill Green. *Shrp* —2D **27**
Millhalf. *H&W* —1D **49**
Milson. *Shrp* —1D **41**
Milton. *N.Sm* —3A **66**
Milton. *Pemb* —2D **53**
Milton Green. *Ches* —2B **18**
Minera. *Wrex* —2D **17**
Minffordd. *Gwyn* —1A **22**
Minllyn. *Gwyn* —3D **23**
Minsterley. *Shrp* —1A **32**
Minton. *Shrp* —2B **32**
Minwear. *Pemb* —1D **53**

Miskin. *Rhon* —1B **64**
Mitcheldean. *Glos* —1D **61**
Mitchel Troy. *Mon* —1B **60**
Mitcheltroy Common. *Mon*
—2B **60**
Moccas. *H&W* —1A **50**
Mochdre. *Cnwy* —3D **7**
Mochdre. *Powy* —3B **30**
Moelfre. *Cnwy* —3A **8**
Moelfre. *IOA* —2A **6**
Moelfre. *Powy* —2C **25**
Mold. *Flin* —1D **17**
Mollington. *Ches* —3A **10**
Monachty. *Cdgn* —2A **36**
Monaughty. *Powy* —2D **39**
Monington. *Pemb* —1A **44**
Monkhide. *H&W* —1D **51**
Monkhopton. *Shrp* —2D **33**
Monkland. *H&W* —3B **40**
Monknash. *V.Gl* —2A **64**
Monkswood. *Mon* —2A **60**
Monkton. *Pemb* —2C **53**
Monmarsh. *H&W* —1C **51**
Monmouth. *Mon* —1C **61**
Monnington on Wye. *H&W*
—1A **50**
Montford. *Shrp* —3B **26**
Montford Bridge. *Shrp*
—3B **26**
Montgomery. *Powy* —2D **31**
Moorcot. *H&W* —3A **40**
Moore. *Ches* —2C **11**
Moorend. *Glos* —2D **61**
Moorhampton. *H&W* —1A **50**
Moortown. *Shrp* —3D **27**
Morda. *Shrp* —2D **25**
Mordiford. *H&W* —2C **51**
More. *Shrp* —2A **32**
Morehouse, The. *Shrp*
—2C **33**
Moreton. *H&W* —2C **41**
Moreton. *Mers* —1D **9**
Moreton Corbet. *Shrp*
—2C **27**
Moreton Jeffries. *H&W*
—1D **51**
Moreton on Lugg. *H&W*
—1C **51**
Moreton Say. *Shrp* —1D **27**
Morfa. *Cdgn* —3C **35**
Morfa Bach. *Carm* —1C **55**
Morfa Bychan. *Gwyn* —1A **22**
Morfa Glas. *Neat* —2D **57**
Morfa Nefyn. *Gwyn* —3B **12**
Morganstown. *Card* —1C **65**
Moriah. *Cdgn* —1B **36**
Morriston. *Swan* —3B **56**
Mortimer's Cross. *H&W*
—2B **40**
Morton. *Shrp* —2D **25**
Morton. *S.Glo* —3D **61**
Morton Mill. *Shrp* —2C **27**
Morvil. *Pemb* —2D **43**
Morville. *Shrp* —2D **33**
Mose. *Shrp* —2D **33**
Moss. *Wrex* —2A **18**
Moss Bank. *Mers* —1C **11**
Mossbrow. *G.Mn* —2D **11**
Mossley Hill. *Mers* —2A **10**
Moss Side. *Mers* —1A **10**
Moston. *Shrp* —2C **27**
Moston Green. *Ches* —1D **19**
Mostyn. *Flin* —2C **9**
Mouldsworth. *Ches* —3C **11**
Moulton. *Ches* —1D **19**
Moulton. *V.Gl* —2B **64**
Mountain Ash. *Rhon* —3B **58**
Mountain Water. *Pemb*
—3C **43**
Mounton. *Mon* —3C **61**
Moylgrove. *Pemb* —1A **44**
Much Birch. *H&W* —2C **51**

Much Cowarne. *H&W* —1D **51**
Much Dewchurch. *H&W*
—2B **50**
Much Marcle. *H&W* —2D **51**
Much Wenlock. *Shrp* —2D **33**
Mucklestone. *Staf* —1D **27**
Muckleton. *Shrp* —2C **27**
Muckley. *Shrp* —2D **33**
Mumbles, The. *Swan* —1B **62**
Munderfield Row. *H&W*
—3D **41**
Munderfield Stocks. *H&W*
—3D **41**
Munsley. *H&W* —1D **51**
Munslow. *Shrp* —3C **33**
Murton. *Swan* —1A **62**
Muxton. *Shrp* —3D **27**
Mwmbwls. *Swan* —1B **62**
Myddfai. *Carm* —2C **47**
Myddle. *Shrp* —2B **26**
Mydroilyn. *Cdgn* —3D **35**
Mynachlog-ddu. *Pemb*
—2A **44**
Mynydd-bach. *Mon* —3B **60**
Mynydd Isa. *Flin* —1D **17**
Mynyddislwyn. *Cphy* —3C **59**
Mynydd Llandegai. *Gwyn*
—1B **14**
Mynydd-y-briw. *Powy* —2C **25**
Mynyddygarreg. *Carm*
—2D **55**
Mynytho. *Gwyn* —1C **21**
Mytton. *Shrp* —3B **26**

Nailbridge. *Glos* —1D **61**
Nailsea. *N.Sm* —2B **66**
Nannerch. *Flin* —1C **17**
Nant-ddu. *Rhon* —1B **58**
Nanternis. *Cdgn* —3C **35**
Nantgaredig. *Carm* —3D **45**
Nantgarw. *Rhon* —1C **65**
Nant Glas. *Powy* —2A **38**
Nantglyn. *Den* —1B **16**
Nantgwyn. *Powy* —1A **38**
Nantlle. *Gwyn* —2A **14**
Nantmawr. *Shrp* —2D **25**
Nantmel. *Powy* —2B **38**
Nantmor. *Gwyn* —3B **14**
Nant Peris. *Gwyn* —2B **14**
Nantwich. *Ches* —2D **19**
Nant-y-bai. *Carm* —1C **47**
Nant-y-Derry. *Mon* —2A **60**
Nant-y-dugoed. *Powy* —3A **24**
Nant-y-felin. *Cnwy* —3B **6**
Nantyffyllon. *Bri* —3D **57**
Nantyglo. *Blae* —1C **59**
Nant-y-meichiaid. *Powy*
—3C **25**
Nant-y-moel. *Bri* —3A **58**
Nant-y-Pandy. *Cnwy* —3B **6**
Narberth. *Pemb* —1A **54**
Narberth Bridge. *Pemb*
—1A **54**
Narth, The. *Mon* —2C **61**
Nasareth. *Gwyn* —3D **13**
Nash. *H&W* —2A **40**
Nash. *Newp* —1A **66**
Nash. *Shrp* —1D **41**
Neath. *Neat* —3C **57**
Neath Abbey. *Neat* —3C **57**
Nebo. *Cdgn* —2A **36**
Nebo. *Cnwy* —2D **15**
Nebo. *Gwyn* —2D **13**
Nebo. *IOA* —1D **5**
Neen Savage. *Shrp* —1D **41**
Neen Sollars. *Shrp* —1D **41**
Neenton. *Shrp* —3D **33**
Nefyn. *Gwyn* —3C **13**
Nelly Andrews Green. *Powy*
—1D **31**
Nelson. *Cphy* —3C **59**

Nempnett Thrubwell. *Bath*
—3C **67**
Nercwys. *Flin* —1D **17**
Ness. *Ches* —3A **10**
Nesscliffe. *Shrp* —3A **26**
Neston. *Ches* —3D **9**
Netchwood. *Shrp* —2D **33**
Netherend. *Glos* —2C **61**
Netherton. *H&W* —3C **51**
Netherton. *Mers* —1A **10**
Netherton. *Shrp* —3D **33**
Netley. *Shrp* —1B **32**
Neuadd. *Carm* —3C **47**
Neuadd. *Powy* —1B **30**
Nevern. *Pemb* —2D **43**
Newborough. *IOA* —1D **13**
Newbridge. *Cphy* —3D **59**
Newbridge. *Cdgn* —3A **36**
Newbridge. *Pemb* —2C **43**
Newbridge. *Wrex* —3D **17**
Newbridge-on-Usk. *Mon*
—3A **60**
Newbridge on Wye. *Powy*
—3B **38**
New Brighton. *Flin* —1D **17**
New Broughton. *Wrex*
—2A **18**
Newcastle. *Bri* —2D **63**
Newcastle. *Mon* —1B **60**
Newcastle. *Shrp* —3D **31**
Newcastle Emlyn. *Carm*
—1C **45**
Newchapel. *Pemb* —2B **44**
Newchapel. *Powy* —3A **30**
Newchurch. *Carm* —3C **45**
Newchurch. *H&W* —3A **40**
Newchurch. *Mon* —3B **60**
Newchurch. *Powy* —3D **39**
New Cross. *Cdgn* —1B **36**
Newent. *Glos* —3D **51**
New Ferry. *Mers* —2A **10**
Newgate. *Pemb* —3B **42**
Newhall. *Ches* —3D **19**
New Hedges. *Pemb* —2A **54**
New Inn. *Carm* —2D **45**
New Inn. *Mon* —2B **60**
New Inn. *Torf* —3A **60**
New Invention. *Shrp* —1D **39**
Newland. *Glos* —2C **61**
New Lane End. *Ches* —1D **11**
New Marton. *Shrp* —1A **26**
New Mills. *Mon* —2C **61**
New Mills. *Powy* —1B **30**
New Moat. *Pemb* —3D **43**
Newnham. *Glos* —1D **61**
Newnham Bridge. *H&W*
—2D **41**
Newport. *Glos* —3D **61**
Newport. *Newp* —1A **66**
Newport. *Pemb* —2D **43**
Newport. *Shrp* —3D **27**
New Quay. *Cdgn* —3C **35**
New Radnor. *Powy* —2D **39**
New Row. *Cdgn* —1C **37**
New Street. *H&W* —3A **40**
Newstreet Lane. *Shrp* —1D **27**
Newton. *Bri* —2D **63**
Newton. *Ches* —1B **18**
(nr. Chester)
Newton. *Ches* —2C **19**
(nr. Tattenhall)
Newton. *H&W* —2A **50**
(nr. Ewyas Harold)
Newton. *H&W* —3C **41**
(nr. Leominster)
Newton. *Mers* —2D **9**
Newton. *Shrp* —2D **33**
(nr. Bridgnorth)
Newton. *Shrp* —1B **26**
(nr. Wem)
Newton. *Swan* —1B **62**
Newton Green. *Mon* —3C **61**

Newton-le-Willows. *Mers*
—1C **11**
Newton on the Hill. *Shrp*
—2B **26**
Newton St Loe. *Bath* —3D **67**
Newtown. *Ches* —3D **19**
Newtown. *Glos* —2D **61**
Newtown. *H&W* —2D **51**
(nr. Ledbury)
Newtown. *H&W* —2C **51**
(nr. Little Dewchurch)
Newtown. *H&W* —1D **51**
(nr. Stretton Grandison)
Newtown. *Powy* —2C **31**
Newtown. *Rhon* —3B **58**
Newtown. *Shrp* —1B **26**
New Tredegar. *Cphy* —2C **59**
Nextend. *H&W* —3A **40**
Neyland. *Pemb* —2C **53**
Nib Heath. *Shrp* —3B **26**
Nicholaston. *Swan* —1A **62**
Niwbwrch. *IOA* —1B **4**
Nobold. *Shrp* —3B **26**
Nolton. *Pemb* —1B **52**
Nolton Haven. *Pemb* —1B **52**
No Man's Heath. *Ches* —3C **19**
Noneley. *Shrp* —2B **26**
Norbridge. *H&W* —1D **51**
Norbury. *Ches* —3C **19**
Norbury. *Shrp* —2A **32**
Nordley. *Shrp* —2D **33**
Norley. *Ches* —3C **11**
Norris Green. *Mers* —1A **10**
North Cornelly. *Bri* —1D **63**
North End. *N.Sm* —3B **66**
North Nibley. *Glos* —3D **61**
Northop. *Flin* —1D **17**
Northop Hall. *Flin* —1D **17**
North Stoke. *Bath* —3D **67**
Northway. *Swan* —1A **62**
North Weston. *N.Sm* —2B **66**
Northwich. *Ches* —3D **11**
North Wick. *Bath* —3C **67**
Northwick. *S.Glo* —1C **67**
North Widcombe. *Bath*
—3C **67**
Northwood. *Shrp* —1B **26**
Northwood Green. *Glos*
—1D **61**
Norton. *Mon* —3B **50**
Norton. *Powy* —2A **40**
Norton. *Shrp* —3B **32**
(nr. Ludlow)
Norton. *Shrp* —1D **33**
(nr. Madeley)
Norton. *Shrp* —1C **33**
(nr. Shrewsbury)
Norton. *Swan* —1B **62**
Norton Canon. *H&W* —1A **50**
Norton Hawkfield. *Bath*
—3C **67**
Norton in Hales. *Shrp* —1D **27**
Norton Malreward. *Bath*
—3D **67**
Nottage. *Bri* —2D **63**
Nox. *Shrp* —3B **26**
Noyadd Trefawr. *Cdgn*
—1B **44**
Nurston. *V.Gl* —3B **64**

Oakdale. *Cphy* —3C **59**
Oakengates. *Shrp* —3D **27**
Oakenholt. *Flin* —3D **9**
Oakford. *Cdgn* —3D **35**
Oaklands. *Powy* —3B **38**
Oakle Street. *Glos* —1D **61**
Oakley Park. *Powy* —3A **30**
Oakmere. *Ches* —1C **19**
Oaks. *Shrp* —1B **32**
Occlestone Green. *Ches*
—1D **19**

Ocle Pychard. *H&W* —1C **51**
Odd Down. *Bath* —3D **67**
Ogmore. *V.Gl* —2D **63**
Ogmore-by-Sea. *V.Gl* —2D **63**
Ogmore Vale. *Bri* —1A **64**
Oldbury. *Shrp* —2D **33**
Oldbury-on-Severn. *S.Glo*
—3D **61**
Oldcastle. *Mon* —3A **50**
Oldcastle Heath. *Ches* —3B **18**
Old Colwyn. *Cnwy* —3D **7**
Old Down. *S.Glo* —1D **67**
Oldfield. *Shrp* —3D **33**
Old Forge. *H&W* —1C **61**
Old Gore. *H&W* —3D **51**
Oldland. *S.Glo* —2D **67**
Old Llanberis. *Gwyn* —2B **14**
Oldmixon. *N.Sm* —3A **66**
Old Park. *Shrp* —1D **33**
Old Radnor. *Powy* —3D **39**
Old Sodbury. *S.Glo* —1D **67**
Old Swan. *Mers* —1A **10**
Oldwalls. *Swan* —3D **55**
Oldwood Common. *H&W*
—2C **41**
Ollerton. *Shrp* —2D **27**
Olmarch. *Cdgn* —3B **36**
Olveston. *S.Glo* —1D **67**
Onen. *Mon* —1B **60**
Ongar Street. *H&W* —2A **40**
Onibury. *Shrp* —1B **40**
Onllwyn. *Neat* —1D **57**
Onneley. *Shrp* —3D **19**
Orcop. *H&W* —3B **50**
Orcop Hill. *H&W* —3B **50**
Oreton. *Shrp* —3D **33**
Orford. *Ches* —1D **11**
Orleton. *H&W* —2B **40**
(nr. Leominster)
Orleton. *H&W* —2D **41**
(nr. Tenbury Wells)
Orleton Common. *H&W*
—2B **40**
Orrell. *Mers* —1A **10**
Osbaston. *Shrp* —2A **26**
Oscroft. *Ches* —1C **19**
Oswestry. *Shrp* —2D **25**
Otterspool. *Mers* —2A **10**
Oughtrington. *Ches* —2D **11**
Over. *Ches* —1D **19**
Over. *S.Glo* —1C **67**
Over Monnow. *Mon* —1C **61**
Overpool. *Ches* —3A **10**
Overton. *Ches* —3C **11**
Overton. *Shrp* —3D **33**
(nr. Bridgnorth)
Overton. *Shrp* —1C **41**
(nr. Ludlow)
Overton. *Swan* —1A **62**
Overton. *Wrex* —3A **18**
Oxenhall. *Glos* —3D **51**
Oxton. *Mers* —2D **9**
Oxwich. *Swan* —3D **55**
Oxwich Green. *Swan* —1A **62**
Oystermouth. *Swan* —1B **62**

Paddington. *Ches* —2D **11**
Paddolgreen. *Shrp* —1C **27**
Padeswood. *Flin* —1D **17**
Painscastle. *Powy* —1C **49**
Pale. *Gwyn* —1A **24**
Palmerstown. *V.Gl* —3C **65**
Pandy. *Gwyn* —2D **23**
(nr. Bala)
Pandy. *Gwyn* —1B **28**
(nr. Tywyn)
Pandy. *Mon* —3A **50**
Pandy. *Powy* —1A **30**
Pandy. *Wrex* —1C **25**
Pandy Tudur. *Cnwy* —1D **15**

Pant. *Shrp* —2D **25**
Pant. *Wrex* —3A **18**
Pantasaph. *Flin* —3C **9**
Pant Glas. *Gwyn* —3D **13**
Pant-glas. *Shrp* —1D **25**
Pantgwyn. *Carm* —3A **46**
Pantgwyn. *Cdgn* —1B **44**
Pant-lasau. *Swan* —3B **56**
Pant-pastynog. *Den* —1B **16**
Pantperthog. *Gwyn* —1C **29**
Pant-teg. *Carm* —3D **45**
Pant-y-Caws. *Carm* —3A **44**
Pant-y-dwr. *Powy* —1A **38**
Pant-y-ffridd. *Powy* —1C **31**
Pantyffynnon. *Carm* —1B **56**
Pantygasseg. *Torf* —2D **59**
Pant-y-llyn. *Carm* —1B **56**
Pant-yr-awel. *Bri* —1A **64**
Pant y Wacco. *Flin* —3C **9**
Parc. *Gwyn* —1D **23**
Parcllyn. *Cdgn* —3B **34**
Parc-Seymour. *Newp* —3B **60**
Parkend. *Glos* —2D **61**
Parkgate. *Ches* —3D **9**
Park Hill. *Mers* —1B **10**
Parkhouse. *Mon* —2B **60**
Parkmill. *Swan* —1A **62**
Parkway. *H&W* —2D **51**
Parr. *Mers* —1C **11**
Parrog. *Pemb* —2D **43**
Partington. *G.Mn* —1D **11**
Patchway. *S.Glo* —1D **67**
Paulton. *Bath* —3D **67**
Peasedown St John. *Bath*
—3D **67**
Peasley Cross. *Mers* —1C **11**
Peaton. *Shrp* —3C **33**
Peckforton. *Ches* —2C **19**
Pedair-ffordd. *Powy* —2C **25**
Pelcomb Bridge. *Pemb*
—1C **53**
Pelcomb Cross. *Pemb*
—1C **53**
Pemberton. *Carm* —2A **56**
Pembrey. *Carm* —2D **55**
Pembridge. *H&W* —3A **40**
Pembroke. *Pemb* —2C **53**
Pembroke Dock. *Pemb*
—2C **53**
Pembroke Ferry. *Pemb*
—2C **53**
Penallt. *Mon* —2C **61**
Penally. *Pemb* —3A **54**
Penalt. *H&W* —3C **51**
Penalum. *Pemb* —3A **54**
Penarth. *V.Gl* —2C **65**
Pen-bont Rhydybeddau. *Cdgn*
—3B **28**
Penbryn. *Cdgn* —3B **34**
Pencader. *Carm* —2D **45**
Pen-cae. *Cdgn* —3D **35**
Pencaenewydd. *Gwyn* —3D **13**
Pencaerau. *Neat* —3C **57**
Pencarnisiog. *IOA* —3C **5**
Pencarreg. *Carm* —1A **46**
Pencelli. *Powy* —3B **48**
Pen-clawdd. *Swan* —3A **56**
Pencoed. *Bri* —1A **64**
Pencombe. *H&W* —3C **41**
Pencraig. *H&W* —3C **51**
Pencraig. *Powy* —2B **24**
Penderyn. *Rhon* —2A **58**
Pendine. *Carm* —2B **54**
Pendoylan. *V.Gl* —2B **64**
Pendre. *Bri* —1A **64**
Penegoes. *Powy* —1C **29**
Penffordd. *Pemb* —3D **43**
Penfro. *Pemb* —2C **53**
Pengam. *Cphy* —3C **59**
Pengam. *Card* —2D **65**
Pengenffordd. *Powy* —2C **49**
Pengorffwysfa. *IOA* —1D **5**

Pengwern. *Den* —3B **8**
Penhelig. *Gwyn* —2B **28**
Penhow. *Newp* —3B **60**
Peniarth. *Gwyn* —1B **28**
Peniel. *Carm* —3D **45**
Penisa'r Waun. *Gwyn* —1A **14**
Penketh. *Ches* —2C **11**
Penley. *Wrex* —1B **26**
Penllech. *Gwyn* —1B **20**
Penllergaer. *Swan* —3B **56**
Pen-llyn. *IOA* —2C **5**
Penmachno. *Cnwy* —2C **15**
Penmaen. *Swan* —1A **62**
Penmaenmawr. *Cnwy* —3C **7**
Penmaenpool. *Gwyn* —3B **22**
Penmaen Rhos. *Cnwy* —3D **7**
Penmark. *V.Gl* —3B **64**
Penmon. *IOA* —2B **6**
Penmorfa. *Gwyn* —3A **14**
Penmynydd. *IOA* —3A **6**
Pennal. *Gwyn* —1C **29**
Pennant. *Cdgn* —2A **36**
Pennant. *Den* —1B **24**
Pennant. *Gwyn* —2A **24**
Pennant. *Powy* —2D **29**
Pennant Melangell. *Powy*
—2B **24**
Pennar. *Pemb* —2C **53**
Pennard. *Swan* —1A **62**
Pennerley. *Shrp* —2A **32**
Pennington. *G.Mn* —1D **11**
Pennorth. *Powy* —3C **49**
Pennsylvania. *S.Glo* —2D **67**
Penparc. *Cdgn* —1B **44**
Penparcau. *Cdgn* —3A **28**
Penpedairheol. *Cphy* —3C **59**
Penperlleni. *Mon* —2A **60**
Penpont. *Powy* —3A **48**
Penprysg. *Bri* —1A **64**
Penrherber. *Carm* —2B **44**
Penrhiw. *Pemb* —1B **44**
Penrhiwceiber. *Rhon* —3B **58**
Pen Rhiwfawr. *Neat* —1C **57**
Penrhiw-llan. *Cdgn* —1C **45**
Penrhiw-pal. *Cdgn* —1C **45**
Penrhos. *Gwyn* —1C **21**
Penrhos. *H&W* —3A **40**
Penrhos. *IOA* —2B **4**
Penrhos. *Mon* —1B **60**
Penrhos. *Powy* —1D **57**
Penrhos garnedd. *Gwyn*
—3A **6**
Penrhyn. *IOA* —1C **5**
Penrhyn Bay. *Cnwy* —2D **7**
Penrhyncoch. *Cdgn* —3B **28**
Penrhyndeudraeth. *Gwyn*
—1B **22**
Penrhyn Side. *Cnwy* —2D **7**
Penrice. *Swan* —3D **55**
Pensarn. *Carm* —1D **55**
Pen-sarn. *Gwyn* —2A **22**
Pensax. *H&W* —2D **41**
Pensby. *Mers* —2D **9**
Pensford. *Bath* —3D **67**
Pente-tafarn-y-fedw. *Cnwy*
—1D **15**
Pentir. *Gwyn* —1A **14**
Pentlepoir. *Pemb* —2A **54**
Pentraeth. *IOA* —3A **6**
Pentre. *Powy* —2D **31**
(nr. Church Stoke)
Pentre. *Powy* —3C **31**
(nr. Kerry)
Pentre. *Powy* —3B **30**
(nr. Mochdre)
Pentre. *Rhon* —3A **58**
Pentre. *Shrp* —3A **26**
Pentre. *Wrex* —1C **25**
(nr. Llanfyllin)
Pentre. *Wrex* —3D **17**
(nr. Rhosllanerchrugog)
Pentrebach. *Carm* —2D **47**

Pentre-bach. *Cdgn* —1A **46**
Pentrebach. *Mert* —2B **58**
Pentre-bach. *Powy* —2A **48**
Pentrebach. *Swan* —2B **56**
Pentre Berw. *IOA* —3D **5**
Pentre-bont. *Cnwy* —2C **15**
Pentrecagal. *Carm* —1C **45**
Pentre-celyn. *Den* —2C **17**
Pentre-clawdd. *Shrp* —1D **25**
Pentreclwydau. *Neat* —2D **57**
Pentre-cwrt. *Carm* —2C **45**
Pentre Dolau Honddu. *Powy*
—1A **48**
Pentre-du. *Cnwy* —2C **15**
Pentre-dwr. *Neat* —3B **56**
Pentrefelin. *Carm* —3A **46**
Pentrefelin. *Cdgn* —1B **46**
Pentrefelin. *Cnwy* —3D **7**
Pentrefelin. *Gwyn* —1A **22**
Pentrefoelas. *Cnwy* —2D **15**
Pentre Galar. *Pemb* —2A **44**
Pentregat. *Cdgn* —3C **35**
Pentre Gwenlais. *Carm*
—1B **56**
Pentre Gwynfryn. *Gwyn*
—2A **22**
Pentre Halkyn. *Flin* —3D **9**
Pentre Hodre. *Shrp* —1A **40**
Pentre-Llanrhaeadr. *Den*
—1B **16**
Pentre Llifior. *Powy* —2C **31**
Pentrellwyn. *IOA* —2A **6**
Pentre-llwyn-llwyd. *Powy*
—3A **38**
Pentre-llyn-cymmer. *Cnwy*
—2A **16**
Pentre Meyrick. *V.Gl* —2A **64**
Pentre-piod. *Gwyn* —1D **23**
Pentre-poeth. *Newp* —1D **65**
Pentre'r Beirdd. *Powy*
—3C **25**
Pentre'r-felin. *Powy* —2A **48**
Pentre-ty-gwyn. *Carm*
—2D **47**
Pentre-uchaf. *Gwyn* —1C **21**
Pen-twyn. *Cphy* —2D **59**
(nr. Oakdale)
Pentwyn. *Cphy* —2C **59**
(nr. Rhymney)
Pentwyn. *Card* —1D **65**
Pentyrch. *Card* —1C **65**
Pentywyn. *Carm* —2B **54**
Penuwch. *Cdgn* —2A **36**
Penwyllt. *Powy* —1D **57**
Penybanc. *Carm* —1B **56**
(nr. Ammanford)
Pen-y-banc. *Carm* —3B **46**
(nr. Llandeilo)
Pen-y-bont. *Carm* —3C **45**
Penybont. *Powy* —2C **39**
(nr. Llandrindod Wells)
Pen-y-bont. *Powy* —2D **25**
(nr. Llanfyllin)
Pen-y-Bont Ar Ogwr. *Bri*
—1A **64**
Penybontfawr. *Powy* —2B **24**
Penybryn. *Cphy* —3C **59**
Pen-y-bryn. *Pemb* —1A **44**
Pen-y-bryn. *Wrex* —3D **17**
Pen-y-cae. *Powy* —1D **57**
Penycae. *Wrex* —3D **17**
Pen-y-cae-mawr. *Mon*
—3B **60**
Penycaerau. *Gwyn* —2A **20**
Pen-y-cefn. *Flin* —3C **9**
Pen-y-clawdd. *Mon* —2B **60**
Pen-y-coedcae. *Rhon* —1B **64**
Penycwm. *Pemb* —3B **42**
Pen-y-darren. *Mert* —2B **58**
Pen-y-fai. *Bri* —1D **63**
Penyffordd. *Flin* —1A **18**
(nr. Mold)

Pen-y-ffordd. *Flin* —2C **9**
(nr. Prestatyn)
Penyffridd. *Gwyn* —2A **14**
Pen-y-garn. *Cdgn* —3B **28**
Pen-y-garnedd. *IOA* —3A **6**
Penygarnedd. *Powy* —2C **25**
Pen-y-graig. *Gwyn* —1A **20**
Penygraig. *Rhon* —3A **58**
Pen-y-groes. *Carm* —1A **56**
Penygroes. *Gwyn* —2D **13**
Penygroes. *Pemb* —2A **44**
Penymynydd. *Flin* —1A **18**
Penyrheol. *Cphy* —1C **65**
Pen-yr-heol. *Mon* —1B **60**
Penyrheol. *Swan* —3A **56**
Pen-yr-Heolgerrig. *Mert*
—2B **58**
Penysarn. *IOA* —1D **5**
Pen-y-stryt. *Den* —2D **17**
Penywaun. *Rhon* —2A **58**
Peplow. *Shrp* —2D **27**
Perthy. *Shrp* —1A **26**
Peterchurch. *H&W* —2A **50**
Peterstone Wentlooge. *Newp*
—1D **65**
Peterston-super-Ely. *V.Gl*
—2B **64**
Peterstow. *H&W* —3C **51**
Petton. *Shrp* —2B **26**
Phocle Green. *H&W* —3D **51**
Pibwrlwyd. *Carm* —1D **55**
Picklenash. *Glos* —3D **51**
Picklescott. *Shrp* —2B **32**
Pickmere. *Ches* —3D **11**
Pickstock. *Shrp* —2D **27**
Picton. *Ches* —3B **10**
Picton. *Flin* —2C **9**
Pie Corner. *H&W* —2D **41**
Pill. *N.Sm* —2C **67**
Pilleth. *Powy* —2D **39**
Pillgwenlly. *Newp* —1A **66**
Pillowell. *Glos* —2D **61**
Pill, The. *Mon* —1B **66**
Pilning. *S.Glo* —1C **67**
Pilton Green. *Swan* —3D **55**
Pinged. *Carm* —2C **55**
Pinsley Green. *Ches* —3C **19**
Pipe and Lyde. *H&W* —1C **51**
Pipe Gate. *Shrp* —3D **19**
Pipton. *Powy* —2C **49**
Pistyll. *Gwyn* —3C **13**
Pitchford. *Shrp* —1C **33**
Pitt Court. *Glos* —3D **61**
Pitton. *Swan* —3D **55**
Pixley. *H&W* —2D **51**
Plain Dealings. *Pemb* —1D **53**
Plaish. *Shrp* —2C **33**
Plaistow. *H&W* —2D **51**
Plas Llwyd. *Cnwy* —3A **8**
Plas yn Cefn. *Den* —3B **8**
Platt Bridge. *G.Mn* —1D **11**
Platt Lane. *Shrp* —1C **27**
Plealey. *Shrp* —1B **32**
Ploughfield. *H&W* —1A **50**
Plowden. *Shrp* —3A **32**
Ploxgreen. *Shrp* —1A **32**
Plumley. *Ches* —3D **11**
Plwmp. *Cdgn* —3C **35**
Ponde. *Powy* —2C **49**
Pontamman. *Carm* —1B **56**
Pontantwn. *Carm* —1D **55**
Pontardawe. *Neat* —2C **57**
Pontardulais. *Swan* —2A **56**
Pontarfynach. *Cdgn* —1C **37**
Pont-ar-gothi. *Carm* —3A **46**
Pont ar Hydfer. *Powy* —3D **47**
Pontarllechau. *Carm* —3C **47**
Pontarsais. *Carm* —3D **45**
Pontblyddyn. *Flin* —1D **17**
Pontbren Llwyd. *Rhon* —2A **58**
Pont Cyfyng. *Cnwy* —2C **15**
Pontdolgoch. *Powy* —2B **30**

Ponterwyd. *Cdgn* —3C **29**
Pontesbury. *Shrp* —1B **32**
Pontesford. *Shrp* —1B **32**
Pontfadog. *Wrex* —1D **25**
Pontfaen. *Pemb* —2D **43**
Pont-faen. *Powy* —2A **48**
Pont-Faen. *Shrp* —1D **25**
Pontgarreg. *Cdgn* —3C **35**
Pont-Henri. *Carm* —2D **55**
Ponthir. *Torf* —3A **60**
Ponthirwaun. *Cdgn* —1B **44**
Pontllanfraith. *Cphy* —3C **59**
Pontlliw. *Swan* —2B **56**
Pont Llogel. *Powy* —3B **24**
Pontllyfni. *Gwyn* —2D **13**
Pontlottyn. *Cphy* —2C **59**
Pontneddfechan. *Rhon*
—2A **58**
Pont-newydd. *Carm* —2D **55**
Pont-newydd. *Flin* —1C **17**
Pontnewydd. *Torf* —3A **60**
Pont Pen-y-benglog. *Gwyn*
—1B **14**
Pontrhydfendigaid. *Cdgn*
—2C **37**
Pont Rhyd-y-cyff. *Bri* —1D **63**
Pontrhydyfen. *Neat* —3C **57**
Pont-rhyd-y-groes. *Cdgn*
—1C **37**
Pontrhydyrun. *Torf* —3D **59**
Pont Rhythallt. *Gwyn* —1A **14**
Pontrilas. *H&W* —3A **50**
Pontrilas Road. *H&W* —3A **50**
Pontrobert. *Powy* —3C **25**
Pont-rug. *Gwyn* —1A **14**
Pontshill. *H&W* —3B **51**
Pont-Sian. *Cdgn* —1D **45**
Pontsticill. *Mert* —1B **58**
Pont-Walby. *Neat* —2D **57**
Pontwelly. *Carm* —2D **45**
Pontyates. *Carm* —2D **55**
Pontyberem. *Carm* —1A **56**
Pontybodkin. *Flin* —2D **17**
Pontyclun. *Rhon* —1B **64**
Pontycymer. *Bri* —3A **58**
Pontyglazier. *Pemb* —2A **44**
Pontygwaith. *Rhon* —3B **58**
Pont-y-pant. *Cnwy* —2C **15**
Pontypool. *Torf* —3D **59**
Pontypridd. *Rhon* —3B **58**
Pontypwl. *Torf* —3D **59**
Pontywaun. *Cphy* —3D **59**
Poole Green. *Ches* —2D **19**
Pool Head. *H&W* —3C **41**
Poolhill. *Glos* —3D **51**
Poolmill. *H&W* —3C **51**
Pool Quay. *Powy* —3D **25**
Pope Hill. *Pemb* —1C **53**
Pope's Hill. *Glos* —1D **61**
Porthbury. *N.Sm* —2C **67**
Port Dinorwig. *Gwyn* —1A **14**
Port-Eynon. *Swan* —1A **62**
Portfield Gate. *Pemb* —1C **53**
Porth. *Rhon* —3B **58**
Porthaethwy. *Per* —3A **6**
Porthcawl. *Bri* —2D **63**
Porthgain. *Pemb* —2B **42**
Porthill. *Shrp* —3B **26**
Porthkerry. *V.Gl* —3B **64**
Porthllechog. *IOA* —1D **5**
Porthmadog. *Gwyn* —1A **22**
Porthmeirion. *Gwyn* —1A **22**
Porth Tywyn. *Carm* —2D **55**
Porth-y-felin. *IOA* —2B **4**
Porthyrhyd. *Carm* —1A **56**
(nr. Carmarthen)
Porthyrhyd. *Carm* —2C **47**
(nr. Llandovery)
Porth-y-waen. *Shrp* —2D **25**
Portishead. *N.Sm* —2B **66**
Port Lion. *Pemb* —2C **53**

Port Mead. *Swan* —3B **56**
Portskewett. *Mon* —1C **67**
Port Sunlight. *Mers* —2A **10**
Port Talbot. *Neat* —1C **63**
Port Tennant. *Swan* —3B **56**
Portway. *H&W* —1B **50**
Post-mawr. *Cdgn* —3D **35**
Pound Bank. *H&W* —1D **41**
Poynton. *Shrp* —3C **27**
Poynton Green. *Shrp* —3C **27**
Prees. *Shrp* —1C **27**
Prees Green. *Shrp* —1C **27**
Prees Higher Heath. *Shrp*
—1C **27**
Prendergast. *Pemb* —1C **53**
Pren-gwyn. *Cdgn* —1D **45**
Prenteg. *Gwyn* —3A **14**
Prenton. *Mers* —2A **10**
Prescot. *Mers* —1B **10**
Prescott. *Shrp* —2B **26**
Prestatyn. *Den* —2B **8**
Presteigne. *Powy* —2A **40**
Presthope. *Shrp* —2C **33**
Preston. *Shrp* —3C **27**
Preston Brockhurst. *Shrp*
—2C **27**
Preston Brook. *Ches* —3C **11**
Preston Cross. *Glos* —2D **51**
Preston Gubbals. *Shrp*
—3B **26**
Preston Marsh. *H&W* —1C **51**
Preston on the Hill. *Ches*
—2C **11**
Preston on Wye. *H&W*
—1A **50**
Preston upon the Weald
Moors. *Shrp* —3D **27**
Preston Wynne. *H&W* —1C **51**
Price Town. *Bri* —3A **58**
Priest Weston. *Shrp* —2D **31**
Primrose Hill. *Glos* —2D **61**
Princes Gate. *Pemb* —1A **54**
Prion. *Den* —1B **16**
Prior's Frome. *H&W* —2C **51**
Priors Halton. *Shrp* —1B **40**
Priorslee. *Shrp* —3D **27**
Priory Wood. *H&W* —1D **49**
Priston. *Bath* —3D **67**
Publow. *Bath* —3D **67**
Pucklechurch. *S.Glo* —2D **67**
Puddinglake. *Ches* —1D **19**
Puddington. *Ches* —3A **10**
Puddlebrook. *Glos* —1D **61**
Pudleston. *H&W* —3C **41**
Puleston. *Shrp* —2D **27**
Pulford. *Ches* —2A **18**
Pulley. *Shrp* —1B **32**
Pulverbatch. *Shrp* —1B **32**
Pumsaint. *Carm* —1B **46**
Puncheston. *Pemb* —3D **43**
Purlogue. *Shrp* —1D **39**
Purslow. *Shrp* —3A **32**
Purton. *Glos* —2D **61**
(nr. Lydney)
Purton. *Glos* —2D **61**
(nr. Sharpness)
Putley. *H&W* —2D **51**
Puxton. *N.Sm* —3B **66**
Pwll. *Carm* —2D **55**
Pwll. *Powy* —1C **31**
Pwllcrochan. *Pemb* —2C **53**
Pwll-glas. *Den* —2C **17**
Pwllgloyw. *Powy* —2B **48**
Pwllheli. *Gwyn* —1C **21**
Pwllmeyric. *Mon* —3C **61**
Pwlltrap. *Carm* —1B **54**
Pwll-y-glaw. *Neat* —3C **57**
Pye Corner. *Newp* —1A **66**
Pyle. *Neat* —1D **63**

Quabbs. *Shrp* —3D **31**

Quarrybank. *Ches* —1C **19**
Quarry, The. *Glos* —3D **61**
Quatford. *Shrp* —2D **33**
Quatt. *Shrp* —3D **33**
Queen Charlton. *Bath* —3D **67**
Queensferry. *Flin* —1A **18**
Quina Brook. *Shrp* —1C **27**

Raby. *Mers* —3A **10**
Rachub. *Gwyn* —1B **14**
Radford. *Bath* —3D **67**
Radyr. *Card* —1C **65**
Ragdon. *Shrp* —2B **32**
Raglan. *Mon* —2B **60**
Rainford. *Mers* —1B **10**
Rainford Junction. *Mers*
—1B **10**
Rainhill. *Mers* —1B **10**
Rangeworthy. *S.Glo* —1D **67**
Rassau. *Blae* —1C **59**
Ratlinghope. *Shrp* —2B **32**
Ravenhills Green. *H&W*
—3D **41**
Ravensmoor. *Ches* —2D **19**
Rease Heath. *Ches* —2D **19**
Redberth. *Pemb* —2D **53**
Redbrook. *Mon* —1C **61**
Redbrook. *Wrex* —3C **19**
Redcliff Bay. *N.Sm* —2B **66**
Redhill. *N.Sm* —3B **66**
Redhill. *Shrp* —3D **27**
Redland. *Bris* —2C **67**
Redmarley D'Abitot. *Glos*
—2D **51**
Rednal. *Shrp* —2A **26**
Red Roses. *Carm* —1B **54**
Red Wharf Bay. *IOA* —2A **6**
Redwick. *Newp* —1B **66**
Redwick. *S.Glo* —1C **67**
Regil. *N.Sm* —3C **67**
Reilth. *Shrp* —3D **31**
Resolven. *Neat* —2D **57**
Reynalton. *Pemb* —2D **53**
Reynoldston. *Swan* —3D **55**
Rhadyr. *Mon* —2A **60**
Rhaeadr Gwy. *Powy* —2A **38**
Rhandirmwyn. *Carm* —1C **47**
Rhayader. *Powy* —2A **38**
Rhewl. *Den* —3C **17**
(nr. Llangollen)
Rhewl. *Den* —1C **17**
(nr. Ruthin)
Rhewl. *Shrp* —1A **26**
Rhewl-Mostyn. *Flin* —2C **9**
Rhigos. *Rhon* —2A **58**
Rhiw. *Gwyn* —2B **20**
Rhiwbina. *Card* —1C **65**
Rhiwbryfdir. *Gwyn* —3B **14**
Rhiwderin. *Newp* —1D **65**
Rhiwlas. *Gwyn* —1A **24**
(nr. Bala)
Rhiwlas. *Gwyn* —1A **14**
(nr. Bangor)
Rhiwlas. *Powy* —1C **25**
Rhodiad-y-Brenin. *Pemb*
—3A **42**
Rhoose. *V.Gl* —3B **64**
Rhos. *Carm* —2C **45**
Rhos. *Neat* —2C **57**
Rhosaman. *Carm* —1C **57**
Rhoscefnhir. *IOA* —3A **6**
Rhoscolyn. *IOA* —3B **4**
Rhos Common. *Powy*
—3D **25**
Rhoscrowther. *Pemb* —2C **53**
Rhos-ddu. *Gwyn* —1B **20**
Rhosdylluan. *Gwyn* —2D **23**
Rhosesmor. *Flin* —1D **17**
Rhos-fawr. *Gwyn* —1C **21**
Rhosgadfan. *Gwyn* —2A **14**
Rhosgoch. *IOA* —2D **5**

Rhosgoch. *Powy* —1C **49**
Rhos Haminiog. *Cdgn*
—2A **36**
Rhos-hill. *Pemb* —1A **44**
Rhoslan. *Gwyn* —3D **13**
Rhoslefain. *Gwyn* —1A **17**
Rhosllanerchrugog. *Wrex*
—3D **17**
Rhosmaen. *Carm* —3B **46**
Rhosmeirch. *IOA* —3D **5**
Rhosneigr. *IOA* —3C **5**
Rhos-on-Sea. *Cnwy* —2D **7**
Rhossili. *Swan* —3D **55**
Rhosson. *Pemb* —3A **42**
Rhos, The. *Pemb* —1D **53**
Rhostrenwfa. *IOA* —3D **5**
Rhostryfan. *Gwyn* —2D **13**
Rhostyllen. *Wrex* —3A **18**
Rhoswiel. *Shrp* —1D **25**
Rhosybol. *IOA* —2D **5**
Rhos-y-brithdir. *Powy*
—2C **25**
Rhos-y-garth. *Cdgn* —1B **36**
Rhos-y-gwaliau. *Gwyn*
—1A **24**
Rhos-y-llan. *Gwyn* —1B **20**
Rhos-y-meirch. *Powy* —2D **39**
Rhuallt. *Den* —3B **8**
Rhuddall Heath. *Ches* —1C **19**
Rhuddlan. *Den* —3B **8**
Rhulen. *Powy* —1C **49**
Rhuthun. *Den* —2C **17**
Rhyd. *Gwyn* —3B **14**
Rhydaman. *Carm* —1B **56**
Rhydargaeau. *Carm* —3D **45**
Rhydcymerau. *Carm* —2A **46**
Rhyd-Ddu. *Gwyn* —2A **14**
Rhydding. *Neat* —3C **57**
Rhyddlan. *Cdgn* —1D **45**
Rhydfudr. *Cdgn* —2A **36**
Rhydlanfair. *Cnwy* —2D **15**
Rhydlewis. *Cdgn* —1C **45**
Rhydlios. *Gwyn* —1A **20**
Rhydlydan. *Cnwy* —2D **15**
Rhyd-meirionydd. *Cdgn*
—3B **28**
Rhydowen. *Cdgn* —1D **45**
Rhyd-Rosser. *Cdgn* —2A **36**
Rhydspence. *Powy* —1D **49**
Rhydtalog. *Flin* —2D **17**
Rhyd-uchaf. *Gwyn* —1A **24**
Rhydwyn. *IOA* —2C **5**
Rhyd-y-clafdy. *Gwyn* —1C **21**
Rhydycroesau. *Shrp* —1D **25**
Rhydyfelin. *Cdgn* —1A **36**
Rhydyfelin. *Rhon* —1C **65**
Rhyd-y-foel. *Cnwy* —3A **8**
Rhyd-y-fro. *Neat* —2C **57**
Rhydymain. *Gwyn* —2D **23**
Rhyd-y-meirch. *Mon* —2A **60**
Rhyd-y-meudwy. *Den* —2C **17**
Rhydymwyn. *Flin* —1D **17**
Rhyd-yr-onnen. *Gwyn*
—1B **28**
Rhyd-y-sarn. *Gwyn* —3B **14**
Rhyl. *Den* —2B **8**
Rhymney. *Cphy* —2C **59**
Rhymni. *Cphy* —2C **59**
Richards Castle. *H&W*
—2B **40**
Rickford. *N.Sm* —3B **66**
Ridgebourne. *Powy* —2B **38**
Ridgeway Cross. *H&W*
—1D **51**
Ridgwardine. *Shrp* —1D **27**
Risbury. *H&W* —3C **41**
Risca. *Cphy* —3D **59**
Risley. *Ches* —1D **11**
Roath. *Card* —2C **65**
Robertstown. *Rhon* —2A **58**
Robeston Back. *Pemb*
—1D **53**

Robeston Wathen. *Pemb*
—1D **53**
Robeston West. *Pemb*
—2B **52**
Roch. *Pemb* —3B **42**
Rock. *H&W* —1D **41**
Rock Ferry. *Mers* —2A **10**
Rockfield. *Mon* —1B **60**
Rockgreen. *Shrp* —1C **41**
Rockhampton. *S.Glo* —3D **61**
Rodd. *H&W* —2A **40**
Roden. *Shrp* —3C **27**
Rodington. *Shrp* —3C **27**
Rodington Heath. *Shrp*
—3C **27**
Rodley. *Glos* —1D **61**
Rodway. *Shrp* —3D **27**
Rogerstone. *Newp* —1D **65**
Rogiet. *Mon* —1B **66**
Roman Bank. *Shrp* —2C **33**
Romers Common. *H&W*
—2C **41**
Rorrington. *Shrp* —1A **32**
Rosebush. *Pemb* —3D **43**
Rosehill. *Shrp* —1D **27**
(nr. Market Drayton)
Rosehill. *Shrp* —3B **26**
(nr. Shrewsbury)
Rosemarket. *Pemb* —2C **53**
Roshirwaun. *Gwyn* —2A **20**
Rossett. *Wrex* —2A **18**
Ross-on-Wye. *H&W* —3D **51**
Rostherne. *Ches* —2D **11**
Roughton. *Shrp* —2D **33**
Round Oak. *Shrp* —3A **32**
Rowberrow. *Som* —3B **66**
Rowen. *Cnwy* —3C **7**
Rowley. *Shrp* —1A **32**
Rowlstone. *H&W* —3A **50**
Rowton. *Ches* —1B **18**
Rowton. *Shrp* —3B **32**
(nr. Ludlow)
Rowton. *Shrp* —3D **27**
(nr. Shrewsbury)
Rowton. *Shrp* —3A **26**
(nr. Telford)
Royal Oak. *Lanc* —1B **10**
Royal's Green. *Ches* —3D **19**
Ruabon. *Wrex* —3A **18**
Ruardean. *Glos* —1D **61**
Ruardean Hill. *Glos* —1D **61**
Ruardean Woodside. *Glos*
—1D **61**
Ruckley. *Shrp* —1C **33**
Rudbaxton. *Pemb* —3C **43**
Rudgeway. *S.Glo* —1D **67**
Rudhall. *H&W* —3D **51**
Rudheath. *Ches* —3D **11**
Rudheath Woods. *Ches*
—3D **11**
Rudry. *Cphy* —1C **65**
Rumney. *Card* —2D **65**
Runcorn. *Ches* —2C **11**
Rushall. *H&W* —2D **51**
Rushbury. *Shrp* —2C **33**
Rushton. *Ches* —1C **19**
Rushton. *Shrp* —1D **33**
Ruspidge. *Glos* —1D **61**
Ruthin. *Den* —2C **17**
Ruthin. *V.Gl* —2A **64**
Ruxton Green. *H&W* —1C **61**
Ruyton-XI-Towns. *Shrp*
—2A **26**
Ryeford. *H&W* —3D **51**
Ryton. *Glos* —2D **51**
Ryton. *Shrp* —1D **33**

Sageston. *Pemb* —2D **53**
Saighton. *Ches* —1B **18**
St Andrews Major. *V.Gl*
—2C **65**

St Arvans. *Mon* —3C **61**
St Asaph. *Den* —3B **8**
St Athan. *V.Gl* —3B **64**
St Briavels. *Glos* —2C **61**
St Brides. *Pemb* —1A **52**
St Bride's Major. *V.Gl* —2D **63**
St Bride's Netherwent. *Mon*
—1B **66**
St Bride's-super-Ely. *V.Gl*
—2B **64**
St Brides Wentlooge. *Newp*
—1D **65**
St Clears. *Carm* —1B **54**
St David's. *Pemb* —3A **42**
St Dogmaels. *Pemb* —1A **44**
St Donat's. *V.Gl* —3A **64**
St Fagans. *Card* —2C **65**
St Florence. *Pemb* —2D **53**
St George. *Cnwy* —3A **8**
St George's. *N.Sm* —3A **66**
St Georges. *V.Gl* —2B **64**
St Harmon. *Powy* —1A **38**
St Helens. *Mers* —1B **10**
St Hilary. *V.Gl* —2B **64**
St Illtyd. *Blae* —2D **59**
St Ishmael. *Carm* —2C **55**
St Ishmael's. *Pemb* —2B **52**
St Lythans. *V.Gl* —2C **65**
St Margarets. *H&W* —2A **50**
St Martin's. *Shrp* —1A **26**
St Mary Church. *V.Gl* —2B **64**
St Mary Hill. *V.Gl* —2A **64**
St Mary's Grove. *N.Sm*
—3B **66**
St Maughan's Green. *Mon*
—1B **60**
St Mellons. *Card* —1D **65**
St Michaels. *H&W* —2C **41**
St Nicholas. *Pemb* —2C **43**
St Nicholas. *V.Gl* —2B **64**
St Owen's Cross. *H&W*
—3C **51**
St Petrox. *Pemb* —3C **53**
St Thomas. *Swan* —3B **56**
St Twynnells. *Pemb* —3C **53**
St Weonards. *H&W* —3B **50**
Salem. *Carm* —3B **46**
Salem. *Cdgn* —3B **28**
Salem. *Gwyn* —2A **14**
Salterswall. *Ches* —1D **19**
Saltford. *Bath* —3D **67**
Saltmead. *Card* —2C **65**
Saltney. *Flin* —1A **18**
Sambrook. *Shrp* —2D **27**
Sandbach. *Ches* —1D **19**
Sandfields. *Neat* —3C **57**
Sandford. *N.Sm* —3B **66**
Sandford. *Shrp* —2A **26**
(nr. Oswestry)
Sandford. *Shrp* —1C **27**
(nr. Whitchurch)
Sandiway. *Ches* —3D **11**
Sandy. *Carm* —2D **55**
Sandycroft. *Flin* —1A **18**
Sandy Cross. *H&W* —3D **41**
Sandy Haven. *Pemb* —2B **52**
Sandylane. *Swan* —1A **62**
Sandyway. *H&W* —3B **50**
Sapey Common. *H&W*
—2D **41**
Sardis. *Carm* —2A **56**
Sardis. *Pemb* —2C **53**
(nr. Milford Haven)
Sardis. *Pemb* —2A **54**
(nr. Tenby)
Sarn. *Bri* —1A **64**
Sarn. *Powy* —2D **31**
Sarnau. *Carm* —3D **45**
Sarnau. *Cdgn* —3C **35**
Sarnau. *Gwyn* —1A **24**
Sarnau. *Powy* —2B **48**
(nr. Brecon)

Sarnau. *Powy* —3D **25**
(nr. Welshpool)
Sarn Bach. *Gwyn* —2C **21**
Sarnesfield. *H&W* —2A **40**
Sarn Meyllteyrn. *Gwyn*
—1B **20**
Saron. *Carm* —1B **56**
(nr. Ammanford)
Saron. *Carm* —2C **45**
(nr. Newcastle Emlyn)
Saron. *Gwyn* —1A **14**
(nr. Bethel)
Saron. *Gwyn* —2D **13**
(nr. Bontnewydd)
Saughall. *Ches* —3A **10**
Saul. *Glos* —2D **61**
Saundersfoot. *Pemb* —2A **54**
Scethrog. *Powy* —3C **49**
School Green. *Ches* —1D **19**
Scleddau. *Pemb* —2C **43**
Scolton. *Pemb* —3C **43**
Scurlage. *Swan* —3D **55**
Seacombe. *Mers* —1A **10**
Seaforth. *Mers* —1A **10**
Sealand. *Flin* —1A **18**
Sea Mills. *Bris* —2C **67**
Sebastopol. *Cphy* —2C **59**
Sebastopol. *Torf* —3D **59**
Sedbury. *Glos* —3C **61**
Sefton. *Mers* —1A **10**
Sefton Park. *Mers* —2A **10**
Selattyn. *Shrp* —1D **25**
Sellack. *H&W* —3C **51**
Senghenydd. *Cphy* —3C **59**
Sennybridge. *Powy* —3A **48**
Seven Sisters. *Neat* —2D **57**
Severn Beach. *S.Glo* —1C **67**
Shakesfield. *Glos* —2D **51**
Sharpness. *Glos* —2D **61**
Shavington. *Ches* —2D **19**
Shawbirch. *Shrp* —3D **27**
Shawbury. *Shrp* —2C **27**
Sheepway. *N.Sm* —2B **66**
Sheinton. *Shrp* —1D **33**
Shelderton. *Shrp* —1B **40**
Shell Green. *Ches* —2C **11**
Shelsley Beauchamp. *H&W*
—2D **41**
Shelsley Walsh. *H&W* —2D **41**
Shelton. *Shrp* —3B **26**
Shelve. *Shrp* —2A **32**
Shelwick. *H&W* —1C **51**
Shelwick Green. *H&W* —1C **51**
Shenmore. *H&W* —2A **50**
Shepperdine. *S.Glo* —3D **61**
Sheriffhales. *Shrp* —3D **27**
Shifnal. *Shrp* —1D **33**
Shipham. *Som* —3B **66**
Shipton. *Shrp* —2C **33**
Shirehampton. *Bris* —2C **67**
Shirenewton. *Mon* —3B **60**
Shirl Heath. *H&W* —3B **40**
Shobdon. *H&W* —2A **40**
Shocklach. *Ches* —3B **18**
Shoot Hill. *Shrp* —3B **26**
Shortwood. *S.Glo* —2D **67**
Shoscombe. *Bath* —3D **67**
Shotton. *Flin* —1D **17**
Shotwick. *Ches* —3A **10**
Shrawardine. *Shrp* —3A **26**
Shrewsbury. *Shrp* —3B **26**
Shucknall. *H&W* —1C **51**
Sibdon Carwood. *Shrp* —3B **32**
Sidbury. *Shrp* —3D **33**
Sidcot. *N.Sm* —3B **66**
Siefton. *Shrp* —3B **32**
Sigingstone. *V.Gl* —2A **64**
Silian. *Cdgn* —3A **36**
Silvington. *Shrp* —1D **41**
Simm's Cross. *Ches* —2C **11**
Simm's Lane End. *Mers*
—1C **11**

Simpson. *Pemb* —1B **52**
Simpson Cross. *Pemb*
—1B **52**
Sirhowy. *Blae* —1C **59**
Siston. *S.Glo* —2D **67**
Six Bells. *Blae* —2D **59**
Sketty. *Swan* —3B **56**
Skewen. *Neat* —3C **57**
Skenfrith. *Mon* —3B **50**
Skyborry Green. *Shrp* —1D **39**
Slade. *Swan* —1A **62**
Sleap. *Shrp* —2B **26**
Slimbridge. *Glos* —2D **61**
Smithies, The. *Shrp* —2D **33**
Smithy Green. *Ches* —3D **11**
Snailbeach. *Shrp* —1A **32**
Snead. *Powy* —2A **32**
Snead Common. *H&W*
—2D **41**
Snitton. *Shrp* —1C **41**
Snodhill. *H&W* —1A **50**
Soar. *Carm* —3B **46**
Soar. *Gwyn* —1B **22**
Soar. *Powy* —2A **48**
Sodom. *Den* —3B **8**
Sollers Dilwyn. *H&W* —3B **40**
Sollers Hope. *H&W* —2D **51**
Solva. *Pemb* —3A **42**
Soudley. *Shrp* —2B **32**
(nr. Church Stretton)
Soudley. *Shrp* —2D **27**
(nr. Market Drayton)
Soughton. *Flin* —1D **17**
Soundwell. *S.Glo* —2D **67**
South Cornelly. *Bri* —1D **63**
Southdown. *Bath* —3D **67**
Southend. *Glos* —3D **61**
Southerndown. *V.Gl* —2D **63**
Southgate. *Cdgn* —3A **28**
Southgate. *Swan* —1A **62**
Southstoke. *Bath* —3D **67**
South Widcombe. *Bath*
—3C **67**
Speke. *Mers* —2B **10**
Spital. *Mers* —2A **10**
Spittal. *Pemb* —3C **43**
Sproston Green. *Ches* —1D **19**
Spurstow. *Ches* —2C **19**
Stableford. *Shrp* —2D **33**
Stackpole. *Pemb* —3C **53**
Stackpole Elidor. *Pemb*
—3C **53**
Stafford Park. *Shrp* —1D **33**
Stamford Bridge. *Ches*
—1B **18**
Standford Bridge. *Shrp*
—2D **27**
Stanford Bishop. *H&W*
—3D **41**
Stanford Bridge. *H&W*
—2D **41**
Stanford on Teme. *H&W*
—2D **41**
Stanley. *Shrp* —3D **33**
Stanley Hill. *H&W* —1D **51**
Stanlow. *Ches* —3B **10**
Stansbatch. *H&W* —2A **40**
Stanthorne. *Ches* —1D **19**
Stanton Drew. *Bath* —3C **67**
Stanton Lacy. *Shrp* —1B **40**
Stanton Long. *Shrp* —2C **33**
Stanton Prior. *Bath* —3D **67**
Stanton upon Hine Heath. *Shrp*
—2C **27**
Stanton Wick. *Bath* —3D **67**
Stanwardine in the Fields. *Shrp*
—2B **26**
Stanwardine in the Wood. *Shrp*
—2B **26**
Stapeley. *Ches* —3D **19**
Stapleton. *Bris* —2D **67**
Stapleton. *H&W* —2A **40**

Stapleton. *Shrp* —1B **32**
Staplow. *H&W* —1D **51**
Star. *Pemb* —2B **44**
Staunton. *Glos* —1C **61**
Staunton on Arrow. *H&W*
—2A **40**
Staunton on Wye. *H&W*
—1A **50**
Staylittle. *Powy* —2D **29**
Steel Heath. *Shrp* —1C **27**
Steen's Bridge. *H&W* —3C **41**
Stepaside. *Pemb* —2A **54**
Steynton. *Pemb* —2C **53**
Stifford's Bridge. *H&W*
—1D **51**
Stinchcombe. *Glos* —3D **61**
Stiperstones. *Shrp* —1A **32**
Stirchley. *Shrp* —1D **33**
Stoak. *Ches* —3B **10**
Stocking. *H&W* —2D **51**
Stockton. *H&W* —2C **41**
Stockton. *Shrp* —2D **33**
(nr. Bridgnorth)
Stockton. *Shrp* —1D **31**
(nr. Chirbury)
Stockton Cross. *H&W* —2C **41**
Stockton Heath. *Ches* —2D **11**
Stockton on Teme. *H&W*
—2D **41**
Stockwood. *Bris* —3D **67**
Stoke Bliss. *H&W* —2D **41**
Stoke Cross. *H&W* —3D **41**
Stoke Edith. *H&W* —1D **51**
Stoke Gifford. *S.Glo* —2D **67**
Stoke Heath. *Shrp* —2D **27**
Stoke Lacy. *H&W* —1D **51**
Stoke on Tern. *Shrp* —2D **27**
Stoke Prior. *H&W* —3C **41**
Stoke St Milborough. *Shrp*
—3C **33**
Stokesay. *Shrp* —3B **32**
Stone. *Glos* —3D **61**
Stoneacton. *Shrp* —2C **33**
Stonebridge. *N.Sm* —3A **66**
Stone-edge-Batch. *N.Sm*
—2B **66**
Stoneley Green. *Ches* —2D **19**
Stoney Stretton. *Shrp* —1A **32**
Stony Cross. *H&W* —1D **51**
(nr. Great Malvern)
Stony Cross. *H&W* —2C **41**
(nr. Leominster)
Storeton. *Mers* —2A **10**
Storridge. *H&W* —1D **51**
Stottesdon. *Shrp* —3D **33**
Stowe. *Glos* —2C **61**
Stowe. *Shrp* —1A **40**
Stowey. *Bath* —3C **67**
Strangford. *H&W* —3C **51**
Strata Florida. *Cdgn* —2C **37**
Street Dinas. *Shrp* —1A **26**
Strefford. *Shrp* —3B **32**
Stretford. *H&W* —3C **41**
Stretton. *Ches* —2B **18**
(nr. Farndon)
Stretton. *Ches* —2D **11**
(nr. Warrington)
Stretton Grandison. *H&W*
—1D **51**
Stretton Heath. *Shrp* —3A **26**
Stretton Sugwas. *H&W*
—1B **50**
Stretton Westwood. *Shrp*
—2C **33**
Stroat. *Glos* —3C **61**
Stryd. *IOA* —2B **4**
Stryt-issa. *Wrex* —3D **17**
Suckley. *H&W* —3D **41**
Suckley Knowl. *H&W* —3D **41**
Sudbrook. *Mon* —1C **67**
Sugwas Pool. *H&W* —1B **50**
Sully. *V.Gl* —3C **65**

Summerhill. *Pemb* —2A **54**
Sutton. *H&W* —2D **41**
Sutton. *Pemb* —1C **53**
Sutton. *Shrp* —3D **33**
  (nr. Bridgnorth)
Sutton. *Shrp* —1D **27**
  (nr. Market Drayton)
Sutton. *Shrp* —2A **26**
  (nr. Oswestry)
Sutton. *Shrp* —3C **27**
  (nr. Shrewsbury)
Sutton Leach. *Mers* —1C **11**
Sutton Maddock. *Shrp*
  —1D **33**
Sutton St Michael. *H&W*
  —1C **51**
Sutton St Nicholas. *H&W*
  —1C **51**
Sutton Weaver. *Ches* —3C **11**
Swainshill. *H&W* —1B **50**
Swainswick. *Bath* —3D **67**
Swanbridge. *V.Gl* —3C **65**
Swan Green. *Ches* —3D **11**
Swansea. *Swan* —3B **56**
Swanwick Green. *Ches*
  —3C **19**
Sweet Green. *H&W* —2D **41**
Swinmore Common. *H&W*
  —1D **51**
Sworton Heath. *Ches* —2D **11**
Swyddffynnon. *Cdgn* —2B **36**
Swyffrd. *Cphy* —3D **59**
Sycharth. *Powy* —2D **25**
Sychdyn. *Flin* —1D **17**
Sychnant. *Powy* —1A **38**
Sychtyn. *Powy* —1A **30**
Sydney. *Ches* —2D **19**
Sylen. *Carm* —2A **56**
Sylfaen. *Powy* —1C **31**
Symonds Yat. *H&W* —1C **61**
Synod Inn. *Cdgn* —3D **35**

Tadwick. *Bath* —2D **67**
Tafarnaubach. *Cphy* —1C **59**
Tafarn-y-bwlch. *Pemb* —2D **43**
Tafarn-y-Gelyn. *Den* —1C **17**
Taffs Well. *Card* —1C **65**
Tafolwern. *Powy* —1D **29**
Taibach. *Neat* —1C **63**
Tai-bach. *Powy* —2C **25**
Tai-Nant. *Wrex* —3D **17**
Tai'n Lon. *Gwyn* —2D **13**
Tairgwaith. *Neat* —1C **57**
Talachddu. *Powy* —2B **48**
Talacre. *Flin* —2C **9**
Talardd. *Gwyn* —2D **23**
Talbenny. *Pemb* —1B **52**
Talbot Green. *Rhon* —1B **64**
Talerddig. *Powy* —1A **30**
Talgarreg. *Cdgn* —3D **35**
Talgarth. *Powy* —2C **49**
Tallarn Green. *Wrex* —3B **18**
Talley. *Carm* —2B **46**
Talog. *Carm* —3C **45**
Talsarn. *Carm* —3C **47**
Talsarn. *Cdgn* —3A **36**
Talsarnau. *Gwyn* —1B **22**
Talwrn. *IOA* —3D **5**
Talwrn. *Wrex* —3D **17**
Tal-y-Bont. *Cdgn* —3B **28**
Tal-y-bont. *Cnwy* —1C **15**
Tal-y-bont. *Gwyn* —3B **6**
  (nr. Bangor)
Tal-y-bont. *Gwyn* —2A **22**
  (nr. Barmouth)
Talybont-on-Usk. *Powy*
  —3C **49**
Tal-y-cafn. *Cnwy* —3C **7**
Tal-y-coed. *Mon* —1B **60**
Tal-y-llyn. *Gwyn* —1C **29**
Talyllyn. *Powy* —3C **49**

Talysarn. *Gwyn* —2D **13**
Tal-y-waenydd. *Gwyn* —3B **14**
Talywain. *Torf* —2D **59**
Talywern. *Powy* —1D **29**
Tanerdy. *Carm* —3D **45**
Tangiers. *Pemb* —1C **53**
Tan-lan. *Cnwy* —1C **15**
Tan-lan. *Gwyn* —3B **14**
Tan-y-bwlch. *Gwyn* —3B **14**
Tan-y-fron. *Cnwy* —1A **16**
Tanyfron. *Wrex* —2D **17**
Tan-y-goes. *Cdgn* —1B **44**
Tan-y-groes. *Cdgn* —1B **44**
Tan-yr-allt. *Den* —2B **8**
Tanygrisiau. *Gwyn* —3B **14**
Tan-y-pistyll. *Powy* —2B **24**
Tan-yr-allt. *Den* —2B **8**
Tarbock Green. *Mers* —2B **10**
Tarporley. *Ches* —1C **19**
Tarrington. *H&W* —1D **51**
Tarvin. *Ches* —1B **18**
Tasley. *Shrp* —2D **33**
Tattenhall. *Ches* —2B **18**
Tavernspite. *Pemb* —1A **54**
Taynton. *Glos* —3D **51**
Tedsmore. *Shrp* —2A **26**
Tedstone Delamere. *H&W*
  —3D **41**
Tedstone Wafer. *H&W*
  —3D **41**
Tegryn. *Pemb* —2B **44**
Telford. *Shrp* —3D **27**
Temple Bar. *Carm* —1A **56**
Temple Bar. *Cdgn* —3A **36**
Temple Cloud. *Bath* —3D **67**
Templeton. *Pemb* —1A **54**
Tenbury Wells. *H&W* —2C **41**
Tenby. *Pemb* —2A **54**
Terfyn. *Cnwy* —3A **8**
Ternhill. *Shrp* —1D **27**
Tetchill. *Shrp* —1A **26**
Thatto Heath. *Mers* —1C **11**
Thelwall. *Ches* —2D **11**
Thingwall. *Mers* —2D **9**
Thomas Chapel. *Pemb*
  —2A **54**
Thomastown. *Rhon* —1B **64**
Thorn. *Powy* —2D **39**
Thornbury. *H&W* —3D **41**
Thornbury. *S.Glo* —1D **67**
Thornhill. *Cphy* —1C **65**
Thornton. *Mers* —1A **10**
Thornton Hough. *Mers*
  —2A **10**
Thornton-le-Moors. *Ches*
  —3B **10**
Threapwood. *Ches* —3B **18**
Three Ashes. *H&W* —3C **51**
Three Cocks. *Powy* —2C **49**
Three Crosses. *Swan* —3A **56**
Thruxton. *H&W* —2B **50**
Thurstaston. *Mers* —2D **9**
Tibberton. *Shrp* —2D **27**
Tickenham. *N.Sm* —2B **66**
Ticklerton. *Shrp* —2B **32**
Tidenham. *Glos* —3C **61**
Tiers Cross. *Pemb* —1C **53**
Tillers Green. *Glos* —2D **51**
Tilley. *Shrp* —2C **27**
Tillington. *H&W* —1B **50**
Tillington Common. *H&W*
  —1B **50**
Tilstock. *Shrp* —1C **27**
Tilston. *Ches* —2B **18**
Tilstone Fearnall. *Ches*
  —1C **19**
Timsbury. *Bath* —3D **67**
Tintern Parva. *Mon* —2C **61**
Tirabad. *Powy* —1D **47**
Tirnewydd. *Flin* —3C **9**
Tirphil. *Cphy* —2C **59**
Tir-y-dail. *Carm* —1B **56**
Titley. *H&W* —3A **40**
Tiverton. *Ches* —1C **19**

Tockington. *S.Glo* —1D **67**
Todding. *H&W* —1B **40**
Ton. *Mon* —3A **60**
Tondu. *Bri* —1D **63**
Tonfanau. *Gwyn* —1A **28**
Tongwynlais. *Card* —1C **65**
Tonmawr. *Neat* —3D **57**
Tonna. *Neat* —3C **57**
Ton-Pentre. *Rhon* —3A **58**
Tonypandy. *Rhon* —3A **58**
Tonyrefail. *Rhon* —1B **64**
Tortworth. *S.Glo* —3D **61**
Tower Hill. *Mers* —1B **10**
Town End. *Mers* —2B **10**
Townhill. *Swan* —3B **56**
Towyn. *Cnwy* —3A **8**
Toxteth. *Mers* —2A **10**
Trallong. *Powy* —3A **48**
Trallwng. *Powy* —1D **31**
Tranmere. *Mers* —2A **10**
Trapp. *Carm* —1B **56**
Trawscoed. *Powy* —2B **48**
Trawsfynydd. *Gwyn* —1C **23**
Trawsgoed. *Cdgn* —1B **36**
Treaddow. *H&W* —3C **51**
Trealaw. *Rhon* —3B **58**
Trearddur. *IOA* —3B **4**
Trebanog. *Rhon* —3B **58**
Trebanos. *Neat* —2C **57**
Trecastle. *Powy* —3D **47**
Trecenydd. *Cphy* —1C **65**
Trecwn. *Pemb* —2C **43**
Trecynon. *Rhon* —2A **58**
Tredegar. *Blae* —2C **59**
Trederwen. *Powy* —3D **25**
Tredogan. *V.Gl* —3B **64**
Tredomen. *Powy* —2C **49**
Tredrissi. *Pemb* —1D **43**
Tredunnock. *Mon* —3A **60**
Tredustan. *Powy* —2C **49**
Trefaldwyn. *Powy* —2D **31**
Trefasser. *Pemb* —2B **42**
Trefdraeth. *IOA* —3D **5**
Trefecca. *Powy* —2C **49**
Trefechan. *Mert* —2B **58**
Trefeglwys. *Powy* —2A **30**
Trefeitha. *Powy* —2C **49**
Trefenter. *Cdgn* —2B **36**
Treffgarne. *Pemb* —3C **43**
Treffynnon. *Flin* —3C **9**
Treffynnon. *Pemb* —3B **42**
Trefil. *Blae* —1C **59**
Trefilan. *Cdgn* —3A **36**
Trefin. *Pemb* —2B **42**
Treflach. *Shrp* —2D **25**
Trefnant. *Den* —3B **8**
Trefonen. *Shrp* —2D **25**
Trefor. *Gwyn* —3C **13**
Trefor. *IOA* —3C **5**
Treforest. *Rhon* —1B **64**
Trefriw. *Cnwy* —1C **15**
Tref-y-Clawdd. *Powy* —1D **39**
Trefynwy. *Mon* —1C **61**
Tregare. *Mon* —1B **60**
Tregaron. *Cdgn* —3B **36**
Tregarth. *Gwyn* —1B **14**
Tregeiriog. *Wrex* —1C **25**
Tregele. *IOA* —1C **5**
Tregoyd. *Powy* —2C **49**
Tre-groes. *Cdgn* —1D **45**
Tregynon. *Powy* —2B **30**
Trehafod. *Rhon* —3B **58**
Treharris. *Mert* —3C **59**
Treherbert. *Rhon* —3A **58**
Trelawnyd. *Flin* —3B **8**
Trelech. *Carm* —2B **44**
Treleddyd-fawr. *Pemb*
  —3A **42**
Trelewis. *Mert* —3C **59**
Trelleck. *Mon* —2C **61**
Trelleck Grange. *Mon* —2B **60**
Trelogan. *Flin* —2C **9**

Trelystan. *Powy* —1D **31**
Tremadog. *Gwyn* —1A **22**
Tremain. *Cdgn* —1B **44**
Tremeirchion. *Den* —3B **8**
Tremorfa. *Card* —2D **65**
Trench. *Shrp* —3D **27**
Treoes. *V.Gl* —2A **64**
Treorchy. *Rhon* —3A **58**
Treorci. *Rhon* —3A **58**
Tre'r-ddol. *Cdgn* —2B **28**
Tresaith. *Cdgn* —3B **34**
Tre Taliesin. *Cdgn* —2B **28**
Trethomas. *Cphy* —1C **65**
Tretio. *Pemb* —3A **42**
Tretire. *H&W* —3C **51**
Tretower. *Powy* —3C **49**
Treuddyn. *Flin* —2D **17**
Trevalyn. *Wrex* —2A **18**
Tre-vaughan. *Carm* —3D **45**
  (nr. Carmarthen)
Trevaughan. *Carm* —1A **54**
  (nr. Whitland)
Trevethin. *Torf* —2D **59**
Trevor. *Den* —3D **17**
Trevor Uchaf. *Den* —3D **17**
Trewern. *Powy* —3D **25**
Trimsaran. *Carm* —2D **55**
Trinant. *Cphy* —3D **59**
Trisant. *Cdgn* —1C **37**
Troedrhiwdalar. *Powy* —3A **38**
Troedrhiwfuwch. *Cphy*
  —2C **59**
Troedrhiwgwair. *Blae* —2C **59**
Troedyraur. *Cdgn* —1C **45**
Troedyrhiw. *Mert* —2B **58**
Trumpet. *H&W* —2D **51**
Tryfil. *IOA* —2D **5**
Tudorville. *H&W* —3C **51**
Tudweiliog. *Gwyn* —1B **20**
Tufton. *Pemb* —3D **43**
Tugford. *Shrp* —3C **33**
Tumble. *Carm* —1A **56**
Tunley. *Bath* —3D **67**
Tupsley. *H&W* —1C **51**
Turnant. *H&W* —3A **50**
Turnastone. *H&W* —2A **50**
Tutsbill. *Glos* —3C **61**
Tweedale. *Shrp* —1D **33**
Twerton. *Bath* —3D **67**
Twinhoe. *Bath* —3D **67**
Twiss Green. *Ches* —1D **11**
Twitchen. *Shrp* —1A **40**
Two Bridges. *Glos* —2D **61**
Twyford Common. *H&W*
  —2C **51**
Twyncarno. *Cphy* —2C **59**
Twynllanan. *Carm* —3C **47**
Twynmynydd. *Carm* —1B **56**
Twyn-y-Sheriff. *Mon* —2B **60**
Tyberton. *H&W* —2A **50**
Tycroes. *Carm* —1B **56**
Tycrwyn. *Powy* —3C **25**
Tyddewi. *Pemb* —3A **42**
Ty Issa. *Powy* —2C **25**
Tyldesley. *G.Mn* —1D **11**
Tyle. *Carm* —3B **46**
Tylorstown. *Rhon* —3B **58**
Tylwch. *Powy* —3A **30**
Ty-nant. *Cnwy* —3A **16**
Tynewydd. *Rhon* —3A **58**
Ty'n-y-bryn. *Rhon* —1B **64**
Tyn-y-celyn. *Wrex* —1C **25**
Tyn-y-cwm. *Swan* —2B **56**
Tyn-y-ffridd. *Powy* —1C **25**
Tynygongl. *IOA* —2A **6**
Tynygraig. *Cdgn* —2B **36**
Tyn-y-groes. *Cnwy* —3C **7**
Ty'n-yr-eithin. *Cdgn* —2B **36**
Tyn-y-rhyd. *Powy* —3B **24**
Tyn-y-wern. *Powy* —2B **24**
Tythegston. *Bri* —2D **63**
Tytherington. *S.Glo* —1D **67**

Tywyn. *Cnwy* —3C **7**
Tywyn. *Gwyn* —1A **28**

Ubley. *Bath* —3C **67**
Uckington. *Shrp* —1C **33**
Uffington. *Shrp* —3C **27**
Ullingswick. *H&W* —1C **51**
Underdale. *Shrp* —3C **27**
Underton. *Shrp* —2D **33**
Undy. *Mon* —1B **66**
Upcott. *H&W* —3A **40**
Uphampton. *H&W* —2A **40**
Uphill. *N.Sm* —3A **66**
Upleadon. *Glos* —3D **51**
Upper Affcot. *Shrp* —3B **32**
Upper Bangor. *Gwyn* —3A **6**
Upper Borth. *Cdgn* —3B **28**
Upper Breinton. *H&W* —1B **50**
Upper Brynamman. *Carm*
  —1C **57**
Upper Chapel. *Powy* —1B **48**
Upper Church Village. *Rhon*
  —1B **64**
Upper Coedcae. *Torf* —2D **59**
Upper Cound. *Shrp* —1C **33**
Upper Cwmbran. *Torf* —3D **59**
Upper Dinchope. *Shrp*
  —3B **32**
Upper Framilode. *Glos*
  —1D **61**
Upper Grove Common. *H&W*
  —3C **51**
Upper Hardwick. *H&W*
  —3B **40**
Upper Hayton. *Shrp* —3C **33**
Upper Heath. *Shrp* —3C **33**
Upper Hengoed. *Shrp*
  —1D **25**
Upper Hergest. *H&W* —3D **39**
Upper Hill. *H&W* —3B **40**
Upper Killay. *Swan* —3A **56**
Upper Langford. *N.Sm*
  —3B **66**
Upper Longwood. *Shrp*
  —1D **33**
Upper Lydbrook. *Glos*
  —1D **61**
Upper Lye. *H&W* —2A **40**
Upper Maes-coed. *H&W*
  —2A **50**
Upper Millichope. *Shrp*
  —3C **33**
Upper Nash. *Pemb* —2D **53**
Upper Netchwood. *Shrp*
  —2D **33**
Upper Rochford. *H&W*
  —2D **41**
Upper Sapey. *H&W* —2D **41**
Upper Soudley. *Glos* —1D **61**
Upper Town. *H&W* —1C **51**
Upper Town. *N.Sm* —3C **67**
Uppington. *Shrp* —1C **33**
Upton. *Ches* —1B **18**
Upton. *Mers* —2D **9**
Upton. *Pemb* —2D **53**
Upton Bishop. *H&W* —3D **51**
Upton Cheyney. *S.Glo*
  —3D **67**
Upton Cressett. *Shrp* —2D **33**
Upton Crews. *H&W* —3D **51**
Upton Heath. *Ches* —1B **18**
Upton Magna. *Shrp* —3C **27**
Urdimarsh. *H&W* —1C **51**
Urmston. *G.Mn* —1D **11**
Usk. *Mon* —2A **60**
Uwchmynydd. *Gwyn* —2A **20**
Uzmaston. *Pemb* —1C **53**

Valley. *IOA* —3B **4**
Van. *Powy* —3A **30**

Varteg. *Torf* —2D **59**
Vauld,The. *H&W* —1C **51**
Vaynol. *Gwyn* —3A **6**
Vaynor. *Mert* —1B **58**
Velindre. *Powy* —2C **49**
Vennington. *Shrp* —1A **32**
Venn's Green. *H&W* —1C **51**
Vernolds Common. *Shrp*
—3B **32**
Viney Hill. *Glos* —2D **61**
Vowchurch. *H&W* —2A **50**
Vulcan Village. *Ches* —1C **11**

Waddicar. *Mers* —1A **10**
Waen. *Den* —1B **16**
(nr. Bodfari)
Waen. *Den* —1C **17**
(nr. Llandyrnog)
Waen. *Den* —1A **16**
(nr. Nantglyn)
Waen. *Powy* —2A **30**
Waen Fach. *Powy* —3D **25**
Waen Goleugoed. *Den* —3B **8**
Walcot. *Shrp* —3C **27**
Walford. *H&W* —1A **40**
(nr. Leintwardine)
Walford. *H&W* —3C **51**
(nr. Ross-on-Wye)
Walford. *Shrp* —2B **26**
Walford Heath. *Shrp* —3B **26**
Walgherton. *Ches* —3D **19**
Walkden. *G.Mn* —1D **11**
Walker's Green. *H&W* —1C **51**
Wallasey. *Mers* —1A **10**
Wallaston Green. *Pemb*
—2C **53**
Wallis. *Pemb* —3D **43**
Wall under Heywood. *Shrp*
—2C **33**
Walterston. *V.Gl* —2B **64**
Walterstone. *H&W* —3A **50**
Walton. *Mers* —1A **10**
Walton. *Powy* —3D **39**
Walton. *Shrp* —3C **27**
Walton East. *Pemb* —3D **43**
Walton-in-Gordano. *N.Sm*
—2B **66**
Walton Park. *N.Sm* —2B **66**
Walton West. *Pemb* —1B **52**
Walwyn's Castle. *Pemb*
—1B **52**
Wanswell. *Glos* —2D **61**
Wapley. *S.Glo* —2D **67**
Warburton. *G.Mn* —2D **11**
Warmingham. *Ches* —1D **19**
Warmley. *S.Glo* —2D **67**
Warren. *Pemb* —3C **53**
Warrington. *Ches* —2D **11**
Waterloo. *Cphy* —1C **65**
Waterloo. *H&W* —1A **50**
Waterloo. *Mers* —1A **10**
Waterloo. *Pemb* —2C **53**
Waterloo. *Shrp* —1B **26**
Waterston. *Pemb* —2C **53**
Waters Upton. *Shrp* —3D **27**
Wattlesborough Heath. *Shrp*
—3A **26**
Wattstown. *Rhon* —3B **58**
Wattsville. *Cphy* —3D **59**
Waun. *Powy* —3D **25**
Waunarlwydd. *Swan* —3B **56**
Waun Fawr. *Cdgn* —3A **28**
Waunfawr. *Gwyn* —2A **14**
Waungilwen. *Carm* —2C **45**
Waunlwyd. *Blae* —2C **59**
Waun-y-Clyn. *Carm* —2D **55**
Waverton. *Ches* —1B **18**

Wavertree. *Mers* —2A **10**
Wdig. *Pemb* —2C **43**
Weaverham. *Ches* —3D **11**
Webton. *H&W* —2B **50**
Wellington. *H&W* —1B **50**
Wellington. *Shrp* —3D **27**
Wellington Heath. *H&W*
—1D **51**
Wellow. *Bath* —3D **67**
Wells Green. *Ches* —2D **19**
Welshampton. *Shrp* —1B **26**
Welsh End. *Shrp* —1C **27**
Welsh Frankton. *Shrp* —1A **26**
Welsh Hook. *Pemb* —3C **43**
Welsh Newton. *H&W* —1B **60**
Welsh Newton Common. *H&W*
—1C **61**
Welshpool. *Powy* —1D **31**
Welsh St Donats. *V.Gl*
—2B **64**
Wem. *Shrp* —2C **27**
Wenallt. *Cdgn* —1B **36**
Wenallt. *Gwyn* —3A **16**
Wentnor. *Shrp* —2A **32**
Wenvoe. *V.Gl* —2C **65**
Weobley. *H&W* —3B **40**
Weobley Marsh. *H&W*
—3B **40**
Wern. *Gwyn* —1A **22**
Wern. *Powy* —1C **59**
(nr. Brecon)
Wern. *Powy* —3D **25**
(nr. Guilsfield)
Wern. *Powy* —3A **24**
(nr. Llangadfon)
Wern. *Powy* —2D **25**
(nr. Llanymynech)
Wernffrwd. *Swan* —3A **56**
Wernyrheolydd. *Mon* —1A **60**
Wervin. *Ches* —3B **10**
West Aberthaw. *V.Gl* —3B **64**
West Bank. *Ches* —2C **11**
Westbrook. *H&W* —1D **49**
Westbury. *Shrp* —1A **32**
Westbury-on-Severn. *Glos*
—1D **61**
Westbury on Trym. *Bris*
—2C **67**
West Cross. *Swan* —1B **62**
West Derby. *Mers* —1A **10**
West End. *N.Sm* —3B **66**
West End. *S.Glo* —1D **67**
Westerleigh. *S.Glo* —2D **67**
West Felton. *Shrp* —2A **26**
West Harptree. *Bath* —3C **67**
West Hewish. *N.Sm* —3A **66**
Westhide. *H&W* —1C **51**
West Hill. *N.Sm* —2B **66**
Westhope. *H&W* —3B **40**
Westhope. *Shrp* —3B **32**
West Kirby. *Mers* —2D **9**
Westleigh. *G.Mn* —1D **11**
Westley. *Shrp* —1A **32**
Weston. *Bath* —3D **67**
Weston. *Ches* —2D **19**
(nr. Crewe)
Weston. *Ches* —2C **11**
(nr. Runcorn)
Weston. *H&W* —3A **40**
Weston. *Shrp* —2C **33**
(nr. Bridgnorth)
Weston. *Shrp* —1A **40**
(nr. Knighton)
Weston. *Shrp* —2C **27**
(nr. Wem)
Weston Beggard. *H&W*
—1C **51**
Westoncommon. *Shrp*
—2B **26**

Weston-in-Gordano. *N.Sm*
—2B **66**
Weston Lullingfields. *Shrp*
—2B **26**
Weston Rhyn. *Shrp* —1D **25**
Weston-super-Mare. *N.Sm*
—3A **66**
Weston under Penyard. *H&W*
—3D **51**
Westra. *V.Gl* —2C **65**
West Town. *Bath* —3C **67**
West Town. *N.Sm* —3B **66**
West Wick. *N.Sm* —3A **66**
West Williamston. *Pemb*
—2D **53**
Wettenhall. *Ches* —1D **19**
Weythel. *Powy* —3D **39**
Wharton. *Ches* —1D **19**
Wharton. *H&W* —3C **41**
Whatmore. *Shrp* —1D **41**
Wheathill. *Shrp* —3D **33**
Wheelock. *Ches* —2D **19**
Wheelock Heath. *Ches*
—2D **19**
Whelston. *Flin* —3D **9**
Whiston. *Mers* —1B **10**
Whitbourne. *H&W* —3D **41**
Whitby. *Ches* —3A **10**
Whitbyheath. *Ches* —3A **10**
Whitchurch. *Bath* —3D **67**
Whitchurch. *Card* —2C **65**
Whitchurch. *H&W* —1C **61**
Whitchurch. *Pemb* —3A **42**
Whitchurch. *Shrp* —3C **19**
Whitcot. *Shrp* —2A **32**
Whitcott Keysett. *Shrp*
—3D **31**
Whitebrook. *Mon* —2C **61**
Whitechurch. *Pemb* —2A **44**
Whitecroft. *Glos* —2D **61**
Whitegate. *Ches* —1D **19**
White Mill. *Carm* —3D **45**
White Rocks. *H&W* —3B **50**
White Stone. *H&W* —1C **51**
Whitfield. *S.Glo* —3D **61**
Whitford. *Flin* —3C **9**
Whitland. *Carm* —1B **54**
Whitney. *H&W* —1D **49**
Whitson. *Newp* —1A **66**
Whittingslow. *Shrp* —3B **32**
Whittington. *Shrp* —1A **26**
Whitton. *Powy* —2D **39**
Whitton. *Shrp* —1C **41**
Whixall. *Shrp* —1C **27**
Whyle. *H&W* —2C **41**
Wibdon. *Glos* —3C **61**
Wick. *S.Glo* —2D **67**
Wick. *V.Gl* —2A **64**
Wick St Lawrence. *N.Sm*
—3A **66**
Wickwar. *S.Glo* —1D **67**
Widnes. *Ches* —2C **11**
Wigmore. *H&W* —2B **40**
Wilcott. *Shrp* —3A **26**
Wilderspool. *Ches* —2D **11**
Wilkesley. *Ches* —3D **19**
Willaston. *Ches* —2D **19**
(nr. Crewe)
Willaston. *Ches* —3A **10**
(nr. Neston)
Willersley. *H&W* —1A **50**
Willey. *Shrp* —2D **33**
Willington Corner. *Ches*
—1C **19**
Willoughbridge. *Staf* —1D **19**
Willsbridge. *S.Glo* —2D **67**
Wilmington. *Bath* —3D **67**
Wilson. *H&W* —3C **51**
Wincham. *Ches* —3D **11**

Windle Hill. *Ches* —3A **10**
Winford. *N.Sm* —3C **67**
Winforton. *H&W* —1D **49**
Winnington. *Ches* —3D **11**
Winnington. *Staf* —1D **27**
Winscombe. *N.Sm* —3B **66**
Winsford. *Ches* —1D **19**
Winsh-wen. *Swan* —3B **56**
Winterbourne. *S.Glo* —1D **67**
Winterley. *Ches* —2D **19**
Winwick. *Ches* —1D **11**
Wirswall. *Ches* —3C **19**
Wistanstow. *Shrp* —3B **32**
Wistanswick. *Shrp* —2D **27**
Wistaston. *Ches* —2D **19**
Wiston. *Pemb* —1D **53**
Withington. *H&W* —1C **51**
Withington. *Shrp* —3C **27**
Withington Marsh. *H&W*
—1C **51**
Wixhill. *Shrp* —2C **27**
Wolferlow. *H&W* —2D **41**
Wolf's Castle. *Pemb* —3C **43**
Wolfsdale. *Pemb* —3C **43**
Wollaston. *Shrp* —3A **26**
Wollerton. *Shrp* —1D **27**
Wolverley. *Shrp* —1B **26**
Wolvesnewton. *Mon* —3B **60**
Womaston. *Powy* —2D **39**
Wood. *Pemb* —3B **42**
Woodbank. *Ches* —3A **10**
Woodchurch. *Mers* —2D **9**
Woodcroft. *Glos* —3C **61**
Woodford. *Glos* —3D **61**
Woodhill. *N.Sm* —2B **66**
Woodhill. *Shrp* —3D **33**
Woodhouses. *Ches* —3C **11**
Woodlane. *Shrp* —2D **27**
Woods Eaves. *H&W* —1D **49**
Woodseaves. *Shrp* —1D **27**
Woodstock Slop. *Pemb*
—3D **43**
Woofferton. *Shrp* —2C **41**
Woolaston. *Glos* —3C **61**
Woolhope. *H&W* —2D **51**
Woollard. *Bath* —3D **67**
Woolley. *Bath* —3D **67**
Woolstaston. *Shrp* —2B **32**
Woolston. *Ches* —1D **11**
Woolston. *Shrp* —3B **32**
(nr. Church Stretton)
Woolston. *Shrp* —2A **26**
(nr. Oswestry)
Woolton. *Mers* —2B **10**
Woonton. *H&W* —3A **40**
(nr. Kington)
Woonton. *H&W* —2C **41**
(nr. Leominster)
Woore. *Shrp* —3D **19**
Wootton. *Shrp* —1B **40**
(nr. Ludlow)
Wootton. *Shrp* —2A **26**
(nr. Oswestry)
Worfield. *Shrp* —2D **33**
Worldsend. *Shrp* —2B **32**
Worle. *N.Sm* —3A **66**
Worleston. *Ches* —2D **19**
Wormbridge. *H&W* —2B **50**
Wormelow Tump. *H&W*
—2B **50**
Wormsley. *H&W* —1B **50**
Worsley. *G.Mn* —1D **11**
Worthen. *Shrp* —1A **32**
Worthenbury. *Wrex* —3B **18**
Wotherton. *Shrp* —1D **31**
Wraxall. *N.Sm* —2B **66**
Wrecsam. *Wrex* —2A **18**
Wrenbury. *Ches* —3C **19**
Wrentnall. *Shrp* —1B **32**

Wrexham. *Wrex* —2A **18**
Wrexham Industrial Estate.
Wrex —3A **18**
Wrickton. *Shrp* —3D **33**
Wrinehill. *Staf* —3D **19**
Wrington. *N.Sm* —3B **66**
Wrockwardine. *Shrp* —3D **27**
Wroxeter. *Shrp* —1C **33**
Wybunbury. *Ches* —3D **19**
Wyesham. *Mon* —1C **61**
Wyke. *Shrp* —1D **33**
Wyken. *Shrp* —2D **33**
Wyke, The. *Shrp* —1D **33**
Wykey. *Shrp* —2A **26**
Wyndham. *Bri* —3A **58**
Wyson. *H&W* —2C **41**

Yanley. *N.Sm* —3C **67**
Yardro. *Powy* —3D **39**
Yarkhill. *H&W* —1D **51**
Yarpole. *H&W* —2B **40**
Yarsop. *H&W* —1B **50**
Yate. *S.Glo* —1D **67**
Yatton. *H&W* —2B **40**
(nr. Leominster)
Yatton. *H&W* —2D **51**
(nr. Ross-on-Wye)
Yatton. *N.Sm* —3B **66**
Yazor. *H&W* —1B **50**
Y Bont-Faen. *V.Gl* —2A **64**
Y Dref. *Gwyn* —1D **21**
Y Drenewydd. *Powy* —2C **31**
Yearsett. *H&W* —3D **41**
Yeaton. *Shrp* —3B **26**
Yerbeston. *Pemb* —2D **53**
Y Felinheli. *Gwyn* —1A **14**
Y Felint. *Flin* —3D **9**
Y Fenni. *Mon* —1A **60**
Y Ffor. *Gwyn* —1C **21**
Y Gelli Gandryll. *Powy*
—1D **49**
Ynysboeth. *Rhon* —3B **58**
Ynysddu. *Cphy* —3C **59**
Ynysforgan. *Swan* —3B **56**
Ynyshir. *Rhon* —3B **58**
Ynyslas. *Cdgn* —2B **28**
Ynysmaerdy. *Neat* —3C **57**
Ynysmaerdy. *Rhon* —1B **64**
Ynysmeudwy. *Neat* —2C **57**
Ynystawe. *Swan* —3B **56**
Ynyswen. *Powy* —1D **57**
Ynys-wen. *Rhon* —3A **58**
Ynys y Barri. *V.Gl* —3C **65**
Ynysybwl. *Rhon* —3B **58**
Yockleton. *Shrp* —3B **26**
Yorkley. *Glos* —2D **61**
Yorton. *Shrp* —2C **27**
Yorton Heath. *Shrp* —2C **27**
Yr Wyddgrug. *Flin* —1D **17**
Ysbyty Cynfyn. *Cdgn* —1C **37**
Ysbyty Ifan. *Cnwy* —3D **15**
Ysbyty Ystwyth. *Cdgn*
—1C **37**
Ysceifiog. *Flin* —3C **9**
Yspitty. *Carm* —3A **56**
Ystalyfera. *Neat* —2C **57**
Ystrad. *Rhon* —3A **58**
Ystrad Aeron. *Cdgn* —3A **36**
Ystradfellte. *Powy* —1A **58**
Ystradffin. *Carm* —1C **47**
Ystradgynlais. *Powy* —1C **57**
Ystradmeurig. *Cdgn* —2C **37**
Ystrad Mynach. *Cphy* —3C **59**
Ystradowen. *Neat* —1C **57**
Ystradowen. *V.Gl* —2B **64**
Ystumtuen. *Cdgn* —1C **37**

Selected Places of Interest and other features

❏ Opening times for Places of Interest vary greatly; while some open all year, others open only for the summer season, some only open certain days or even part days.   We recommend, to avoid disappointment, you check with the nearest Tourist Information Centre (see pages 95/96) before starting your journey.

❏ This is an index to selected features shown on the map pages, it is not a comprehensive guide.

❏ To keep the maps as clear as possible, descriptive words like 'Castle', 'Museum' etc. are omitted, a key to the various map symbols used can be found on page 1 in the reference.   Features within very congested areas and town centres are indicated as space allows, wherever possible, at least with the appropriate symbol; in some instances the text may fall into an adjacent map square.

❏ Every possible care has been taken to ensure that the information given is accurate and whilst the publishers would be grateful to learn of any errors, they regret they cannot accept any responsibility for loss thereby caused.

Abbey/Friary/Priory

Abbey Dore Abbey Church
—2A 50
Basingwerk Abbey, Greenfield
(Maes-Glas)—3C 9
Bath Abbey Church—3D 67
Belmont Abbey, Hereford
—2B 50
Buildwas Abbey—1D 33
Caldey Island Priory—3A 54
Craswall Priory, Michaelchurch
Escley—2D 49
Cwmhir Abbey, Abbey-cwm-
hir—1B 38
Cymer Abbey, Llanelltyd
—3C 23
Denbigh Friary—1B 16
Ewenny Priory—2A 64
Haughmond Abbey, Haughton
—3C 27
Haverfordwest Priory—1C 53
Leominster Priory Church
—3B 40
Lilleshall Abbey—3D 27
Llanthony Priory—3D 49
Margam Abbey—1D 63
Neath Abbey—3C 57
Norton Priory, Halton—2C 11
Penmon Priory—2B 6
St Dogmaels Abbey—1A 44
Shrewsbury Abbey Church
—3B 26
Strata Florida Abbey—2C 37
Talley Abbey—2B 46
Tintern Abbey—2C 61
Valle Crucis Abbey,
Llangollen—3D 17

Wenlock Priory, Much Wenlock
—1D 33
Woodspring Priory, Worle
—3A 66

Aquarium

Aberaeron Sea Aquarium
—2D 35
Anglesey Sea Zoo,
Brynsiencyn—1D 13
Beaumaris Marine World—3B 6
Conwy Aquarium—3C 7
Oceanarium, St David's
(Tyddewi)—3A 42
Rhyl Sea Life Centre—2B 8
St David's Marine Life Centre
—3A 42
Silent World Aquarium, Tenby
(Dinbych-y-Pysgod)—2A 54
Weston-super-Mare Sea Life
Centre—3A 66

Arboretum

See also Garden
Afan Forest Park Forest
Garden, Pontrhydyfen—3D 57
Cae'n y Coed Forest Garden,
Betws-y-Coed—2C 15
Eastnor Castle Arboretum
—2D 51
Gelli Aur Country Park
Arboretum, Golden Grove
—1A 56
Glasdir Forest Garden,
Llanfachreth—2C 23
Queenswood Arboretum, Hope

under Dinmore—3C 41
Speech House Arboretum,
Cinderford—1D 61

Aviary/Bird Garden

See also Farm Park, Wildlife Park,
Zoo
Anglesey Birds of Prey &
Conservation Centre,
Llanrhyddlad—2C 5
Brean Down Tropical Bird
Garden—3D 65
Dyfed Bird of Prey Centre,
Cilgerran—1B 44
National Birds of Prey Centre,
Newent—3D 51
Welsh Hawking Centre, Barry
(Barri)—3B 64

Botanical Garden

Ness Botanic Gardens—3A 10
Swansea Plantasia—3B 56
University of Bristol Botanical
Gardens—2C 67

Butterfly Farm

Berkeley Castle Butterfly
Farm—3D 61
Conwy Butterfly House—3C 7
Felinwynt Rainforest & Butterfly
Centre—3B 34
Jubilee Park World of
Butterflies, Symonds Yat
(West)—1C 61
Pili Palas Butterfly & Bird

Palace, Menai Bridge
(Porthaethwy)—3A 6

Dolaucothi Gold Mines,
Pumsaint—1B 46
Gloddfa Ganol Slate Mine,
Blaenau Ffestiniog—3B 14
Great Orme Mines, Llandudno
—2C 7
King Arthur's Cave & Merlins
Cave, Crocker's Ash—1C 61
Kynaston's Cave, Nesscliffe
—3A 26
Llanfair Slate Caverns—2A 22
Llechwedd Slate Caverns,
Blaenau Ffestiniog—3c 15
Llywernog Silver-Lead Mine
—3C 29
Porth'yr-Ogof Cavern,
Ystradfellte—1A 58
Sygun Copper Mine, Beddgelert
—3B 14

Afan Argoed Country Park,
Cynonville—3D 57
Alyn Waters Country Park,
Gwersyllt—2A 18
Arrowe Country Park,
Woodchurch—2D 9
Avon Valley Country Park,
Keynsham—3D 67
Breakwater Country Park,
Holyhead (Caergybi)—2B 4
Bryn Bach Country Park,
Tredegar—2C 59
Bryngarw Country Park,
Brynmenyn—1A 64
Caldicot Castle Country Park
—1B 66
Clyne Valley Country Park, Lower
Sketty—3B 56
Colemere Country Park—1B 26
Cosmeston Lakes Country Park
—3C 65
Craig Gwladus Country Park,
Cilfrew—3C 57
Craig-y-nos Country Park—1D 57
Croxteth Country Park, West
Derby—1B 10
Dare Valley Country Park,
Aberdare (Aberdar)—2A 58
Eastham Woods Country Park,
Eastham Ferry—2A 10
Erddig Park Country Park,
Wrexham (Wrecsam)—3A 18
Forest Farm Country Park,
Whitchurch—1C 65

Gelli Aur Country Park, Golden
Grove—3B 46
Glynllifon Country Park,
Llandwrog—2D 13
Gnoll Estate Country Park, Neath
(Castell-nedd)—3C 57
Granville Country Park, Muxton
—3D 27
Great Orme Country Park,
Llandudno—2C 7
Greenfield Valley Heritage Park,
Greenfield (Maes-Glas)—3C 9
Halewood Triangle Country
Park—2B 10
Henblas Country Park, Capel
Mawr—3D 5
Joys of Life Country Park,
Bethesda—1B 14
Little Budworth Common Country
Park—1C 19
Llyn Llech Owain Country Park,
Gorslas—1A 56
Llys-y-fran Reservoir Country
Park—3D 43
Loggerheads Country Park,
Cadole—1C 17
Lyth Hill Country Park, Great
Lyth—1B 32
Marbury Park Country Park,
Comberbach—3D 11
Margam Park—1D 63
Moel Famau Country Park,
Llanbedr-Dyffryn-Clwyd—1C 17
Nesscliffe Hill Country Park
—3A 26
Padarn Country Park, Llanberis
—1A 14
Parc Cefn Onn Country Park,
Thornhill—1C 65
Parc Cwm Darran Country Park,
Deri—2C 59
Pembrey Country Park—2D 55
Pennington Flash Country Park
—1D 11
Pen-y-fan Pond Country Park,
Pen-twyn—2C 59
Pex Hill Country Park, Cronton
—2C 11
Pickering's Pasture Country Park,
Hale Bank—2B 10
Porthkerry Country Park—3B 64
Queenswood Country Park, Hope
under Dinmore—3C 41
Rivacre Valley Country Park,
Overpool—3A 10
Sankey Valley Park, Newton-le
-Willows / St Helens—1C 11

Scolton Manor Country Park
—3C 43
Severn Valley Country Park,
Highley—3D 33
Sirhowy Valley Country Park,
Crosskeys—3C 59
Stadt Moers Country Park,
Whiston—1B 10
Stanney Woods Country Park,
Whitbyheath—3A 10
Tatton Country Park, Knutsford
—2D 11
Tredegar House Country Park,
Newport (Casnewydd)—1D 65
Ty Mawr Country Park,
Newbridge—3D 17
Waun-y-Llyn Country Park,
Caergwrle—2D 17
Wepre Country Park, Connah's
Quay—1D 17
Wirral Country Park, Thurstaston /
Willaston—2D 9

See also Wildlife Park
Acton Scott Historic Working
Farm—3B 32
Bunny Farm Park, Corwen
—3B 16
Cae Dafydd Rare Breeds Farm,
Nantmor—3B 14
Cardiff City Farm—2C 65
Cardigan Island Coastal Far,
Park, Gwbert—3A 34
Carreg Cennen Castle Farm Park,
Trapp—1B 56
Court Farm, Stonebridge—3A 66
Croxteth Home Farm, West
Derby—1B 10
Dan-yr-Ogof Shire Horse Centre,
Glyntawe—1D 57
Dwyfor Ranch Rabbit Farm &
Farm Park, Llanystumdwy
—1D 21
Dyfed Shire Horse Farm,
Eglwyswrw—2A 44
Farm World (Wrexham),
Rhostyllen—3A 18
Fferm Glyneithinog, Penrherber
—2B 44
Foel Farm Park, Brynsiencyn
—1D 13
Folly Farm, Begelly—2A 54
Gigrin Farm Trail, Rhayader
(Rhaeadr Gwy)—2A 38

Green Acres Farm Park,
 Mancot—1A 18
Greenmeadow Community Farm,
 Cwmbran—3D 59
Gwaynynog Country World,
 Gwaenynog Bach—1B 16
Hall Farm Park, Pengwern—3B 8
Henblas Farm Park, Capel
 Mawr—3D 5
Hoo Farm Animal Kingdom,
 Preston upon the Weald
 Moors—3D 27
Llangloffan Farmhouse Cheese
 Centre—2C 43
Margam Park Farm Park—1D 63
Moors Collection, Buttington
 —1D 31
Noah's Ark Farm Park, Cribyn
 —3D 35
Oaklands Small Breeds Farm,
 The, Kingswood—3D 39
Oldown Farm & Forest,
 Olveston—1D 67
Rays Farm Country Matters, High
 Green—3D 33
St Augustine's Farm, Arlingham
 —1D 61
St David's Farm Park—3A 42
Salem Farm Rural Resource
 Park—3B 46
Shortwood Working Farm,
 Pencombe—3C 41
Stockley Farm, Arley—2D 11
Tatton Dale Home Farm,
 Knutsford—2D 11
Trefeinon Open Farm,
 Llangorse—2C 49
Wernlas Collection, Onibury
 —1B 40
Windmill Hill City Farm,
 Bedminster—2C 67
Woodlands Farm Park, Wiston
 —1D 53
Wye Valley Farm Park,
 Goodrich—1C 61

Forest Parks

See also National Parks
Afan Forest Park—3D 57
Coed y Brenin Forest Park—2C23
Delamere Forest Park—3C 11
Forest of Dean—2D 61
Gwydyr Forest Park—2C 15

Forest Enterprise Visitor Centres

*See also National Park and
 Tourist Information Centres*
NOTE: Telephone numbers are
 given in Italics
Afan Argoed Countryside Centre,
 Cynonville—3D 57
 01639 850564
Betws-y-Coed Y Stablau Visitor
 Centre—2C 15   *01690 710426*
Bod Petrual Visitor Centre,
 Clawdd-newydd—1B 16
Coed y Brenin Forest Park Visitor
 Centre, Bryn Eden—2C 23
Cwmcarn Visitor Centre—3D 59
 01495 272001
Delamere Forest Visitor Centre,
 Hatchmere—3C 11
Garwnant Forest Centre, Llwyn-
 on Village—1B 58
 01685 723060
Nant-yr-Arian Visitor Centre,
 Llywernog—3C29
Wyre Forest Visitor Centre,
 Callow Hill—1D 41
 01299 266302

Fortress

Gun Tower, The, Pembroke Dock
 (Doc Penfro)—2C 53
Perch Rock Fort, New Brighton
 —1A 10

Garden

See also Historic Building & Garden
Abbey Dore Court Gardens
 —2A 50
Bath Georgian Garden—3D 67
Bodnant Garden—3D 7
Bridgemere Garden World,
 Woore—3D 19
Brobury House Garden—1A 50
Bro Meigan Gardens, Llanfair
 -Nant-Gwyn—2A 44
Burford House Gardens—2C 41
Cholmondeley Castle Gardens,
 Hampton Heath—2C 19
Colby Woodland Garden,
 Stepaside—2A 54
Dunraven Park, Southerndown
 —2D 63
Dyffryn Gardens—2B 64
Festival Park, Ebbw Vale (Glyn

Ebwy)—2C 59
Gerddi Gardens, Pontfaen
 —2D 43
Goldstone Hall Garden—2D 27
Happy Valley, Llandudno—2C 7
Haulfre Gardens, Llandudno
 —2C 7
Hergest Croft Gardens, Kington
 —3D 39
Hill Court Gardens, Walford
 —3C 51
Hodnet Hall Gardens—2D 27
How Caple Court Gardens
 —2D 51
Kenchester Water Garden, Pipe
 and Lyde—1C 51
Liverpool Festival Gardens,
 Otterspool—2A 10
Llanerchaeron, Llanaeron—2D 35
Lydney Park Gardens—2D 61
Maenllwyd Isaf Garden,
 Llanmerwig—2C 31
Penlan-uchaf Gardens,
 Crymych—2B 44
Penpergwm Lodge Garden,
 Llanvihangel Gobion—1A 60
Picton Gardens (Old Court
 Nurseries), Colwall Stone
 —1D 51
Plas Brondanw Gardens,
 Garreg—3B 14
Plas Tan-y-Bwlch Gardens, Tan
 -y-Bwlch—3B 14
Prior Park, Bath—3D 67
Ryelands House Garden,
 Taynton—3D 51
Stammers Gardens,
 Saundersfoot—2A 54
Stapeley Water Gardens, Butt
 Green—2D 19
Staunton Park Gardens, Staunton
 on Arrow—2A 40
Upton Castle Grounds—2D 53
Walton Hall Gardens, Higher
 Walton—2D 11
Weir, The, Swainshill—1B 50
Westbury Court Garden,
 Westbury-on-Severn—1D 61
Wye Valley Herb Garden,
 Tintern—2C 61

Hill Fort

Bury Ditches Hill Fort, Lower
 Down—3A 32
Cadbury Camp, Tickenham
 —2B 66

Caer Caradoc, Chapel Lawn
—1A 40
Caer Caradoc, Church Stretton
—2B 32
Caer y Twr Hill Fort, Holyhead
(Caergybi)—2B 4
Carn Goch Hill Fort, Bethlehem
—3B 46
Castell Henllys Iron Age Fort,
Felindre Farchog—2A 44
Cilifor Top Hill Fort, Llanrhidian
—3A 56
Coed-y-Bwynydd Hill Fort, Bettws
Newydd—2A 60
Croft Ambrey Hill Fort, Yatton
—2B 40
Dinedor Camp, Dinedor Cross
—2C 51
Herefordshire Beacon Hill Fort,
Ledbury—1D 51
Llanmelin Hill Fort, Llanvair
-Discoed—3B 60
Midsummer Hill Hill Fort,
Ledbury—2D 51
Moel Goedog Hill Fort,
Eisingrug—1B 22
Nordy Bank Hill Fort,
Cockshutford—3C 33
Norton Camp, Craven Arms
—3B 32
Old Oswestry Hill Fort, Oswestry
(Croesoswallt)—1D 25
Pen-y-crug Hill Fort, Brecon
(Aberhonddu)—2B 48
Pen-y-Gaer Hill Fort, Llanbedr-y
-cennin—1C 15
Rath, The, Crundale—1C 53
Sutton Walls, Sutton St Michael
—1C 51
Tre'r Ceiri Hill Fort,
Llanaelhaearn—3C 13

Dudmaston Hall, Quatford—3D 33
Dunham Massey, Dunham
Town—2D 11
Dyrham Park—2D 67
Erddig, Wrexham (Wrecsam)
—3A 18
Gregynog, Tregynon—2B 30
Gwydir Castle, Llanrwst—1C 15
Hawkstone Hall, Weston—2C 27
Highgate Cottage,
Llanystumdwy—1D 21
Kinnersley Castle—1A 50
Littledean Hall—1D 61
Penrhyn Castle, Llandegai—3B 6
Plas Newydd, Llanfair
Pwllgwyngyll—1A 14
Plas yn Rhiw—2B 20
St Fagans Castle—2C 65
Shipton Hall—2C 33
Speke Hall—2B 10
Tatton Park, Knutsford—2D 11
Tredegar House, Newport
(Casnewydd)—1D 65
Tretower Court—3C 49
Walcot Hall, Lydbury North
—3A 32

Historic Building

Dylan Thomas' Boathouse,
Laugharne—1C 55
Eastnor Castle—2D 51
Garway Dovecote—3B 50
Great Aberystwyth Camera
Obscura—3A 28
Great Castle House, Monmouth
(Trefynwy)—1C 61
Gwrych Castle, Abergele—3A 8
Hellen's, Much Marcle—2D 51
Hereford Old House—1C 51
King Charles Tower, Chester
—1B 18
Kingswood Abbey Gatehouse
—3D 61
Lamphey Bishop's Palace—2D 53
Longnor Moat House—1B 32
Lower Brockhampton, Bringsty
Common—3D 41
Moccas Court—1A 50
Much Wenlock Guildhall—2D 33
Nantyglo Roundhouse Towers
—1C 59
Old Beaupre Castle, St Hilary
—2B 64
Oxwich Castle—3D 55
Penarth Fawr Medieval House,
Chwilog—1D 21
Penmon Dovecot—2B 6
Penrhos Cottage, Maenclochog
—3A 44
Plas Mawr, Conwy—3C 7
Plas Newydd, Llangollen—3D 17
Red Lodge, Bristol—2C 67
Rosehill House, Coalbrookdale
—1D 33
Royal Crescent, No. 1, Bath
—3D 67
St David's Bishop's Palace
—3A 42
St Georges Hall, Liverpool
—1A 10
Smallest House, The, Conwy
—3C 7
Sufton Court, Mordiford—2C 51
Tabley House Collection,
Knutsford—3D 11
Tudor Merchant's House, Tenby
(Dinbych-y-Pysgod)—2A 54
Ty Mawr Wybrnant,
Penmachno—2C 15
Ty'n-y-coed, Penmachno—2D 15
Upton Cressett Hall—2D 33
Wilderhope Manor, Longville in
the Dale—2C 33

Horse Racecourse

Aintree Racecourse—1A 10
Bangor Racecourse, Bangor-is-y-coed—3A 18
Bath & Somerset County Racecourse—3D 67
Chepstow Racecourse—3C 61
Chester (Roodee) Racecourse—1A 18
Haydock Park Racecourse, Ashton-in-Makerfield—1C 11
Hereford Racecourse—1C 51
Ludlow Racecourse, Bromfield—1B 40

Industrial Monument

See also Windmill
Aberdulais Falls Watermills—3C 57
Anderton Boat Lift—3D 11
Audlem Lock Flight—3D 19
Bedlam Furnaces, Ironbridge—1D 33
Bersham Ironworks—3A 18
Blackpool Mill & Caverns, Canaston Bridge—1D 53
Blaenavon Ironworks—2D 59
Brynkir Woollen Mill, Golan—3A 14
Bunbury Staircase Locks—2C 19
Bunbury Watermill—2C 19
Carew Tidal Mill—2D 53
Cefn Cribbwr Ironworks, Cefn Cribwr—1D 63
Cenarth Falls Flour Mill—1B 44
Clydach Ironworks—1D 59
Cochwillan Mill, Tal-y-bont—1B 14
Daniel's Mill, Bridgnorth—2D 33
Denant Mill Inn, Dreenhill—1C 53
Dunham Massey Sawmill, Dunham Town—2D 11
Dyfi Furnace—2B 28
Felin Crewi Watermill, Penegoes—1C 29
Felin Faesog Watermill, Tai'n Lon—2D 13
Felin Geri Watermill, Cwm-cou—1C 45
Felin Isaf Watermill, Pentrefelin—3D 7
Felin Newydd Watermill, Crugybar—2B 46
Felin yr Aber, Llanwnnen—1A 46

Fourteen Locks, Rogerstone—1D 65
Gelligroes Old Mill, Pontllanfraith—3C 59
Hay Inclined Plane, Coalport—1D 33
Ironbridge—1D 33
Melin Howell, Llanddeusant—2C 5
Melin Teifi, Drefach—2C 45
Middle Mill Woollen Mill, Whitchurch—3B 42
Mortimer's Cross Watermill—2B 40
Penmachno Woollen Mill—2D 15
Pentre Watermill, Cadole—1C 17
Priston Mill—3D 67
Rock Mills Woollen Mill, Capel Dewi—1D 45
Salt House, The, Port Eynon—1A 62
Shore Road Pumping Station, Birkenhead—2A 10
Stretton Watermill—2B 18
Tintern Abbey Furnace—2C 61
Tintern Abbey Mill—2C 61
Trefriw Woollen Mills—1C 15
Tregwynt Woollen Mill, Granston—2B 42
Welsh Frankton Lock Flight—1A 26
Y Felin, St Dogmaels—1A 44

Motor Racing Circuit

Llandow Motor Circuit—2A 64
Oulton Park Motor Circuit, Little Budworth—1C 19
Pembrey Motor Circuit—2D 55

Museum & Art Gallery

1st The Queen's Dragoon Guards Museum, Cardiff (Caerdydd)—2C 65
Abbey Farm Museum, Greenfield (Maes-Glas)—3C 9
Aberaeron Honey Bee Exhibition—2D 35
Abergavenny & District Museum—1D 59
Aberystwyth Arts Centre—3A 28
Aberystwyth Yesterday—3A 28
Albion Art Gallery, St David's (Tyddewi)—3A 42
Andrew Logan Museum of

Sculpture, Berriew—1C 31
Anglesey Heritage Gallery, Llangefni—3D 5
Bangor Museum & Art Gallery—3A 6
Barmouth Lifeboat Museum—3B 22
Bath Book Museum—3D 67
Bath Postal Museum—3D 67
Bath Roman Bath Museum—3D 67
Beaumaris Gaol—3B 6
Beaumaris Museum of Childhood Memories—3B 6
Beckford's Tower Museum, Bath—3D 67
Bersham Heritage Centre—3A 18
Betws-y-Coed Motor Museum—2C 15
Big Pit Mining Museum, Blaenavon—2D 59
Birkenhead Priory Interpetive Centre—2A 10
Birkenhead Tramway Museum—2A 10
Bishop's Castle Railway Museum—3A 32
Blaise Castle House Museum, Henbury—2C 67
Blists Hill Open Air Museum—1D 33
Bluecoat Chambers Art Gallery, Liverpool—1A 10
Boat Museum, The, Ellesmere Port—3B 10
Brecknock Museum, Brecon (Aberhonddu)—3B 48
Bridgnorth Childhood & Costume Museum—2D 33
Bristol City Museum & Art Gallery—2C 67
Bristol Industrial Museum—2C 67
British Folk Art Collection, Bath—3D 67
Bromyard Heritage Centre—3D 41
Building of Bath Museum—3D 67
Button Museum, The, Ross-on-Wye—3C 51
Caerleon Roman Legionary Museum—3A 60
Caernarfon Air World, Dinas Dinlle—2D 13
Carmarthen Heritage Centre—1D 55
Carmarthen Museum, Abergwili—3D 45

Magical Machines, Museum of, Cardiff (Caerdydd)—2C 65

Margam Stones Museum—1D 63

Merseyside Maritime Museum, Liverpool—2A 10

Midland Motor Museum, Bridgnorth—2D 33

Milford Haven Museum—2C 53

Model Farm Folk Collection, Wolvesnewton—3B 60

Mold Museum & Art Gallery —1D 17

Mouldsworth Motor Museum —3C 11

Mr Bowler's Business, Bath —3D 67

Much Wenlock Museum—2D 33

Nantgarw China Works Museum—1C 65

Nantwich Museum—2D 19

Nant-y-Coy Mill Museum, Wolf's Castle—3C 43

National Coracle Centre, Cenarth—1B 44

National Library of Wales, Aberystwyth—3A 28

National Museum of Wales (Main Building), Cardiff (Caerdydd) —2C 65

Neath Museum & Art Gallery —3C 57

Nelson Museum & Local History Centre, Monmouth (Trefynwy)—1C 61

Newport Museum & Art Gallery —1A 66

Newtown Textile Museum—2C 31

Norchard Steam Centre Museum, Lydney—2D 61

Norton Priory Museum, Halton —2C 11

Old Bell Museum, Montgomery (Trefaldwyn)—2D 31

Old Chapel Gallery, Pembridge —3A 40

Old Welsh Country Life, Museum of, Tai'n Lon—2D 13

'On the Air' The Broadcasting Museum, Chester—1B 18

Oriel Mostyn, Llandudno—2C 7

Oriel Pendeitsh Gallery, Caernarfon—1D 13

Oswestry Transport Museum —2D 25

Outward Bound Museum, Aberdovey (Aberdyfi)—2B 28

Owain Glyndwr Museum

(Parliament House), Machynlleth—1C 29

Owen Memorial Museum, Newtown (Y Drenewydd) —2C 31

Parc Howard Museum & Art Gallery, Llanelli—2A 56

Park Hall Working Farm Museum, Oswestry (Croesoswallt) —1A 26

Pembroke Farm Museum—2C 53

Pembrokeshire Motor Museum, Keeston—1B 52

Penbontbren Countryside Collection, Glynarthen—1C 45

Penrhyn Castle Industrial Railway Museum, Llandegai—3B 6

Pilkington Glass Museum, St Helens—1B 10

Pontypridd Historical & Cultural Centre—3B 58

Porthmadog Harbour Station Railway Museum—1A 22

Porthmadog Maritime Museum —1A 22

Port Sunlight Heritage Centre —2A 10

Powysland Museum & Montgomery Canal Centre, Welshpool (Trallwng)—1D 31

Prescot Museum of Clock & Watch Making—1B 10

Presteigne (Shire Hall) Museum —2A 40

Primitive Methodism, Museum of, Englesea-brook—2D 19

Railway Age, The, Crewe—2D 19

Rainhill Trails Exhibition—1B 10

Rhondda Heritage Park, Trehafod—3B 58

River & Visitor Centre, Museum of the, Ironbridge—1D 33

Rob Piercy Gallery, Porthmadog—1A 22

Rowley's House Museum, Shrewsbury—3B 26

Royal Cambrian Academy, The, Conwy—3C 7

Royal Forest of Dean Mining Museum, Clearwell—2C 61

Royal Photographic Society, The, Bath—3D 67

Royal Welch Fusiliers Museum, Caernarfon—1D 13

Ruthin Craft Centre Gallery —2C 17

St Helens Museum & Art

Gallery—1C 11

St Helens Transport Museum —1C 11

St John Medieval Museum, Hereford—1C 51

Sally Lunn's House, Bath—3D 67

Salt Museum, The, Northwich —3D 11

Scolton Manor Museum—3C 43

Sea Historic Gallery & Marine Life Aquarium, Pembroke (Penfro)—2C 53

Segontium Roman Fort Museum, Caernarfon—1D 13

Seiont II Maritime Museum, Caernarfon—1D 13

Selvedge Farm Museum, Clarbeston Road—3D 43

Seven Sisters Museum—2D 57

Shambles Museum, The, Newent—3D 51

Shropshire Regimental Museum, Shrewsbury—3B 26

South Wales Borders Museum, Brecon (Aberhonddu)—3B 48

South Wales Miners Museum, Cynonville—3D 57

South Wales Police Museum, Bridgend (Pen-y-bont ar Ogwr)—2A 64

Stapeley's Yesteryear Museum, Butt Green—2D 19

Stone Science, Llanddyfnan —3D 5

Sudley House, Mossley Hill —2A 10

Swansea Maritime & Industrial Museum—3B 56

Swansea Museum—3B 56

Talyllyn Narrow Gauge Railway Museum, Tywyn—1A 28

Tate Gallery Liverpool—2A 10

Tenbury Museum, Tenbury Wells—2C 41

Tenby Museum & Picture Gallery—2A 54

Thornbury Museum—1D 67

Tre'r-ddol Local Folk Museum —2B 28

Turner House Gallery, Penarth —2C 65

Turnpike Gallery, Leigh—1D 11

University of Liverpool Art Gallery—1A 10

University of Wales School of Art Museum & Gallery, Aberystwyth—3A 28

Vale of Glamorgan Railway Visitor
Centre, Barry Island (Ynys y
Barri)—3C 65
Valley Inheritance Museum, The,
Pontypool (Pontypwl)—2D 59
Victoria Art Gallery, Bath—3D 67
Wales Aircraft Museum,
Tredogan—3B 64
Walker Art Gallery, Liverpool
—1A 10
Warrington Museum & Art
Gallery—2D 11
Water Folk Canal Centre
Museum, Llanfrynach—3B 48
Welch Regiment Museum of The
Royal Regiment of Wales, The,
Cardiff (Caerdydd)—2C 65
Welsh Folk Museum, St Fagans
—2C 65
Welsh Industrial & Maritime
Museum, Cardiff (Caerdydd)
—2C 65
Welsh Slate Museum, Llanberis
—1A 14
Welsh Woollen Industry, Museum
of the, Drefach—2C 45
W.H.Smith Museum, Newtown (Y
Drenewydd)—2C 31
Williamson Art Gallery & Museum,
Birkenhead—2A 10
Wilson Museum of Narberth
—1A 54
Wonderful World of Welsh Wool,
Llanwrtyd Wells—1D 47
Woodspring Museum, Weston
-super-Mare—3A 66
Wrexham Maelor Heritage Centre,
Wrexham (Wrecsam)—2A 18
Wroxeter Roman City Museum
—1C 33
Ynysfach Iron Heritage Centre,
Merthyr Tydfil—2B 58
Y Tabernacl (The Museum of
Modern Art, Wales),
Machynlleth—1C 29

See also Forest Parks
Brecon Beacons National Park
—3B 48 / 1D 57 / 1A 58
Pembrokeshire Coast National
Park—2D 53 / 1B 52 / 2D 43
Snowdonia National Park—2B 14
/ 1C 23

National Park Information Centre

See also Forest Park and Tourist
Information Centres
NOTE: Telephone Numbers are
given in Italics
Aberdovey (Aberdyfi) Information
Centre—2B 28   01654 767321
Abergavenny (Y Fenni)
Information Centre—1A 60
01873 853254
Betws-y-Coed Y Stablau Visitor
Centre—2C 15   01690 710426
Blaenau Ffestiniog Information
Centre—3C 15   01766 830360
Brecon (Aberhonddu) Information
Centre—3B 48   01874 623156
Broad Haven Information
Centre—1B 52   01437 781412
Craig-y-nos Information Centre
—1D 57   01639 730395
Dolgellau Information Centre
—3C 23   01341 422888
Harlech Information Centre
—1A 22   01766 780658
Haverfordwest (Hwlffordd)
Information Centre—1C 53
01437 760136
Llandovery (Llanymddyfri)
Information Centre—2C 47
01550 20693
Mountain Centre Visitor Centre,
Libanus—3A 48   01874 623366
Newport Information Centre
(Pembrokeshire)—2D 43
01239 820912
Pembroke (Penfro) Information
Centre—2C 53   01646 682148
St David's (Tyddewi) Information
Centre—3A 42   01437 720392
Saundersfoot Information
Centre—2A 54   01834 811411

Natural Attraction

Aberdulais Falls—3C 57
Aberedw Rocks—1B 48
Aber Falls, Abergwyngregyn
—1B 14
Afon Arddu Waterfall, Llanberis
—2A 14
Afon Gamlan Cataracts,
Ganllwyd—2C 23
Afon Mellte & Afon Hepste
Waterfalls, Pontneddfechan
—1A 58

Afon Pyrddin Waterfall,
Pontneddfechan—2D 57
Arthog Waterfalls—3B 22
Avon Gorge, Bristol—2C 67
Bala Lake (Llyn Tegid)—1A 24
Bethania Waterfalls—2B 14
Black Mountain, Upper
Brynamman—1C 57
Bleadon Hill—3A 66
Blue Lagoon, Abereiddy—2A 42
Brecon Beacons, Libanus—3B 48
Brockley Combe—3B 66
Brown Clee Hill, Hillside—3C 33
Buck Stone, The, Staunton
—1C 61
Burrington Combe—3B 66
Caldey Island—3A 54
Cenarth Falls—1B 44
Chew Valley Lake, Chew Stoke
—3C 67
Claerwen Reservoir, Elan
Village—2D 37
Conwy Falls, Betws-y-Coed
—2D 15
Devil's Bridge—1C 37
Dinefwr Deer Park, Llandeilo
—3B 46
Dolgoch Falls—1B 28
Elan Valley, Elan Village—2A 38
Elegug Stacks, Merrion—3C 53
Fairy Glen, Betws-y-Coed—2D 15
Flat Holm—3D 65
Forest of Dean, Parkend—2D 61
Garw Fechan Woodland Park,
Pontycymer—3D 57
Gethin Woodland Park,
Pentrebach—2B 58
Gower (Gwyr), Swansea
(Abertawe)—3D 55
Great Orme, Llandudno—2C 7
Grey Mare's Tail, The, Llanrwst
—1C 15
Hatch Mere, Hatchmere—3C 11
Henrhyd Falls, Coelbren—1D 57
Horseshoe Falls, Berwyn—3C 17
Lake Vyrnwy (Llyn Efyrnwy),
Llanwddyn—2A 24
Llwyn-on Reservoir, Llwyn-on
Village—1B 58
Llyn Alaw, Llanbabo—2C 5
Llyn Brenig, Pentre-llyn-cymmer
—2A 16
Llyn Clywedog, Llanidloes—3A 30
Llyn Mair, Tan-y-bwlch—3B 14
Llyn Trawsfynydd—1B 22
Llyn-y-Fan Fach Escarpment,
Llanddeusant—3D 47

Long Mynd, Church Stretton
  —2B 32
Machno Falls, Betws-y-Coed
  —2D 15
Melincourt Waterfall—2D 57
Mere, The, Ellesmere—1B 26
Moel Famau, Llanbedr-Dyffryn
  -Clwyd—1C 17
Mynach Falls, Devil's Bridge
  (Pontarfynach)—1C 37
Nedd Fechan Waterfall,
  Pontneddfechan—2A 58
Penpych Woodland Park,
  Blaencwm—3A 58
Pistyll Cain, Ganllwyd—2C 23
Pistyll Rhaeadr, Tan-y-pistyll
  —2B 24
Ramsey Island—3A 42
Rhaeadr Cynfal, Ffestiniog
  —3C 15
Rhaeadr Ddu, Ganllwyd—2C 23
Rhaeadr Mawddach, Ganllwyd
  —2C 23
Rhaeadr y Cwm, Ffestiniog
  —3C 15
Rheidol Falls, Aberffrwd—1C 37
Rodneys Pillar, Criggion—3D 25
Shell Island (Mochras),
  Llanbedr—2A 22
Skokholm Island—2A 52
Skomer Island—2A 52
Snowdon, Llanberis—2B 14
Stiperstones, The Bog—2A 32
Sugar Loaf, Llwyn-du—1D 59
Swallow Falls, Betws-y-Coed
  —2C 15
Symonds Yat—1C 61
Talybont Reservoir, Aber
  Village—1B 58
Titterstone Clee Hill, Angelbank
  —1C 41
Water-break-its-neck Waterfall,
  Llanfihangel-Nant-Melan
  —2C 39
Wenlock Edge, Presthope—2C 33
Wentwood Forest, Llanvair
  -Discoed—3B 60
Wrekin, The, Little Wenlock
  —1D 33
Wyre Forest, Bewdley—1D 41

*R.S.P.B., English Nature &
  Wildfowl Trust only.*
Arthog Bog Bird Sanctuary
  —3B 22

Avon Gorge Nature Reserve,
  Bristol—2C 67
Cadair Idris Nature Reserve, Tal
  -y-llyn—3C 23
Carngafallt Common Nature
  Reserve, Elan Village—2A 38
Coed Garth Gell Bird Sanctuary,
  Penmaenpool—3B 22
Coedydd Aber Nature Reserve,
  Abergwyngregyn—3B 6
Coedydd Maentwrog (Llyn Mair)
  Nature Reserve, Tan-y-bwlch
  —3B 14
Cors Caron Nature Reserve,
  Tregaron—2B 36
Craig-y-Cilau Nature Reserve,
  Darren—1C 59
Crymlyn Bog Nature Reserve,
  Pentre-dwr—3B 56
Cwm Clydach Bird Sanctuary,
  Craig-cefn-parc—2B 56
Cwm Idwal & Glydeiriau Nature
  Reserve, Pont Pen-y-benglog
  —2B 14
Cwm Wood Nature Reserve, Elan
  Village—2A 38
Dinas Bird Sanctuary, Ystradffin
  —1C 47
Dyffryn Wood Bird Sanctuary,
  Rhayader (Rhaeadr Gwy)
  —2A 38
Dyfi Nature Reserve, Ynyslas
  —2B 28
Gayton Sands Bird Sanctuary,
  Neston—3D 9
Gower Coast Nature Reserve,
  Pitton—3D 55
Gwenffrwd Bird Sanctuary, Nant
  -y-Bai—1C 47
Highbury Wood Nature Reserve,
  Redbrook—2C 61
Lake Vyrnwy Bird Sanctuary,
  Llanwddyn—2A 24
Llanelli Wildfowl & Wetlands
  Centre—3A 56
Morfa Dyffryn Nature Reserve,
  Llanenddwyn—2A 22
Nagshead Bird Sanctuary,
  Parkend—2D 61
Nant Irfon Nature Reserve,
  Abergwesyn—3D 37
Newborough Warren Nature
  Reserve—1D 13
Ogof Ffynon Ddu Nature Reserve,
  Craig-y-nos—1D 57
Oxwich Nature Reserve—1A 62
Penhow Woodlands Nature

Reserve—1B 66
Penmoelallt Forest Nature
  Reserve, Llwyn-on Village
  —2A 58
Point of Ayr Bird Sanctuary,
  Talacre—2C 9
Ramsey Island Nature Reserve
  —3A 42
Rhinog Nature Reserve, Pentre
  Gwynfryn—2B 22
Skomer Island Nature Reserve
  —2A 52
Slimbridge Wildfowl & Wetlands
  Centre—2D 61
Snowdon (Yr Wyddfa) Nature
  Reserve, Bethania—2B 14
South Stack Cliffs Bird Sanctuary,
  Holyhead (Caergybi)—2B 4
Stackpole & Bosherston Ponds
  Nature Reserve, Bosherston
  —3C 53
Stanner Rocks Nature Reserve,
  Walton—3D 39
Stiperstones Nature Reserve,
  The—2A 32
Ty Canol Nature Reserve,
  Felindre Farchog—2D 43
Valley Lakes Bird Sanctuary,
  Llanfihangel yn Nhowyn—3C 5
Whiteford Nature Reserve,
  Llanmadoc—3D 55
Worms Head Nature Reserve,
  Rhossili—3C 55
Wyre Forest Nature Reserve,
  Bewdley—1D 41
Ynys-Hir Bird Sanctuary, Eglwys
  Fach—2B 28

Admiralty Arch, Holyhead
  (Caergybi)—2B 4
Alice in Wonderland Visitor
  Centre, Llandudno—2C 7
Anglesey Column, Llanfair
  Pwllgwyngyll—3A 6
Anglesey Model Village,
  Newborough (Niwbwrch)
  —1D 13
Animation World, Liverpool
  —2A 10
Atcham Bridge—1C 33
Avondale Glass, Kilgetty
  (Cilgeti)—2A 54
Babell Chapel, Cwmfelinfach
  —3C 59
Bath Pump Room—3D 67

Prehistoric Monument

Bryn Celli Ddu Burial Chamber,
Llanddaniel Fab—3A 6
Caer Leb Earthwork,
Brynsiencyn—1D 13
Capel Garmon Burial Chamber
—2D 15
Carn Llechart Burial Chamber,
Rhyd-y-fro—2B 56
Carn Llechart Cairn Circle, Rhyd
-y-fro—2B 56
Carreg Coetan Arthur Burial
Chamber, Newport—2D 43
Castell Bryn Gwyn Earthwork,
Brynsiencyn—1D 13
Cefn Coch Stone Circle (`Druids
Circle'), Penmaenmawr—3C 7
Din Dryfol Burial Chamber,
Bethel—3C 5
Din Lligwy Settlement (Capel
Lligwy Hut Group), Moelfre
—2D 5
Dyffryn Ardudwy Burial
Chamber—2A 22
Hangstone Davey, Broadway
—1B 52
Harold's Stones, Trelleck—2B 60
Holyhead Mountain Hut Group,
Holyhead (Caergybi)—2B 4
Llech Idris Standing Stone,
Bronaber—1C 23
Lligwy Burial Chamber, Moelfre
—2A 6
Maen Ceti (Arthur's Stone) Burial
Chamber, Reynoldston—3D 55
Maen-y-bardd Burial Chambers,
Rowen—3C 7
Mitchell's Fold Stone Circle, Priest
Weston—2A 32
Offa's Dyke, Craignant—1D 25
Offa's Dyke, Knighton (Tref-y-
Clawdd)—1D 39
Offa's Dyke, Tintern—2C 61
Parc Le Breos Burial Chamber
(Giant's Grave), Parkmill
—1A 62
Penmaen Burial Chamber—1A 62
Penrhos Feilw Standing Stones,
Holyhead (Caergybi)—2B 4
Pentre Ifan Burial Chamber,
Felindre Farchog—2D 43
Porth Dafarch Hut Circles,
Holyhead (Caergybi)—2B 4
Presaddfed Burial Chambers,
Bodedern—2C 5
St Lythans Burial Chamber
—2C 65
Samson's Jack Standing Stone,

Oldwalls—3D 55
Stanton Drew Cove—3C 67
Stanton Drew Stone Circles
—3C 67
Stoney Littleton Long Barrow,
Wellow—3D 67
Three Leaps, The, Pentraeth
—3A 6
Tinkinswood Burial Chamber, St
Nicholas—2B 64
Trefignath Burial Chamber,
Holyhead (Caergybi)—2B 4
Ty Mawr Standing Stone,
Holyhead (Caergybi)—2B 4
Ty Newydd Burial Chamber,
Llanfaelog—3C 5

Railway

Preserved, Steam, Narrow Gauge
Aberystwyth Cliff Railway—3A 28
Avon Valley Railway,
Willsbridge—2D 67
Bala Lake Railway,
Llanuwchllyn—1D 23
Birkenhead Tramway—2A 10
Brecon Mountain Railway,
Pontsticill—1B 58
Bridgnorth Castle Hill Railway
—2D 33
Bristol Harbour Railway—2C 67
Cat Funicular Railway, The,
Pantperthog—1C 29
Corris Railway—1C 29
Dean Forest Railway, Lydney
—2D 61
Eirias Park Railway, Colwyn Bay
(Bae Colwyn)—3D 7
Fairbourne & Barmouth Steam
Railway, Fairbourne—3B 22
Ffestiniog Railway, Porthmadog
—1A 22
Great Orme Tramway,
Llandudno—2C 7
Gwili Railway, Bronwydd Arms
—3D 45
Halton Miniature Railway—2C 11
Llanberis Lake Railway—1A 14
Llangollen Railway—3C 17
Mydlewood Railway, Marton
—2B 26
Pontypool & Blaenavon Railway,
Blaenavon—2D 59
Rhyl Miniature Railway—2A 8
Saundersfoot Steam Railway,
Stepaside—2A 54

Severn Valley Railway,
Bridgnorth—2D 33
Snowdon Mountain Railway,
Llanberis—2A 14
Swansea Vale Railway,
Llansamlet—3B 56
Talyllyn Railway, Tywyn—1A 28
Teifi Valley Railway, Henllan
—1C 45
Telford Steam Railway,
Horsehay—1D 33
Vale of Rheidol Railway,
Aberystwyth—3A 28
Welsh Highland Railway,
Porthmadog—1A 22
Welshpool & Llanfair Light
Railway, Llanfair Caereinion
—1C 31

Roman Remains

Blackpool Bridge Roman Road,
Upper Soudley—2D 61
Brecon Gaer Roman Fort (Y
Gaer/Cicucium), Aberyscir
—3B 48
Caer Gybi Roman Fortlet,
Holyhead (Caergybi)—2B 4
Canovium Roman Fort, Ty'n-y
-groes—3C 7
Carmarthen Roman
Amphitheatre—3D 45
Castell Collen, Llandrindod
Wells—2B 38
Chester Roman Amphitheatre
—1B 18
Chester Roman Garden—1B 18
Cold Knap Roman Building, Barry
(Barri)—3B 64
Deva Roman Experience,
Chester—1B 18
Isca (Caerleon) Fortress Baths,
Caerleon (Caerllion)—3A 60
Isca (Caerleon) Roman
Amphitheatre, Caerleon
(Caerllion)—3A 60
Isca (Caerleon) Roman Fortress,
Caerleon (Caerllion)—3A 60
Roman Steps, Pentre Gwynfryn
—1B 22
Segontium Roman Fort,
Caernarfon—1D 13
Tomen-y-mur Roman
Amphitheatre, Gellilydan
—1C 23
Venta Silurum Roman Town

(Caerwent)—3B 60
Viroconium Roman Town,
Wroxeter—1C 33

Theme Park

Gullivers World, Warrington
—1C 11
Oakwood, Canaston Bridge
—1D 53
Pleasure Island Theme Park,
Otterspool, Liverpool—2A 10

Tourist Information Centres

OPEN ALL YEAR

*NOTE: Telephone Numbers are
given in Italics*
Aberaeron—2D 35 *01545 570602*
Abergavenny (Y Fenni)—1A 60
01873 857588
Aberystwyth—3A 28
01970 612125
Bala—1A 24   *01678 521021*
Bath—3D 67   *01225 462831*
Betws-y-Coed—2C 15
01690 710426
Birkenhead—2A 10
0151 647 6780
Bishop's Castle—3A 32
01588 638467
Brecon (Aberhonddu)—3B 48
01874 622485
Bridgnorth—2D 33 *01746 763358*
Bristol—2C 67   *0117 9260767*
Bristol Airport, Lulsgate Bottom
—3C 67   *01275 474444*
Bromyard—3D 41
01885 482038 / 482341
Builth Wells (Llanfair-ym-Mualt)
—3B 38   *01982 553307*
Caerleon (Caerllion)—3A 60
01633 430777
Caernarfon—1D 13
01286 672232
Caerphilly (Caerffili)—1C 65
01222 851378
Cardiff (Caerdydd)—2C 65
01222 227281
Cardigan (Aberteifi)—1A 44
01239 613230
Carmarthen (Caerfyrddin)—3D 45
01267 231557
Chepstow (Cas-gwent)—3C 61

01291 623772
Chester (Railway Station)—1B 18
01244 322220
Chester (Town Hall)—1B 18
01244 317962
Chester Visitor Centre—1B 18
01244 351609 / 318916
Cinderford—1D 61
01594 822581
Coleford—1C 61   *01594 836307*
Colwyn Bay (Bae Colwyn)—3D 7
01492 530478
Conwy—3C 7   *01492 592248*
Cwmcarn—3D 59   *01495 272001*
Dolgellau—3C 23   *01341 422888*
Eardisland—3B 40
01544 388226
Ewloe (Ewlo) Services—1D 17
01244 541597
Fishguard Harbour (Abergwaun
Porthladd), Goodwick (Wdig)
—2C 43   *01348 872037*
Fishguard Town (Tref
Abergwaun)—2C 43
01348 873484
Haverfordwest (Hwlffordd)
—1C 53   *01437 763110*
Hay-on-Wye (Y Gelli Gandryll)
—1D 49   *01497 820144*
Hereford—2C 51   *01432 268430*
Holyhead (Caergybi)—2B 4
01407 762622
Ironbridge—1D 33   *01952 432166*
Kington—3D 39   *01544 230778*
Knighton (Tref-y-Clawdd)—1D 39
01547 528753
Knutsford—3D 11
01565 632611 / 632210
Lake Vyrnwy (Llyn Efyrnwy),
Llanwddyn—3B 24
01691 870346
Ledbury—2D 51   *01531 636147*
Leominster—3B 40
01568 616460
Liverpool—1A 10
0151 709 3631
Liverpool (Albert Dock)—2A 10
0151 708 8854
Llandrindod Wells—2B 38
01597 822600
Llandudno—2C 7   *01492 876413*
Llanelli—2A 56   *01554 772020*
Llanfair Pwllgwyngyll—3A 6
01248 713177
Llangollen—3D 17 *01978 860828*
Llanidloes—3A 30 *01686 412605*
Llanwrtyd Wells—1D 47

01591 610666
Ludlow—1C 41   *01584 875053*
Machynlleth—1C 29
01654 702401
Magor (Magwyr) Services—1B 66
01633 881122
Market Drayton—1D 27
01630 652139
Merthyr Tydfil—2B 58
01685 379884
Mold (Yr Wyddgrug)—1D 17
01352 759331
Nantwich—2D 19
01270 610983 / 610880
Narberth (Arberth)—1A 54
01834 860061
Newent—3D 51   *01531 822145*
Newport (Casnewydd)(Newport)
—1A 66   *01633 842962*
Newport (Shropshire)—3D 27
01952 814109
Newtown (Y Drenewydd)—2C 31
01686 625580
Oswestry Mile End (Croesoswallt
Mile End)—2A 26
01691 662488
Oswestry Town (Croesoswallt
Tref)—2D 25   *01691 662753*
Pembroke (Penfro)—2C 53
01646 622388
Pont Abraham Services,
Pontardulais—2A 56
01792 883838
Pontneddfechan—2A 58
01639 721795
Pontypridd—3B 58
01443 409512
Porthcawl—2D 63
01656 786639
Porthmadog—1A 22
01766 512981
Pwllheli—1C 21   *01758 613000*
Queenswood, Hope under
Dinmore—3C 41
01568 797842
Rhayader (Rhaeadr Gwy)—2A 38
01597 810591
Rhyl—2B 8   *01745 355068*
Ross-on-Wye—3D 51
01989 562768
Runcorn—2C 11   *01928 576776*
Ruthin (Rhuthun)—2C 17
01824 703992
Sarn Park Services—1A 64
01656 654906
Shrewsbury—3B 26
01743 350761

Swansea (Abertawe)—3B 56
  01792 468321
Telford—1D 33 *01952 291370*
Tenbury Wells—2C 41
  01584 810136
Tenby (Dinbych-y-Pysgod)
  —2A 54 *01834 842402*
Thornbury—1D 67 *01454 281638*
Tregaron—3B 36 *01974 298144*
Warrington—2D 11
  01925 442180 / 444400
Welshpool (Trallwng)—1D 31
  01938 552043
Weston-super-Mare—3A 66
  01934 626838
Whitchurch—3C 19
  01948 664577
Widnes—2C 11 *0151 424 2061*
Wrexham (Wrecsam)—2A 18
  01978 292015

OPEN SUMMER SEASON ONLY

Abercraf, Glyntawe—1D 57
  01639 730284
Aberdovey (Aberdyfi)—2B 28
  01654 767321
Bangor Services, Llandegai
  —1A 14 *01248 352786*
Barmouth (Abermaw)—3B 22
  01341 280787
Barry Island (Ynys y Barri)
  —3C 65 *01446 747171*
Blaenau Ffestiniog—3C 15
  01766 830360
Borth—2B 28 *01970 871174*
Church Stretton—2B 32
  01694 723133
Corris—1C 29 *01654 761244*
Crickhowell (Crughywel)—1D 59
  01873 812105
Elan Valley (Cwm Elan), Elan
  Village—2A 38 *01597 810898*
Ellesmere—1B 26 *01691 622981*

Harlech—1A 22 *01766 780658*
Kilgetty (Cilgeti)—2A 54
  01834 813672
Llanberis—1A 14 *01286 870765*
Llandarcy—3C 57 *01792 813030*
Llandovery (Llanymddyfri)—2C 47
  01550 720693
Milford Haven (Aberdaugleddau)
  —2C 53 *01646 690866*
Monmouth (Trefynwy)—1C 61
  01600 713899
Much Wenlock—2D 33
  01952 727679
Mumbles (Mwmbwls),
  Oystermouth—1B 62
  01792 361302
Newcastle Emlyn (Castell Newydd
  Emlyn)—1C 45
  01239 711333
New Quay (Ceinewydd)—2C 35
  01545 560865
Pembroke Dock (Doc Penfro)
  —2C 53 *01646 622246*
Penarth—2C 65 *01222 708849*
Prestatyn—2B 8 *01745 889092*
Presteigne (Llanandras)—2A 40
  01544 260193
Rhos-on-Sea (Llandrillo yn
  Rhos)—2D 7 *01492 548778*
St David's (Tyddewi)—3A 42
  01437 720392
Tywyn—1A 28 *01654 710070*

Vineyard

Brecon Court Vineyard, Llansoy
  —2B 60
Broadfield Gardens & Vineyards,
  Bowley—3C 41
Cwm Deri Vineyard, Martletwy
  —1D 53
Gwinllan Ffynnon Las Vineyard,

Aberaeron—2D 35
Llanerch Vineyard, Clawdd-coch
  —2B 64
Three Choirs Vineyards, Botloe's
  Green—3D 51
Wroxeter Roman Vineyard
  —1C 33

Wildlife Park

*See also Aviary/Bird Garden,
  Farm Park, Zoo*
Aberaeron Wildlife & Leisure
  Park—2D 35
Manor House Wildlife & Leisure
  Park, St Florence—2D 53
Penscynor Wildlife Park, Cilfrew
  —3C 57
Stepaside Bird & Animal Park
  —2A 54

Windmill

Llynnon Towermill,
  Llanddeusant—2C 5

Zoo/Safari Park

*See also Bird Garden, Farm Park,
  Wildlife Park*
Borth Animalarium—3B 28
Bristol Zoo, Clifton—2C 67
Chester Zoo, Upton Heath
  —3B 10
Knowsley Safari Park, Prescot
  —1B 10
Welsh Mountain Zoo, Colwyn Bay
  (Bae Colwyn)—3D 7